T0295614

What Workers Say

ROBERTA REHNER IVERSEN

What Workers Say

Decades of Struggle and
How to Make Real Opportunity Now

TEMPLE UNIVERSITY PRESS
Philadelphia • *Rome* • *Tokyo*

TEMPLE UNIVERSITY PRESS
Philadelphia, Pennsylvania 19122
tupress.temple.edu

Library of Congress Cataloging-in-Publication Data

Names: Iversen, Roberta Rehner, author.
Title: What workers say : decades of struggle and how to make real
opportunity now / Roberta Rehner Iversen.
Description: Philadelphia : Temple University Press, 2022. | Includes
bibliographical references and index. | Summary: "Presents American
workers discussing their jobs as they have experienced them between 1980
and today to illustrate the challenges of changed work in the labor
market. The final chapter offers potential policy solutions"—Provided
by publisher.
Identifiers: LCCN 2021051882 (print) | LCCN 2021051883 (ebook) | ISBN
9781439922361 (cloth) | ISBN 9781439922378 (paperback) | ISBN
9781439922385 (pdf)
Subjects: LCSH: Working class—United States—Interviews. | Working
class—United States—Attitudes. | Quality of work life—United States.
| Labor market—Social aspects—United States. | United States—Social
conditions—1980–2020. | LCGFT: Interviews.
Classification: LCC HD8072.5 .I94 2022 (print) | LCC HD8072.5 (ebook) |
DDC 305.5/620973—dc23/eng/20220215
LC record available at https://lccn.loc.gov/2021051882
LC ebook record available at https://lccn.loc.gov/2021051883

Printed in the United States of America

9 8 7 6 5 4 3 2 1

Contents

Dedication and Funding
Acknowledgments

W*hat Workers Say* is dedicated to the millions of workers who keep people and countries going. I am particularly grateful to the workers who generously shared their struggles and hopes about work as they knew and experienced it during the years of research study. I hope that their participation means that the workers who come after them will also benefit.

What Workers Say is also dedicated to my beloved, supportive family: Gudmund, Doris, John, Chris, and Jack; Kirsten (Dave), Eric (Catherine), John (Chikako), Gretchen (Luke); my grandchildren, Anna, Audrey, Chisato, Elizabeth, Glenn, Ivan, Owen, and Sonja, who are the next generation who can foster initiatives like compensated civil labor. I also thank my longtime friends, especially Nancy Patchen, Karen Berry, Linda M. Fisher, Mary Gergen, Kenneth Gergen, and others whom I hope to see more often now that this book is finished.

In addition to the colleagues identified in the appendix who helped and inspired me as we collaborated on the research projects in this book, these others sustained me in many important ways: Leslie Alexander, Sara Bachman, Jerri Bourjolly, Frank F. Furstenberg, Jr., Richard Gelles, Mark Granovetter; Lina Hartocollis, Robert Inman, Allan Irving, John Jackson, Carole Joffe, Arne Kalleberg, Hans-Uwe Otto, John Pencavel, Andy Rosen, Susan Sorenson, Marty Spiegel, Karen Staller, Stanley Witkin, and University of Pennsylvania students, faculty, and administrative staff. I also thank the many other colleagues who have labored with me on work, family, and mobility issues over the years—particularly Naomi Farber, Anna Haley, Julia Henly, Cheryl Hyde, Susan Lambert, and Daniel Meyer.

Finally, I gratefully acknowledge Lois Maharg's expert editorial contributions to this book's clarity, crispness, and depth. Her efficiency, perspective, experience, and enthusiasm enabled a final manuscript after my years of solo writing. I also deeply appreciate that Aaron Javsicas, editor in chief at Temple Press, remained patient, encouraging, and convinced of the importance of this book throughout my years of writing. The TUP production and marketing team were also always very responsive, thorough, and helpful. Similarly, I appreciate the thoughtful comments and suggestions offered by the reviewers.

Funding Acknowledgments

My deep gratitude goes to the following people and organizations for generously supporting my research. Their support has already enabled the research to positively affect scholarly knowledge, social policy, and social programs.

- The Fahs-Beck Fund for Research and Experimentation for two grants for my dissertation research (the Teen Study Follow-Up: 1989 to 1990)
- The University of Pennsylvania Faculty Research Fund and the 1199C Training and Upgrading Fund for two studies on women in welfare-to-work programs (the Welfare-to-Work Studies: 1990s)
- The Annie E. Casey Foundation for four years of funding for the Ethnographic Study: 2000 to 2005, and a fifth year of funding for book preparation (Iversen and Armstrong 2006)
- The Russell Sage Foundation to Frank F. Furstenberg Jr. for support of the team of investigators, interviewers, and analysts for the Philadelphia suburb portion of the Families in the Middle Study (the Family Study: 2008 to 2015 and Beyond)
- A generous gift award in 2018 from an anonymous donor who is similarly interested in ideas about work in the future. This gift enabled travel for interviews with experts and helped greatly with costs associated with research and preparation of this book.

What Workers Say

1

Hard Work Hasn't Been Paying Off

Creating Real *Opportunity for Millions of Workers*

W hat's the real story about today's jobs? What have jobs really been like for the past 40 years and what do the workers themselves say about them? What do most of us know about the work that millions of people do—the manufacturing, construction, printing, clerical, healthcare, retail, food service, grocery, real estate, and automotive service jobs that have employed nearly two-thirds of the U.S. workforce since 1980 (BLS 2019f; Rose 2018; Plunkert 1990)? These are the day and night jobs that are important to society as a whole and that keep most people's families and communities strong, healthy, and surviving. But they're also the jobs that seldom enable families and communities to thrive and are often first to go in a recession. None of us can do without these jobs, but the reality is that these jobs don't pay off, they are often discriminatory by gender and race/ethnicity, they don't provide advancement opportunity, they are sometimes dangerous and exploitative, and they too seldom utilize people's full range of capabilities. It is the latter—utilizing capabilities—that ultimately benefits the worker, the community, and the nation, as all benefit when people are able to utilize their capabilities and strengths in their work.[1]

Accordingly, the aim of this book is twofold: first, to present workers' stories about their labor market jobs during the past 40 years of major changes in the labor market so that we learn what their jobs were and are

---

1. I explicitly do not use the terms *skills* and *skill levels*, thanks to a reviewer's comments. Even though those terms are widely used, they may be subjective and contested and are here better indicated by terms such as capabilities, interests, and capacities.

really like and, second, to suggest ways that ideas about work could be usefully expanded in order to benefit workers, communities, and the nation. In fact, the ranks of these workers have swelled over the past 40 years to include individuals with occupations formerly associated with four-year college degrees and professional or semiprofessional status. The impact of recessions over the 40 years that culminated in the Great Recession in 2007–2009 and its decadelong aftermath of labor market constriction were then magnified by the economic downturn resulting from the COVID-19 pandemic and its high level of unemployment and financial stress. In a word, sole reliance on the labor market for workers' economic security and meaningful activity needs serious consideration, which this book aims to provide.

Foundational Beliefs about Work

Underneath the economic and labor market changes and challenges reviewed in the next sections, foundational beliefs held by most in the United States, such as America is the land of opportunity and that hard work pays off, are called into question. Workers whose stories appear in this book, whose hard work has not paid off since the 1980s, and others who are still out of work raise their voices against the view that today's United States is a land of opportunity and unlimited possibility. The high value placed on labor market work in the United States, above all other kinds of work, as Kathi Weeks (2011) has richly documented, underlies these workers' hopes and struggles alike.

Historically, the land of opportunity characterization began in the frontier days, even though much of the opportunity was achieved at the expense of indigenous peoples. Early on, colonial governments took Native Americans' lands and sent Native children away to boarding schools to eliminate their indigenous culture and assimilate them to white Christian culture. In the 1700s and 1800s, famine in Europe and Scandinavia inspired large-scale migration to the United States because of the new country's ample arable land, much of which was originally the indigenous peoples' land, and agricultural success was achieved in large part at the expense of enslaved persons primarily from Africa. After industrial work supplanted agricultural work in the economy of the late 1800s, labor market work in goods-producing manufacturing industries, often enhanced by unions, became the locus of wage and advancement opportunity for millions of workers and their families in the United States. From the 1960s, however, and expanding in the 1970s, manufacturing industries receded as the dominant source of unionized, family-sustaining, higher-waged jobs. Today, although productivity in some parts of the manufacturing industry is still substantial, it mostly occurs in the computer and electronics sectors (Baily and Bosworth 2014) or results from management practices that require overtime instead of engaging in additional hiring. As a result, by the late 1900s, the number of job possibilities in manufacturing were massively reduced and superseded by an increasing number of jobs in service industries, which generally did not match manufacturing in productivity or wages. And while productivity and wages had grown in parallel before the 1970s, the great decoupling of wages from productivity in virtually all U.S. industries since the 1970s remains the case today, to some extent a result of declining unionization and greater managerial focus on short-term gains and the accompanying cuts in the cost of wages (Kenworthy and Marx 2017, 18).

The historic view of opportunity in the United States has also been based on economic criteria in contrast to class or caste differences. Nevertheless, as in today's more "developed" society—in quotes because philosophically and theoretically, development implies far more than economic development—the notion of opportunity in this book draws less on economic metrics and more on Nobelist Amartya Sen's (1999) ideas about human freedoms and human flourishing. Freedom and flourishing occur in a social, economic, political, and moral environment that values and aims for "good and flourishing lives" for all community members through the freedom to develop and enact one's capabilities and interests in ways that are meaningful for both persons and society. From the standpoint of Sen and this book, community signifies "the relations of mutual engagement" (Wenger 1999, 73). This does not mean unanimity, but implies "people who are engaged in actions whose meanings they negotiate with one another" (73).

Regarding the foundational belief that hard work pays off, the fastest-growing service jobs in the United States today are healthcare support positions such as home health aide, medical assistant, personal care aide, physical or occupational therapy aide, pharmacy aide, and phlebotomist, with median[2] annual wages in 2019[3] of $28,470 (BLS 2020i). This annual wage barely exceeds the poverty line for a family of four (110%), and doesn't come close to 200% of the poverty line, which is considered barebones self-sufficiency by many scholars and policymakers (e.g., Jiang, Ekono, and Skinner 2016, 1). The number of these positions was projected to increase by almost 30% between 2018 and 2028 in the United States (BLS 2019f) as a result of the

---

2. For labor market and employment metrics, the Bureau of Labor Statistics regularly uses the *median*, defined as the middle number in a range of numbers; in other words, the "typical" or "average" number. In this book, the terms *median* and *average* are used as equivalent. If another metric, such as *mean* is used in BLS or other research cited, we will identify that accordingly.

3. In many places I use 2019 as a baseline metric for wage-related information (e.g. BLS 2020b) because it was the most recent normal or typical period before the COVID-19 pandemic and its resultant economic and labor market tumult.

growing size of the aging population. Wages are not projected to rise significantly, however, which means that these hard-work positions will continue to not pay off.

Other fast-growing service jobs with a similar range of annual wages in 2019 include waiters; retail salespersons; bicycle repairers; derrick operators in oil and gas; roustabouts in oil and gas; service unit operators in oil, gas, and mining; and operations managers. Service jobs in the oil, gas, and mining areas, in contrast, yield median annual wages from the high $30,000s to the low $40,000s. By comparison, the median household income in the United States in 2019 was $63,000, barely surpassing the pre–Great Recession figure of $60,664 in 2001 (BLS 2019i). Worse, according to the Consumer Price Index (CPI) Inflation Calculator, an income of $60,664 in 2001 is the equivalent of just over $89,000 in buying power today, which is roughly $26,000 more than the actual median household income in 2019. Thus, hard work does not seem to be paying off for most service workers, even though the country vitally needs what they contribute.

Nevertheless, beliefs that hard work pays off and that the United States is the land of opportunity remain recognizable symbols of the perceived economic potential of labor market work for persons in the United States. Historically, the idea of opportunity in the labor market was founded on these premises: wage work is available to all who seek it, a person's hard work will be rewarded by regular wage increases, education and employer-provided skill training will lead to promotion, and parents' efforts will be rewarded by their children's future mobility, which will surpass theirs. These ideas and beliefs about opportunity through work and wages are still held by many in the general public and by many workers, even though they are not fully applicable or achievable for countless millions today.

In fact, as noted earlier, throughout U.S. history, opportunity has never been available to all, or even to most people (Ingraham 2016), and today it is increasingly less available to lower- and even middle-income workers (Kalleberg 2018; Willis 2015). By 1980, labor market work had changed for the worse for virtually all workers to some extent (Kalleberg 2009; Kochan and Barley 1999; Vallas 2012), particularly for those without postsecondary education and those with below-sufficiency earnings (Dodson 2009; Iversen and Armstrong 2006; Shipler 2004), despite the short period in the late 1990s (Kenworthy and Marx 2017). Not surprisingly, the workers whose stories appear in this book, most of whom are also parents and many of whom are female, people of color, or both, expressed both belief and disbelief about opportunity in labor market work. One critical reason for workers' disbelief in both opportunity and the payoff of hard work is that there are not enough jobs in the United States today for all who need and want one.

Hard Work: What It's Like Today for Millions

More than 10 years after the Great Recession officially ended, and until the coronavirus pandemic in early 2020, news media reported daily that the U.S. economy was on the upswing and unemployment was down. In fact, for most of 2019, the unemployment rate fell below 4% (BLS 2020b), the usual signifier of full employment in the United States. That perspective was completely upended in April 2020 when more than 16 million workers, more than one in ten, filed unemployment claims during the coronavirus pandemic (Soergel 2020, 2). Even before the pandemic, however, glowing numbers about the country's general economic health and unemployment rates under 4% told only part of the story about today's workers, and to a great extent it was a misleading story.

The real story about the hard work that hasn't been paying off for millions of lower-wage earners involves both economic and employment conditions and numbers. In this book, numbers clarify what's happening now, and narratives present workers' experiences in manufacturing, construction, printing, clerical, retail, healthcare, and semiprofessional service jobs since the 1980s. Both the numbers and four decades of people's everyday work experiences suggest that work available in the U.S. labor market alone is not sufficient now, nor will it be in the coming decades, to support the millions of people in the United States who want to work hard, want their work to pay off, and want real opportunity for their futures.

Let's look at the numbers first. Five recessions since January 1980, including the Great Recession (officially lasting from 2007 to 2009) and longer postrecession unemployment periods than in earlier decades, have resulted in punishing, higher-than-average-unemployment rates for some workers. Specifically, the downturn in employment accompanying the Great Recession was notable for its "prolonged length, for affecting an especially wide range of industries, and for being deeper than any other downturn since World War II" (Goodman and Mance 2011, 3). The recession and its aftermath have also disproportionately disadvantaged workers of color and younger workers. For example, unemployment rates in December 2019 were higher for African Americans (5.9%) and Hispanics (4.2%) than for whites (3.2%) or Asians (2.5%) (BLS 2020d). Pandemic-related poverty rates for the same groups were predicted to be 15.2%, 13.7%, and 6.6%, respectively (Giannarelli, Wheaton, and Acs, 2020), despite the help from the stimulus checks and increased SNAP (Supplemental Nutrition Assistance Program) allotment.

In addition, the jobless rate for over a half-million youth aged 16 to 24 years, which is a prime period for labor market entry, was 11.2% for whites and nearly double that (20.6%) for African Americans (BLS 2020d). Worse, in December 2019, almost one in five unemployed persons overall (1.2 million) had been unemployed for more than 27 weeks (BLS 2020d), which made them ineligible for unemployment compensation in all but two states— *if* they had been eligible for the unemployment insurance program to begin with. Extended unemployment compensation under the federal CARES Act in March 2020 helped roughly 13.3 million people, but the act was set to expire in December 2020. At that point, the Pandemic Unemployment Assistance (PUA) Act extended benefits for new applicants to March 14, 2021, and the Pandemic Relief Act extended the CARES act compensation up to 50 weeks (Staller 2022). Under the new administration in January 2021, the American Rescue Plan authorized another round of stimulus payments, extended the time frame for unemployment benefits, and vastly expanded aid to children in lower-income families. Even earlier, however, a historically low one in four jobless workers actually received unemployment insurance benefits in 2015 (Buffie and Rawlins 2017; West et al. 2021), a situation that disadvantaged a number of workers reporting in this book.

Importantly, the unemployment numbers do not include the epic and lasting withdrawal of millions of workers from the labor force, those who are not counted as officially unemployed. Since 1994, the U.S. Census Bureau has designated and counted workers that are "not in the labor force" in total and in three subgroups: "marginally attached to the labor force," "discouraged," or "other" (BLS 2020b). The subgroups are further described as persons who have looked but cannot find work ("marginally attached"); persons who believe that no work is available for them ("discouraged"); and persons who lack schooling or training, are viewed as too young or too old by employers, or are the target of some type of discrimination ("other"). In 2009, the official end of the Great Recession, 5.9 million persons were not in the labor force but wanted a job, yet that number had fallen by only about 1.3 million, to 4.6 million, 10 years later, by December 2019. It is clear, then, that if those 4.6 million persons were considered officially unemployed and added to the 5.5 million actually counted as officially unemployed, which constituted a 3.5% unemployment rate (AARP Public Policy Institute 2019), the *actual* unemployment rate would be at least 7%. Moreover, these figures preceded the major economic downturn in spring 2020, when the economy essentially ground to a halt during the coronavirus pandemic. It will be years before we know the full effects of that downturn on workers and businesses.

The numbers above, of course, reflect only the workers' side of the equation. Unfortunately, the employer-side numbers—the number of jobs available—are equally concerning. Rates of employment in the total nonfarm and total private categories, which encompass the initially mentioned occupations in this book, fell 21% and 23%, respectively, between December

2018 and December 2019 (BLS 2020c). Average weekly hours of work remained the same over the year at 34.5 hours, but average hourly and weekly wages across all employers also stayed the same. As Gould (2019) has found, although a low unemployment rate in the past has generally benefited lower-wage workers, workers at the lower end of the income distribution today have experienced a slowdown in the rate of wage growth since the Great Recession. In contrast, wages at the top end have skyrocketed, a sign of growing income inequality. Treuhaft and Hamilton (2020, 2) report similar findings: "Forty-four percent of American workers earn less than $18,000 a year, while the executives of the largest 350 companies earn $18.9 million on average."

Overall, then, given the pattern of frequent economic recessions in the United States, persistent wage stagnation in lower-paying jobs since the 1970s (Benmelech, Bergman, and Kim 2019), and greater income inequality, the long-term prognosis for employment stability and racial/ethnic equity in the labor market for those below the top echelon of earners seems poor. In addition, glacial increases in U.S. productivity between 2009 and 2021, as evidenced by gross domestic product (GDP) growth of −1% to +2% or slightly more, are paralleled by similarly slow hiring practices and minimal job creation by most U.S. employers.

Expanding the hard-work-doesn't-pay-off lens to expose the everyday conditions and experiences of those who hold labor market jobs forces us to train our attention on changes imposed by upper management, such as just-in-time scheduling, where employees are told to come and go at the last minute; the elimination of on-the-job training; the reduction or making of nonwage benefits unaffordable; and the deemphasis of employer-employee loyalty, as rigorously documented elsewhere (e.g., Autor 2019; Kalleberg 2018; Eberstadt 2016; Kochan and Dyer 2017; Lambert, Fugiel, and Henly 2014; Weeks 2011; Beck 2000). Such neoliberal managerial actions have greatly compounded the struggles resulting from broader economic patterns for millions of workers like those in this book, as the next section elaborates.

On-the-Ground Challenges in Today's Labor Market

Autor (2019) describes one labor market change as job polarization, meaning that current jobs and those projected to be created over the next decade or so are either at the top of the occupational ladder, for workers with professional or semiprofessional credentials and those with four years of education, or at the lower end of the ladder, for workers without postsecondary education and credentials. In Autor's view, polarization largely results from two demand-side forces: (1) the decline of manufacturing production work as a result of automation and rising trade pressure and (2) the proliferation of office computing that has diminished the ranks of clerical and administrative workers, in favor of those with four-year college degrees (2019, 21). In contrast, Holzer (2011) and Holzer and Lerman (2009) contend that employment in jobs that require education or training beyond high school but less than a four-year bachelor's degree has remained quite strong.

Autor and Holzer agree, however, that wages for millions of men have either decreased or stagnated since 1980, particularly in manufacturing but also in other occupational areas. In contrast to earlier decades when workers could provide financially for their families, often regardless of their education level, wages today are tightly tied to schooling. The most common message employers give lower-earning job seekers now is "not enough skills" (Rushing 2019). In other words, the presumption is that there are plenty of jobs, but today's job seekers lack sufficient training to do them. Others (Weyrich 2006; Holzer 1998) suggest that employers use lack of schooling as a way to discriminate against job seekers because of their race, geographic location, gender, age, or sexual orientation.

Automation and globalization (Stern and Kravitz 2016) are often cited as other labor market changes that have cut down on work opportunities in recent decades, particularly evident in the severe downturn in manufacturing and related industry jobs such as construction and printing. Union membership among workers has declined from 20.1% (17.7 million workers), in the initial census measurement taken in 1983, to 10.3% (14.6 million workers, most of whom are in public-sector workplaces) in 2021 (BLS 2022). New forms of strategic collective influence at both management and employee levels are part of today's labor discourse (Stern and Kravitz 2016). Some of the new forms of management, however, such as employee groups, are attempts to use the new form of employer-employee relations to *discourage* unionization efforts (e.g., the Sam Gates Family Story, in Iversen and Armstrong 2006, 137–39).

Another labor market challenge that particularly affects workers like those in this book is the frequency of nonfatal occupational injuries and illnesses in private industry every year (BLS 2019h). The frequency of injury in manufacturing and related industries is well known, but data from the increase in service industry jobs in healthcare, retail, and other service venues such as business call centers reveal that they are also sites of physical strain, falls, carpal tunnel syndrome, back injuries, eye injuries, and emotional stress for many everyday workers (BLS 2018; Iversen and Armstrong 2006, 2007; Guendelsberger 2019). In 2017, nearly one-third of nonfatal occupational injuries and illnesses resulted in days away from work (BLS 2018, 1). Considering the projected increase in the country's aging population, the number of nonfatal injuries in 2018 to workers in the healthcare and social assistance sectors is particularly worrisome. Workers in these sectors experienced about 550,000 nonfatal occupational injuries, the highest number of all labor market industries. Nonfatal healthcare and social assistance injuries in 2018 outnumbered those in manufacturing, at about 400,000; retail trade, at almost 200,000; accommodation and food service, at 270,000; and construction, at almost 200,000 (BLS 2019h, 1). The jobs held by most of the workers in this book, and millions like them across the United States, are not only the lowest paid, often earning below poverty-level wages, and the most vulnerable to economic downturn, but are also associated with the highest risk of nonfatal occupational injury (BLS 2019h, 4).

More Job Seekers but Not Enough Jobs

Here are some recent numbers about how many jobs are actually available. The total U.S. population reached 329.4 million persons in March 2020 (U.S. Census Bureau 2020). Earlier estimates indicated that in 2020, approximately 74 million would be children under the age of 18, about 56 million would be adults 65 years or older, and a little over 200 million would be adults in the prime working ages of 18 to 64 years (Vespa, Armstrong, and Medina 2018, 5). At the same time, the notion of "prime working years" for some women now extends into the late 60s and 70s (Goldin and Katz 2018).

Official employment numbers in March 2020, revised in September 2020, showed that 155.8 million persons were employed full-time (34.5 hours or more a week) and 5.8 million were employed part-time for economic reasons, meaning they were working 1 to 34 hours a week but wanted full-time employment. A total of 20.6 million were employed part-time for noneconomic reasons, including childcare problems, family or personal obligations, school or training, and social security limits on earnings (BLS 2020d). Almost 8 million held multiple jobs (5% of the total number of individuals employed) and 9.5 million persons were listed by the BLS as self-employed, unincorporated (BLS 2020d). Overall, 162.9 million persons held paying jobs (BLS 2020d).

At the same time, approximately 152.3 million jobs were available in the U.S. labor market (Department of Numbers 2019) for the 200 million potential prime-age workers in 2020 noted earlier. The discrepancy in the number of people who want to work versus the number of jobs available became even greater in 2021 than it was at the end of 2019, as pandemic-related unemployment raged on. In April 2020, for example, out of 22 million jobs lost during the pandemic, only 9 million had been regained (Bartash 2020). Opportunity rhetoric such as "anyone can work if they want it enough" or "people who are unemployed are just too lazy to work" did not jibe with the number of jobs available, either as the economy inched forward after the Great Recession and during the pandemic or today, in 2021–2022.

And, of course, numbers alone don't account for the low wages that far too many jobs pay, as noted earlier about occupations in the service sector, the glacial pace of post–Great Recession wage increases more than 10 years after the recession technically ended, and the pandemic's effects on job loss. Ultimately, millions of counted and uncounted people who describe their life activities as work but are not paid or not paid enough figure centrally in the need to create *real* opportunity for the workers in the United States.

Creating *Real* Opportunity through Expanding Ideas about Work

Since the dominant narratives about hard work paying off and opportunity being available for all do not square with the numbers, another question emerges: What can be done so that 12 million full-time workers at ages 25 to 64 do not live in poverty or have incomes below 200% of the federal poverty threshold (PolicyLink 2019)? Forty years ago, in 1980, fewer than 7 million people were working but still poor; today, 12.4 million workers struggle in that category. Many noted scholars have rigorously explored the causes and consequences of the past 40 years of labor market changes using statistical analyses (e.g., Kochan and Barley 1999; Beck 2000; Ciulla 2000; Clogg, Eliason, and Leicht 2001; Levy and Murnane 2006; Blank, Danziger, and Schoeni 2006; Bartik and Houseman 2008; Kalleberg 2009, 2018), and the experiences recounted by the workers in this book add another dimension to the numbers. They help us understand in greater detail how workers' lives have been affected by changes in labor market jobs and clarify the kinds of opportunity that could create meaningful change in their lives.

In brief, the workers here speak of having to substitute lower-wage service jobs for the higher-wage manufacturing, construction, printing, and automotive positions they held before their companies moved from urban centers to the suburbs or out of the country or closed down completely. They speak of increasingly stressful physical and emotional working conditions in offices, foundries, healthcare facilities, and customer service and other call centers where workforce flexibility for employers is experienced as insecurity for the workers (McCall 2000) and workplace efficiency strategies take the form of intrusive surveillance. They speak of the declining value of their wages, limited union possibilities, and wage-reduction practices at work that are surreptitiously presented as an increase in paid hours. Such practices are often accompanied by reduction or elimination of nonwage benefits.

In addition, higher percentages of these workers are underemployed, defined officially as working part-time but wanting full-time work (Stevens, Huff, and Pihl 2017), or have stopped looking for work. Worse, these workers' narratives show that even when their incomes reach 200% of the federal poverty level, which is barebones family economic sufficiency as noted earlier, making ends meet is a daily struggle wherein the fragile balance is easily upended by a medical bill, a car repair, a child's need for special services, or a layoff. The workers here illustrate what it's like to be among the 12.4 million full-time workers between the ages of 25 and 64 in the United States who are considered *economically insecure*, a term parallel to *low-income*, because these workers earn less than 200% of the poverty line (PolicyLink 2019). More than half of such workers, like many whose stories are featured in this book, are persons of color, and a high percentage are women. The narratives in this book also demonstrate how repeated recessions over the decades since the 1980s have resulted in neoliberal employer practices that disadvantage many workers. For example, cost-saving practices such as *outsourcing* (contracting some roles or whole departments, such as human resources, to organizations outside the business); using *contingent workers* (hiring short-term workers on an as-needed basis rather than hiring more full-time employees) (Sweet and Meiksins 2017); and *offshoring* (sending some tasks out of the country, where labor is cheaper) have cumulatively lowered or eliminated work opportunity for millions of workers in the United States.

Why Are Workers' Accounts Important?

Workers' narrative accounts that touch on these issues are particularly important because their actual experiences on the job are often not reflected in employment policies or workplace practices, which may then result in continual exclusion from an opportunity path. As noted, workplace conditions in many jobs have become increasingly inhospitable or downright dangerous, which can easily truncate opportunity. Second, worker accounts are important because policymakers and the public often characterize lower-income workers as lacking motivation, being lazy, or not working hard enough, and solutions to the perceived problem are then directed at changing individual behaviors rather than toward creating innovative and supportive policies, programs, and organizational structures. Specifically, the individualistic default path to mobility and higher earnings is understood to be more education, even though only about 35% of jobs in the United States actually require a four-year college education (Carnevale, Smith, and Strohl 2019) and 34% of working-age people in the United States have a four-year college degree (Voice of America 2018). Third, in contrast to pejorative characterizations of many workers, their own accounts provide vivid evidence that work is still deeply meaningful to them, even when their daily dedication and future hopes are being sorely challenged by employers' policies and practices or by inadequately funded public workforce retraining and supports. Their vivid accounts may then reach policymakers' hearts and minds to suggest more equitable policy improvements. Fourth, worker accounts are important because some government officials in the prior administration had raised the hopes of workers in industries such as steel and coal, where work opportunities are actually decreasing, attempting to revive a bygone period in U.S. labor market history rather than envisioning new ways to foster opportunity for workers in the future. Fifth, without public and policymaker understanding of what *real* opportunity means to workers and would-be workers, now and in the foreseeable future, workers' visions of their own futures are less likely to be realized. As Sennett (1998, 30) reminds us, "Narratives are more than simple chronicles of events; they give shape to the forward movement of time, suggesting reasons why things happen, showing their consequences." Finally, the workers in this book, as elsewhere, express strong desires to work at least some of the time at what they love, do what is meaningful to them and others, and have the opportunity to utilize their capabilities (Sen 1992; Nussbaum and Sen 1993; Fleurbaey 2018; Ferguson and Li 2018). These six reasons for paying attention to narrative accounts suggest they are critical for informing policy change and to the book's aim of expanding what is considered work and compensating it.

In particular, despite many television and internet reality shows, the U.S. public does not seem to know much more today about what many workers' jobs are like than they did in Studs Terkel's (1974) book, *Working*, which was situated in the old job market of the 1960s and early 1970s under the "old employment contract" (Kochan and Dyer 2017), before the major changes in the 1980s that continue today. That such changes in the labor market have taken place in basically a single generation makes it even more imperative to challenge the exclusive valuation of labor market work as "work," as Kathi Weeks (2011), Ulrich Beck (2000), and Karl Marx (1933) have done. Although some of the new work forms, such as gig work, are considered to be outside the formal labor market, most are affiliated with larger businesses, though usually without nonwage benefits. More broadly, the experiences that workers in this book relate raise questions about labor market inequality, stratification, and limited opportunity or life chances (Weber 1978 [1922]). Pragmatically, workers' accounts have broad implications for themselves and their families, especially their children; for workforce and employment-related education and policy; for the health of communities; and for the very way the U.S. populace thinks about what work is today and will be in the future.

Considering the needs of people and the social and physical environment in the 2020s and that "60% of jobs we have today will see more than 30% of tasks fundamentally transformed" (Sneader 2019, 2), the following chapters showcase workers' experiences in their jobs and occupations and their struggles and occasional small successes, which cumulatively herald the need for changes in thinking. Even current policy efforts, such as raising the minimum wage and other wage movements, such as the Fight for $15, valuably address wages but remain embedded in labor market jobs. The Earned Income Tax Credit similarly enhances income for labor market workers through the tax system. Only the Universal Basic Income (UBI) pilot programs (e.g., West, Baker, et al. 2021) are separate from need assessment, means testing, or job participation but, to date, UBI programs are limited in scope and length as well. Acknowledging the plusses of these policy efforts and expanding upon them, the final chapter in this book presents new ways to think about defining and compensating work beyond the labor market in order to benefit workers and families, foster community and civic engagement, and improve the country's failing infrastructure (American Society of Civil Engineers 2021).

The Book in Brief

This book puts a human face on the work experiences of a broad range of workers from the early 1980s to today, the 2020s, and aims to let their voices illustrate the challenges of the changes to work in the labor market and make them more visible and known. Importantly, the workers describe not only what they did or do as work, but also what they would like to do: in one worker's terms, their "heart-string." Chapter 2 shows what manufacturing, construction, and printing industry jobs have been like over the decades as they shifted by geography, workplace practices, and size of workforce. Subsequent chapters then explore the industry shift from manufacturing to services, detailing what service jobs entailed yesterday and entail today through workers' experience of them over the decades. Because the content of today's most common service jobs has not been broadly discussed beyond the low wages and the little mobility opportunity they afford, the chapters here examine the details of workers' experiences in the most common and highly populated service sector jobs: clerical (Chapter 3), healthcare (Chapter 4), food service and retail (Chapter 5), and in less common but still widespread service areas such as real estate, architecture, and automotive service (Chapter 6). In each sector, workers' descriptions and analytic commentary illuminate job content, working conditions, wage adequacy, and workers' feelings about their work and future work opportunity. Hearing directly from these workers and would-be workers enables us to more fully understand "the relations between the transformations within working life and workers' subjectivities [which] have been relatively under-explored" (Gill and Pratt 2008, 2).

The in-person knowledge and understanding we gained talking with our interlocutors, observing them at work, and talking with their coworkers and supervisors enable us to assess the relevance of existing policy and program solutions to the work-related struggles that so many workers and communities experience. For example, President Donald Trump's 2018 executive order (White House 2018, 1) aimed to remedy the so-called skills crisis through "fostering an environment of lifelong learning and skills-based training, and to cultivate a demand-driven approach to workforce development." The executive order asked companies to create training opportunities, which most had already begun, but no reliable information exists about how many jobs were created or filled (Kessler 2019), largely because the companies were not required to hire those they trained. Demonstrating the president's preference for business solutions over policy ones, in 2018 he also proposed a 39% budget cut to the main federal workforce policy, the Workforce Innovation and Opportunity Act of 2014. Although the cut was ultimately not approved by Congress, the president's views were in line with the ongoing decline in federal funding for workforce training and education that has taken place over the past 20 years: from $4.68 billion in 2001 to $2.79 billion in 2019 and $2.79 billion proposed for 2020 (Campaign to Invest in America's Workforce 2019). Similarly, the administration's proposal to add work requirements for persons needing temporary food assistance (Supplemental Nutrition Assistance Program, known as SNAP), housing assistance (Housing Choice Voucher Program), or childcare assistance, often coming from redirected Temporary Assistance for Needy Families (TANF) funds, particularly disadvantages those who are unemployed because of mental or physical disabilities but need such supports *before* they are able to look for work. Although these assistance programs are officially oriented to supporting parents' work and, occasionally, workforce training, they are less accessible than expected. Relatedly, the relevance of wage policies and income movements noted earlier is also part of the conversation.

The final chapter (Chapter 7) proposes new ways to create *real* opportunity for workers, including the importance of revising ideas about what work is and how some work can be transformed into civil labor and compensated in various ways, such as by money, time, or exchange. Examples of success with civil labor programs in European countries and others outside the United States add our imperative of compensation to Ulrich Beck's (2000) idea of civil labor. This work expansion effort we propose is oriented both to combining civil labor with labor market work and also to enabling workers to pursue the kind of work or activity that is meaningful to them and similarly benefits others. Teresa[4] is an example. Teresa's automotive service position in Seattle, which she achieved after a period of workforce

4. Most organization and all person names are pseudonyms, with the exception of two community respondents in Chapter 7 (see footnote 2 in Chapter 7). Pseudonyms were selected by the participants in the Ethnographic and Family Studies, and by the author in the other two studies.

development training, paid the bills. But her passion and talent, what she so aptly called "my heart-string," lay in catering, which she had time to do only occasionally, uncompensated, for her church and community organizations. If she could job-share her automotive position and be compensated for it and for part-time catering, perhaps by federal funds to communities for compensated civil labor initiatives, Teresa, her family, the job-sharing worker, and her community could all benefit. We return to Teresa's story in Chapter 7.

The final chapter also suggests ways that creating new, compensated ways of working could dramatically benefit towns and neighborhoods. One way we propose is through enhanced civic engagement activities that the community values. Some might be compensated by philanthropists or foundations, as can be seen in the examples of artists in North Philadelphia and horticulture in Swarthmore, Pennsylvania. A second way could enable more people to spend some of their time outdoors working on widespread improvements in roads, bridges, and other local structural needs, now that decades of labor market changes have resulted in an insufficient workforce to solve the severe infrastructure problems throughout the United States. Groups of supervisors and managers could oversee less-trained workers, who could then advance their capabilities while improving community safety. Finally, Chapter 7 suggests how new ways of working can provide greater intergenerational opportunity for the workers' children. Creating real opportunity through compensated civil labor, then, is what Phills, Deiglmeier, and Miller (2008, 36) might view as "a novel solution to a social problem that is more effective, efficient, sustainable, or just than existing solutions and for which the value created accrues primarily to society as a whole rather than to private individuals." In sum, the focus in the last chapter of this book is the generation and expansion of compensated civil labor.

A Word about the People and Research in This Book

The workers' stories in this book are drawn from several research studies I conducted alone or with colleagues [see Appendix] between the late 1980s and 2019. I have talked with the study participants about their work experiences in seven locations across the United States: Milwaukee, Wisconsin; New Orleans, Louisiana; Philadelphia, Pennsylvania; a Philadelphia suburb in Pennsylvania; St. Louis, Missouri; Seattle, Washington; and Tacoma, Washington. The workers were racially and ethnically diverse and represented earners in both lower- and middle-income categories.[5] Table A.1 in

---

5. We follow the many scholars and policymakers today who define "lower income" as income below 200% of the federal poverty line. For "middle income," we use the range other scholars employ, which is family income that falls within 75% to 125% of the national median family income (Gauthier 2015).

the Appendix summarizes the studies and the workers whose interviews I revisited and reanalyzed for this book.[6]

In all, I have interviewed more than 1,200 workers and would-be workers since the 1980s, including hundreds more family members, community members, workforce and welfare-to-work trainers, K–12 school personnel, employers, religious figures, and others relevant to the workers themselves. In most of these studies, the conversations took place multiple times over many years. For this book, I rereviewed the transcripts and data collected during these studies—at least fifteen thousand pages in all—and plumbed aspects of the workers' experiences and perceptions in addition to those examined in and reported following the original studies. Chamberlayne, Bornat, and Wengraf (2000) call this analytic method the biographical-interpretive method, which extends qualitative methods such as oral history, biography, and ethnography with analytic interpretation and reflexive positioning. As they note, "Biographies, which are rooted in analysis of both social history and the wellsprings of individual personality, reach forwards and backwards in time, documenting processes and experiences of social change" (2). Relatedly, use of multiple studies connected by researcher positionality, but not necessarily related by time or original intent, has become more common (for example, Burawoy 2009; Dodson 1998; Kanter 1989), even though it is still quite novel. Technically, this method can also be called an ethnographic reanalysis, which Burawoy (2009, 76) has identified as very rare among sociologically inclined ethnographers.

Overall, the labor market context over the past 40 years has been increasingly challenging for nearly two-thirds of the workers in the United States. While some workers could indeed benefit from more education and training, many of those with such advantages have not been thriving in the changed labor market environment. Worse yet, wage and salary projections for the labor market occupations explored in this book do not look as if they will pay off or offer real opportunity for at least the rest of the 2020s. We see this first in Chapter 2, in the experiences of workers whose hard work in manufacturing, construction, and printing jobs has met wage and opportunity challenges from both employers and the larger economy.

---

6. Research partners and the relevant studies are identified in full in the Appendix.

2

The Whir of Machines

Manufacturing, Construction, and Printing Jobs, 1980s to Today

I ndustrial-era task-specific capabilities,[1] such as those required for jobs in manufacturing, construction, and printing, provided *real* mobility opportunity for nearly four decades for high school graduates in the United States without postsecondary education. Initial postwar hiring in these industries primarily consisted of white men, but hiring of African American men began to increase in 1960 and by 1980 matched that of white men (Gould 2018). Also during those decades (1945 to 1980), productivity and hourly compensation rose together: 96.7% and 91.3%, respectively (Collins 2016, 1), to some extent a result of postwar union strength in the 1940s and 1950s. But after the high point of manufacturing employment in 1979 (Ghanbari and McCall 2016, 4) and the post-1980s decline in industrial unions, industrial productivity rose 74.4% while hourly compensation rose only 9.2% (Collins 2016, 1). This wage stagnation from the later 1980s onward occurred simultaneously with the shift from manufacturing and related industry jobs to a higher number of lower-paying service industry jobs. The shift is commonly referred to as *postindustrialization* and continues today.

---

1. Industrial-era task-specific capabilities are often called "hard skills" in contrast to more interpersonal, relational, and emotional capabilities, known as "soft skills." In this book, however, we primarily use *capabilities*, *interests*, and *activities* rather than *skills*, as we contend that virtually all types of work increasingly require multiple types of capabilities. When study participants used the term *skills* in the quotes we present, we have left their words as they are.

The workers' stories in this chapter are lodged in the first recession period in the 2000s (2001–2002), based on observations and interviews conducted in Milwaukee and New Orleans, two of the five U.S. cities in the Ethnographic Study[2] (Iversen and Armstrong 2006). The narratives reveal specifics about workers' workplace contexts, including safety, wages, benefits, learning and promotion opportunities, and utilization of their capabilities, as well as employers' views of them and of changing industry practices. The stories deal also with how the workers contended with the fluctuation or decrease in jobs in manufacturing, construction, and printing overall, resulting in fewer or more insecure labor market work opportunities. The four stories, which were typical of many others in the Ethnographic Study as well as the experiences of thousands in the United States at that time (Rank 2014), exemplify how the post-1980s realities in product manufacturing, construction, and printing jobs both benefited and limited many workers' lives and goals for their work. The stories also illustrate the dreams and hopes such workers had for their future work opportunities. Such opportunities could be realized in the form of compensated civil labor, whether as sole jobs or in addition to labor market jobs, a possibility we will examine further in Chapter 7.

Tisha: Product Manufacturing Jobs, Early 2000s, Milwaukee

In the late 1990s, 33-year-old Tisha was a Latina high school dropout, who later achieved her high school diploma, and the mother of two teenagers and a preteen. Participation in a weeklong workforce development manufacturing training program enabled her to obtain a union position as an assembler in a manufacturing company (Product Manufacturing Company [PMC]) that made propane gas tanks for small appliances. As an assembler, Tisha characteristically worked with schematics and blueprints, used hand tools or machines to assemble parts, conducted quality control checks as she went along, and worked with others in product development. Most of Tisha's job tasks were replaced by robots by 2010.

Before this job, Tisha only had "odd jobs and I took a job and I would keep a job two weeks and it wasn't paying enough money." In an earlier full-time, three-month cashier position, for example, she earned $6.25 an hour with no benefits ($9.96 in 2021 dollars). By the early 2000s, however, Tisha had worked full-time for PMC for more than a year. She described her work pathway with details that illustrate both remnants of the "old social contract" of the 1970s (Kochan and Dyer 2017), that include on-the-job advancement training and long-term job stability, and the scheduling and

---

2. See the Appendix for descriptions of the studies.

mobility challenges that have become so problematic for so many workers today:

I moved around that factory so fast. When I first started, I started at something minor and then my supervisor came and asked me to do something harder. I said, "I don't know but I will try," and he moved me around and I guess I moved fast. I got higher in my pay now and so I am always asking, "Is there anything open, is there anything else you want me to do or try?" I think there is still more there. There was an assistant supervisor position open but I didn't feel confident about it yet, so I didn't apply. I was kind of scared a little bit and I know a lot of people had seniority, but a girl that started there a year after I did, she got a higher position.

The factory makes propane canisters. We fill the canisters, so we have had bomb threats. For Y2K, a shorthand term for the year 2000, we had an order out of this world. We were working overtime every weekend, but now I've slowed down a little bit. I work third shift, 10:30 P.M. to 6:30 A.M. I like it. Well, I worked second shift for a while [2:30 P.M. to 10:30 P.M. and then I went to third shift, but I am not a morning person (which would be first shift, 6:30 A.M. to 2:30 P.M.] Leaving at six in the morning, I tried that for a while, and it didn't work and I went back to second [shift].

At the start, Tisha was paid $7.86 an hour ($12.58 in 2021 dollars), was offered health benefits for her family, and, through union efforts, was offered opportunities for promotions and regular wage increases. In her words, "They offered the best money for you to survive and not to struggle." The security and mobility of the job in the tight labor market of the late 1990s were reminiscent of manufacturing jobs before the 1980s. Three months after she began, Tisha was promoted to the position of cell operator, which is now more commonly called production operator. It involves more aspects of product manufacturing than just assembly and also involves working in a team, which the industry calls a *cell*. As a cell operator, Tisha saw her wage increase to $8.40 per hour and, after a year of employment, Tisha's hourly wage in 2000 was almost $10 ($15.39 in 2021 dollars). As good as her wages seemed, Tisha's annual income for full-time, full-year work was just under $20,738 (in 2000 dollars), only 22% over the federal poverty level of $17,050 for a family of four. That Tisha was earning $14.81 an hour in 2019 dollars and her family was still living close to the federal poverty level also makes us wonder whether today's $15-an-hour minimum wage movement would really enable workers to prosper as they did half a century ago.

When the research team accompanied Tisha to her plant worksite after she had moved to third shift (10:30 P.M. to 6:30 A.M.), it was clear that she was well liked by her coworkers and knew a lot about her manufacturing area. She described the propane gas manufacturing equipment in detail and also noted that she had done several other tasks because it was customary to rotate workers from one machine to the next for cross-training. At the same time, company attendance policies seemed excessively strict. According to a coworker, "Even with a doctor's confirmation that the worker's absence was health related, an employee's absence is counted against them."

In addition to wage increases, even if still not fully sufficient, Tisha was gaining considerable on-the-job supervisory experience through the factory's mentoring program. In fact, she helped to form the program, which was fostered by a partnership between her manufacturing employer and the mentor advisers in the workforce intermediary that sponsored Tisha's preemployment training. This active engagement of multiple actors—preemployment trainers, new workers, and employers—on behalf of new or returning workers is optimal but rare. The quality and ongoing success of a multiactor mentoring program revolve around establishing structures within the firm, such as union workforce education centers, that are accountable to each other and dedicated to a continuing relationship. Measuring the outcomes of its mentor programs, which Tisha's employer did, also helps to sustain the programs. In fact, Tisha's mentor program was found to have saved $2,000 in reduced turnover in the first year of its existence.

INTERVIEWER: How did you get involved in the mentoring program?
TISHA: There was no mentoring program. My supervisor told me I should develop a program because I am friends with everybody at the job and I speak with everybody. Every time somebody has a problem, I am always an ear, and he said, "I think you would be good for that," and I like working with people and I am a people person. We had training in getting along with people, like mediation. It's kind of like peer mediation. There is a meeting every week. This is when I was working second shift, so by me getting off at 10:30 P.M., having meetings afterward meant I didn't get to bed until like 2:00 A.M. The program involved bringing in new people and making them feel comfortable and that is what mentoring is. It is not just a program, it is a pattern, and now they just broke it down to certain individuals, even though everybody else is still friendly.

When Tisha's former training program helped to set up the workplace mentor program at PMC, the employer expected that five to seven people would be interested, but between 30 and 60 showed up at the initial meeting. Even so, a long-time employee expressed a more old-fashioned, industrial-era view about new workers: "Training and pre-training are coddling them." His solution was to "throw 'em into the pool and see if they drown." In contrast, the driving philosophy of the mentoring program, which by early 2000 had been vastly expanded, was that "the key to retaining employees and building a better environment in a facility, whether factory, shop floor, or hotel, is to bring together varied individuals, create good system communication, and recognize the contributions of incumbent workers," according to the founder of the workforce training program.

Tisha's future hopes at PMC revolved around the mentoring program:

> I really do like it. For one thing, the managers get really involved and I like that. They are really good about it. I like to work with people. For the supervisor's job I mentioned before, I thought you needed experience so I didn't apply for it. I wished now that I had. I'd like to find some way to get experience or education or something to help along those lines.

In fact, through the union's outreach and its established workplace education structure, Tisha was engaged both as a peer mentor in the factory and as an inspirational speaker in the community to encourage female youth to consider nontraditional employment. These community efforts were particularly satisfying for Tisha, who felt she had lacked such encouragement as a teen.

By May 2000, however, eighteen months after starting, Tisha was laid off from PMC: "Last week I was laid off, there weren't enough orders. We have had layoffs before, but not so many and not in the same departments." Tisha's layoff was a feature of the general ups and downs of the manufacturing industry and an early sign of the 2001 recession to come. She wasn't sure whether the slowdown was a permanent sign for the company or only temporary. In fact, Tisha was laid off for only one week, but she had to change to first shift, which did not work well with her family responsibilities, and found that "people from our department are bumping people from the stovetop assembly department and everyone is getting pretty nervous and upset about it. Also, we lost our night shift premium, which is an extra 45 cents an hour" (70 cents in 2021 dollars). Today, only about 1 in 10 jobs across all occupations offers extra pay for working specific shifts (Currier, Key, and Sattelmeyer 2016, 5). Tisha also had to turn down inspirational speaking invitations during that period, thus denying community teens her valuable contribution to their thoughts about their futures and satisfying her heartfelt desire to contribute to youth development.

Two months later (July 2000) Tisha was still working at PMC, but since she was still on the daytime shift, she was less enthusiastic about her job than she had been earlier. By September, Tisha expressed additional concern about PMC's precarious position and began to recognize that greater employment stability was a lost cause as the 2001 recession neared and production manufacturers like hers were either closing or moving to just-in-time production:

> I'm trying to escape PMC. There have been a lot of changes. Once you're laid off, your mind starts checking. When you get extended days off, like holidays, you start thinking about somewhere else. I've been there 16 months. As it turned out, after the stockpiling for Y2K, there were a lot of layoffs. So many companies ordered propane that we got overstocked. There were eighty thousand tanks waiting to be shipped. There was a flood in Mississippi—so we had a lot of orders. Then the parent company was bought by Europeans several months ago. The parent company has nine companies. There were new owners. The rules changed—for better and for worse. They got a contract for satellite dishes which led to a lot of overtime, then we lost that contract. The one good thing was that PMC kept the employees informed. Personally, I think that if employers let the employees know the high and low points, it makes them work harder. But I was afraid if there was ever another layoff, since I have such low seniority, I'd lose my job. The whole point of my doing this work is to have stability.

But job stability in the 2000s had become a rare commodity in the manufacturing industry, as in most other industries and occupations populated by lower-earning workers. In October 2000, Tisha reported her new job as a spot welder that she had found on her own: "It's a factory, a day job. It's for Steel Company. I will be earning $10.93 an hour to start" ($16.88 in 2021 dollars), which was an increase over her final wage at PMC. A few days later, Tisha expressed great enthusiasm about the new position: "I love it. I'm working nine and a half hours a day and eight hours on Saturdays. I don't think I'll get burned out. I need the money. You know, when I was at PMC, I was just barely getting by. There was hardly any overtime. That's when I can make the money. Steel Company is not union."

In fact, Steel Company provided a form of pre-1980 stability that Tisha would never experience again. The long hours foreshadowed a regular practice in product manufacturing companies that is common today, requiring existing employees to work long hours and overtime rather than hiring additional employees.

Too soon, Steel Company was actively struggling with the 2001 recession. In April 2001, Tisha reported that company workers were being laid off. The layoffs hadn't hit her yet, but she was concerned. She also wasn't getting much overtime at that point, which made her financial situation particularly stressful. In fact, Tisha survived six company layoffs but anticipated being included in the seventh round, as an alert from her supervisor suggested. Surviving the seventh layoff, Tisha and a friend accepted a speaking invitation, this time to a group of scouts in the greater Milwaukee area. Tisha's talk was persuasive and inspirational, which was evident in her report of the event:

> The talk was to Brownies and Girl Scouts, 3,426 of them! We talked about our jobs, why we liked them, why we picked them. We told them that we picked them partly because we didn't see any women doing our jobs. Their eyes widened open when we said we didn't see women doing it. They wanted to know who was most encouraging to us. Maria [Tisha's 13-year-old daughter] came along too; she handed out pencils.

Still, as is consistent with the national manufacturing scene during times of recession, Tisha was eventually laid off from Steel Company in May 2001. She related the layoff experience with considerable understanding:

> The company hit a brick wall. Everything stopped. No overtime. The first layoffs were mandatory layoffs. The next six were voluntary. The last one I missed by four days. Every two weeks I tell the kids I may be laid off. There's another rumor that more will be laid off next week. Every rumor has been true so far. Our department is new—we're the only people who know the job. All manufacturing companies are experiencing this right now.

Tisha expected to receive unemployment insurance for one year, anticipating that she might remain jobless for that long. As became typical in recessions during the first decade of the 2000s, unemployment after the 2001 recession (which lasted officially from March 2001 to November 2001) was more protracted than had been the case in earlier recessions, starting a trend that grew dramatically after the Great Recession later in the decade. In fact, unemployment after the 2001 recession did not peak until June 2003, about 19 months after the recession technically ended, and was accompanied by a high rate of permanent job separations (Vroman 2005). As one expert reported, "Securing work with a new employer presents challenges for many, but it was especially difficult during 2002–2004, when employment growth was very low" (Vroman 2005, 63). Such challenges often include a loss of earnings that can last several years or more (Jacobson, Lalonde, and Sullivan 1993; Quintini and Venn 2013).

Unemployment compensation after the 2001 recession was extended beyond the usual 26 weeks in March 2002 through the Temporary Extended Unemployment Compensation program (National Employment Law Project 2002). But the extension was phased out in December 2003 (Shapiro 2004), six months after the peak unemployment date and well before the labor market resumed hiring. As noted in Chapter 1, recovery from recessions often takes several years, particularly in an industry such as manufacturing, which by 2000 had lost considerable ground to offshoring and globalization, even in Milwaukee, where manufacturing was stronger and longer lasting than in most other cities. But recovery periods do not last forever.

Tisha had earlier covered her bases by enrolling in a carpentry apprenticeship, and she returned to that commitment after the Steel Company layoff. She had passed the nonunion carpentry apprenticeship test and was proud of the copy of the acceptance letter the nonunion facility had sent her to show to prospective employers. But Tisha had not passed the union test, having passed every part but the spatial mechanics portion. She could retake that portion after a six-month wait, but she would have to take more classes in the interim. She had already begun to look for a nonunion apprenticeship, despite knowing that the wage scale was considerably lower than the union scale: "T&C Electric. I sent an application this week. That's where my friend works. Hopefully they'll call. I'd start at half the journeyman wage, which is $26 to $28. Painters and drywall. The test I took allows me to go into any trade."

Tisha expected her apprenticeship wage would be $13 or $14 an hour, which meant she would not experience a wage drop from her Steel Company job. Nor would she experience a wage increase, which used to happen when workers moved to a new firm, although this pattern was more common among higher-earning workers. In addition, Tisha's income at Steel Company had been $43 above the monthly income eligibility level for food stamps (what the Supplemental Nutrition Assistance Program, SNAP, was called then): "Forty-three dollars can't feed five people! If it wasn't for my boyfriend, I don't know how I would make it food-wise. If I had to do it myself, I'd have to call Mom." Actually, Tisha had lost her previous food stamp allotment of about $234 a month (U.S. Department of Agriculture 2001) after the $43 a month raise, making the policy on food stamps seem like a catch-22 policy at best. In addition, the taxes and insurance fees for her mortgage had increased, even though the mortgage itself was fixed. With these fee increases, policy ceilings, and debt from an early period in cosmetology school, Tisha felt very stressed about her income. Adding to the stress, she was unable to complete the nonunion apprenticeship course because she'd been diagnosed with gout and instructed to stay off her feet.

Six months later, in October 2001, with the country in the throes of recession, Tisha was working in retail as an assistant manager in a clothing store, an outcome consistent with the likelihood that "workers who find new full-time employment on average experience significantly decreased earnings relative to what they earned before they lost employment" (Whittaker and Isaacs 2013, 1). Tisha found herself in the same situation when she obtained a position at Brass Company, a metal fixtures manufacturer, in March 2002. Her hourly wage of $9.80 ($14.50 in 2021 dollars) was $2.29 an hour less than her wage at Steel Company a year earlier and less than $2 above her starting wage at PMC, her first job almost five years earlier. As the aftermath of the recession wore on, Tisha's employment and financial situation got even worse. Sometime between April 2002 and April 2003, Tisha lost her house. To make ends come even close to meeting, she substituted for a friend part-time as a bartender for three months. Food stamps and the limited health insurance for those eligible for food stamps were the only work supports she was eligible for, since a brush with the law years earlier left her ineligible to apply for housing assistance.

In late 2003, Tisha was still working at Brass Company for $9.80 an hour, which meant she had not received a raise in more than 18 months. She was also about to receive a "Justice Award of Honor" from a community justice center in Milwaukee that is "an interfaith nonprofit agency working with victims, offenders, and the community to achieve a system of criminal justice that is fair and treats every person involved with dignity and respect," in the words of the center's website. Tisha's award was given for her "personal achievement in volunteer work with the Women's Harm Reduction Program." She had been coleading workshops that focused on reading, mathematics, General Educational Development (GED) attainment, and arts and crafts instruction, which she felt supported and encouraged participants to develop achievable life goals. Tisha felt very honored to receive the award: "I'm so excited. A television station will be there and everything." In terms of *real* opportunity, Tisha's service work, including her inspirational youth work, could be extremely valuable as civil labor that, if compensated, could buffer the negative influences of recession and industry change on the manufacturing career she also relished.

Construction Jobs: Joseph and Randy

The construction industry has suffered more business-cycle employment fluctuation over the past 40-plus years (Goodrum and Gangwar 2004) than the manufacturing industry has, but simultaneously it has experienced lower productivity (Teicholz 2015). Another feature of the construction industry in many states is its historical exclusion of African American workers, although access and share of employment vary by state and locality and are higher in union than in nonunion firms (Mishel 2013; Iversen and Armstrong 2006). At the same time, the construction industry has been historically a pipeline to middle incomes for workers without postsecondary education, which made it a favorite of people who enrolled in workforce development programs in many U.S. cities at the beginning of the twenty-first century, as the stories of Joseph and Randy will illustrate.

Joseph: Construction Industry Jobs, Early 2000s, New Orleans

A 23-year-old African American married father of two, Joseph participated in a workforce development program in New Orleans in the early 2000s to realize his dream of entering the construction industry and eventually having his own construction business. Joseph grew up in a public housing community in New Orleans, where its after-school learning programs helped to counterbalance the poor quality of his neighborhood schools. As a teen, Joseph had active mentors at the housing community's youth center, and they helped him develop both hope and a tangible direction for his desire to escape intergenerational poverty, as he explained:

> The youth center was developed for the housing development as an after-school learning center where you could also learn about your culture. They had study programs on the African man and African history, and they also had a free enterprise class; that's why I was at the center. The leader was my star and my role model; he taught us how to be leaders. He took our minds way further than where they was at, and the whole mission was just to help others. You didn't want to go home after school because you knew what was at home, so you came straight to the youth center. The struggles in the project were just sickening, the poverty and the schools, you just got tired of going to school the next day and you just wanted to get away. That's why I'm glad we had the youth center; you could stay away [from the difficulties] longer.

The youth center programs also provided Joseph with a foundation for his spirited church involvement and community commitments, as well as his vision of becoming a successful carpenter with his own business. A pathway to the historically discriminatory construction industry in New Orleans (Keegan 2020) that his workforce program offered was thus extremely appealing to Joseph: "I never was an indoor person. I couldn't stand to be inside. I had to be out in the open. In construction, you get to see everything. When I was in other jobs, I was just missing the whole world. With doing construction, I wake up happy, I wake up excited."

The 12-week workforce program reinforced Joseph's already well-developed motivation for working in the construction field. He hoped that the one-month postprogram training in construction methods provided by the work-force program's local community college partner would lead to a formal construction apprenticeship. The college training was a generic, preapprenticeship type of course that included instruction in carpentry, painting, and electrical and masonry work.

Despite feeling that the quality of his training was excellent, Joseph felt his union apprenticeship placement was extremely disappointing and even exploitive. A training program source reported that Joseph had been required to pay extravagant union dues up front, just to be placed on an "out of work" list. After waiting for weeks, the one job he was given was to set up bleachers and display tables at a convention center. Worse, the actual assignment was to pick up garbage for an entire day, as Joseph described with distress: "I did not go to all this training and take two months out of my life [without any pay] so that I could go pick up trash." A workforce program administrator confirmed that it was typical for graduates not to receive immediate placement in the construction field after they had completed training—to some extent, the administrator said, because the insufficient public transportation in New Orleans made it difficult for new workers to travel great distances to worksites. The lack of placement was also commonly thought to be a result of the post-9/11 economic downturn in the industry. A local construction expert, however, offered an alternative explanation, a view that is even more commonly held today: "You see new buildings, but they are in certain phases. Since 9/11, builders use this as an excuse to slow down. So do financial institutions backing the projects. For example, one local building had a large hotel contract that was supposed to start March 2002. It's on hold for a year. The contract will likely fail to come through."

Sherman, a white apprentice and local college graduate who tried to access a carpentry position, also recounted his experiences in the complex construction world of New Orleans. Sherman provided a similar perspective on the carpenters' union to that of the workforce program administrator, with details about the expenses Joseph had likely faced when he joined: "I joined the carpenters' union local as an apprentice in late August, early September 2001. I was required to pay three months of dues in advance [$90–$129 in 2021 dollars], buy a workbook [$21–$29 in 2021 dollars], buy a number of tools [approximately $312–$444 in 2021 dollars], and encouraged to get a cell phone." By 2020, construction companies required workers, including carpenters, to buy and use cell phones, simultaneously warning them about the dangers of distraction on the job (Selbst and Ticona 2017).

Sherman also spoke in detail about what being a new union member entailed and what the union's view of carpentry actually was, shedding more light on Joseph's situation:

> Upon joining the union one's name is put on the "out-of-work list" and he or she will be contacted when work becomes available. Most of the jobs to come up were at the convention center setting up or dismantling for trade shows and conventions. One of the contracted decorating companies will call the union and request a number of workers. The union then contacts members from the out-of-work list and gives them a time to report to the center. The carpenter must get a work slip from the union hall before proceeding to the convention center. Setup work might include putting up pole-and-curtain partitions, laying carpet, setting up lighting, unloading tractor-trailers, assembling display booths or setting up folding tables with plastic covers and colored cloth skirts. Dismantling would involve the inverse actions. A shift might be four and a half hours long. Apparently there are about 100 union members who make 40 hours a week or more at the center. All other workers essentially work part time, except during sporadically busy periods. The work at the convention center is essentially stagehand work, not carpentry. Aside from convention center work, the union has contracts with companies involved in heavy construction, but the jobs become available infrequently, even though, when they do, they are full time. There is little or no work in the light construction [home building] sector.

In contrast, the carpenters' union website describes the types of jobs done by carpenters as follows: "Carpenters measure, saw, level and nail wood along with other building materials. They install tile, insulation, acoustical ceilings, cabinets, siding and much more. They work with many tools and materials to build houses, schools, churches and hotels. They erect skyscrapers, hospitals, office buildings and prisons. They construct bridges, tunnels and highways. Carpenters make up the largest group of skilled workers in the country" (New Orleans Carpenters Union 2016).

But neither Joseph nor Sherman nor other construction hopefuls in New Orleans whom we interviewed were called on to use capabilities or perform tasks such as those in the job description on the carpenters' union website, regardless of how long they had been union members, and some had belonged for more than five years. Sherman's experience was the most common we encountered and was replicated in our research interviews in Milwaukee, Seattle, Philadelphia, and St. Louis, even years afterward.

After Joseph's unsatisfying initiation into the union apprenticeship program, he left both the workforce program and the community college training system. He then took a food service and informal construction job at a downtown hotel (see further in Chapter 5). A year later, Joseph left the hotel for a construction position with an informal construction company, Church Construction Company (CCC), run by members of his church.

As was consistent with the church mission, the construction company was oriented to property development and redevelopment, a mission Joseph fully appreciated. Over time, he learned about a number of building trades from various church members involved in construction, which was similar to a formal union apprenticeship but with a societal rather than a profit-dominant orientation. His initial CCC mentor, George, who held a state mechanical license for air conditioning, heating, and ventilation; a builder's license; and a building construction license, helped Joseph expand his portfolio, as Joseph explained:

> I'm working with one guy, he's in air conditioning. I help him work on his own house for now until something else comes up. Really, I do this to jump to my own construction business, and he's just assisting me until I get on my feet. My first [independent] business job was when he called and asked me to do this, so I want to keep that and make my name known. That's why I want to do the job right, because I really want to start my own career, my own construction company. . . . I'm the first person in my family that started my own business. I feel like a man now, and I know I'm gifted.

George, Joseph's CCC mentor, first described his impetus for working with Joseph and with other young men at the church as a way to "provide them entrepreneurial working opportunities." George was impressed with Joseph's diligence, noting that "he took the identity of carpentry with such fervor that he would work into the night and literally not take off the work clothes to sleep." George himself had learned carpentry through his father, who was "a bus driver but did electrical work on the side. The side jobs pulled our family through the 1978–1980 bus strike." While in a formal job situation Joseph would earn an hourly wage, under George's tutelage he received a weekly wage regardless of the number of hours he worked, as George explained.

> GEORGE: I started Joseph out at $250 a week [$365 in 2021 dollars] and just brought him up to $300 a week [$444 in 2021 dollars] a few weeks ago. It's not about how much time is spent on the worksite, but about profitability. It is about performance, not re-

sults, and not being on an hourly mentality is the first step. Joseph's next step is to work at a subcontractor level, naming a price for his own work. In order to keep workers like Joseph on a lower weekly salary and on track for completion, I give them bonuses.

INTERVIEWER: Benefits?

GEORGE: No, unfortunately, I would have to pay for it out of my own pocket. Benefits will come when they can be paid for.

A later conversation with the church pastor revealed that George's payment philosophy was consistent with that of other mentors at the church, including the pastor himself, who spoke of the longer-run need to prioritize experience and learning over money for new trainees.

Joseph's passion and diligence were evident on the several tours he conducted of projects that ranged from "completed" to "in progress" to "visionary." One site visit featured a house that had originally consisted of three rooms but had now doubled in size. The walls were torn down and the new floor plan included three bedrooms, an office, a big living room, a utility room for laundry, and a den-kitchen combination. The walls were nicely floated, meaning constructed to shift slightly when the floor or ceiling within the space expands or contracts, and freshly painted. Joseph proudly went through the details of his accomplishments:

What I have to do right here, we had an electrical inspection and we failed. The reason was because they had to have a fixture outlet up here [pointing to wall]. I had to make this electrical connection here using this wire to hook in this one, which goes into the house, bring it back, and come out on this side. They'll come back to reinspect it on Monday. Over here, this is the sink and we got the countertops there, and this is the first bedroom right here. This is going to be carpet, and this right here is going to be a bathroom that is almost finished; we just have to get back and put the toilets in. This is the master bedroom, I just built this, and right here there used to be a wall [that we took out]. So, I just hang Sheetrock and built this bedroom and then painted it, and they'll come back and do little touch-ups, like adding the little shelves.

While extremely valuable for Joseph's carpentry skill development, the informal relationship he had with George and the CCC also constrained Joseph's income and job security. Because George's payment philosophy was to pay by the profitability of the job, not by the hour, the jobs in which Joseph participated during the first year of their partnership in 2002 yielded an annual income of about $9,000 ($13,292 in 2021 dollars), which was well below

the poverty level of $15,020 in 2002 for his family of three. Even more prob-
lematic, because Joseph was paid under the table, he could not access work
supports such as the earned income tax credit because eligibility required
official income statements. This left the family in an even more precarious
financial position. Nevertheless, the network of contracting connections Joseph was making was right in line with his dream for the CCC, which he
envisioned as a self-sustaining group or internal partnership: "The Church
Company will be a group. Like my best friend next door, he's in the real estate
so whatever house he gets, I'll get a call. Then we have the air conditioner
contractor [who can connect us to work also], and we've got somebody to do
Sheetrock too, so, when our contract is out, I'll know who to call. You can say
it's a partnership; it's really like a circle partnership." Being in a group, rather
than being a single licensed contractor, would also enable Joseph to share the
$10,000 cost of materials, such as a van and tools, that licensure requires.

Over time, however, Joseph saw that his goal of being a licensed contractor and owning a business was pushed further into the future than he originally expected, although he also saw that he could add to his capabilities as
he worked toward the goal. Therefore, he added proficiency in "installation
of ceramic tiles, installation of vinyl floors and vinyl siding, trim work, add-
ons, pouring concrete, and electrical work," which he acquired through the
apprentice-like relationship with George. Moving toward establishing a
business, though, is a significantly larger step that often is not supported by
the business community or knowledgeable mentors. Fortunately for Joseph,
such was not the case in New Orleans.

A year later, in 2003, Joseph enrolled in a 12-week entrepreneurship
class run by the University of New Orleans to learn about the various aspects of running a business. He found the class enormously stimulating and
helpful: "It's like 20, 25 people, so you're seeing all kinds of interesting stuff
about going on with their businesses. I make sure I don't make their mis-
takes. They have homework; you write up business plans." The class included a valuable individual development account voucher plan, funded by an
area nonprofit that partnered with the University, which matched the participant's savings four to one and was designated solely for tools and materials that
would help establish the business. As Joseph explained, "OK, I have my $1,000,
then they match the $4,000, and that's as far as you can go. I can't go in there
and just get cash. If I want to purchase a tool, I just tell them the price of the
tool and they give me a voucher, so I go with that voucher to Supply Store."

Several years later, Joseph's enthusiasm for carpentry and construction
remained strong, as he indicated during another worksite visit:

It's something that's gonna last, just like the bookstore at the church
[which he helped to build]. You gotta pass that every day. Then you

start getting a personal touch and people say, this is what I want you to do, like I had to do right there. I had to patch up holes. That's why I got that Sheetrock over there. I had to patch that. It's fun, man. You're on your own. You ain't got nobody on your back. You're doing a good deed. It looks beautiful. It really lights you up, you know.

To some extent, Joseph's experiences illustrate how a workforce development program can help a person like Joseph find a career direction: "I finally found out what was my destiny. I found out what I was finally called to do, so I started giving myself a pledge, this is what I want to do, this is what I want to require myself as being this new character. That was the door opening. Like I said, even though I didn't get the job [apprenticeship], it still made me realize who I am. No matter what you do, do it as your business."

At the same time, one of the main dilemmas posed by industry-sector-based workforce programs is their market volatility. In Seattle, for example, the workforce program and a major company partnered to teach participants computerized numerical control machine tool operation, which the partnership did very effectively. By the end of the program, however, in conjunction with the 2001 recession, neither the partner company nor other similar companies needed more numerical control-trained operators. Thus, no positions were available for those who were promised employment.

Likewise, in Joseph's case, the construction industry also constricted in the early 2000s and did not return until after Hurricane Katrina in 2005–2006. But, at that point, the industry became populated predominantly by experienced white and Hispanic construction workers from other southern states who saw opportunity in New Orleans, which meant there was little room for construction learners in New Orleans. In addition, Joseph's problems with the carpentry union apprenticeship suggest that it would be helpful if workforce programs could establish in advance that particular labor unions provide real paths for worker advancement. Unions are perhaps the only institution in society that has been able to procure a livable wage with a family benefits package for entry-level workers. While union membership may also involve challenges and idiosyncrasies, such as the type of hazing practices Joseph experienced during the convention center trash pickup, the CCC alternative to a union position did not offer a structured path to state contractor licensure, which was Joseph's goal. Worse, when we visited New Orleans five months after Katrina, Joseph and his family could not be located.

Another visit to Joseph's former address in 2017 revealed that the house had been completely removed. No building stood on the site. Joseph's downtown church also was still abandoned and empty and no one at the branch church in the New Orleans suburbs knew anything about CCC or Joseph.

Although Joseph found it impossible to afford the business training he would need to be self-employed, it is not clear that the union organization would have provided training superior to what he received at CCC. What the union could have given him, though, was a formal stamp of approval and licensure in a highly regulated occupation. The union's long-standing racial discrimination and hazing-like practices, however, led many workers, like Joseph, to reject the union path to a construction career. Short of that, the opportunity to partner with others in his church company, many of whom had achieved licenses, might also have proven satisfying in the event that Joseph could not find a path to self-employment.

Randy: Construction Industry Jobs, Early 2000s, Milwaukee

Coming from a past of significant academic, student government, and sports achievement in his African homeland where his father served as village chief, Randy emigrated to the United States in the late 1980s with high hopes of pursuing a professional career in medicine or law. Subsequently, however, his goals were constrained by policy limitations, financial responsibilities he faced as a sole family earner with a wife and two elementary-school-age children, and workforce programs oriented to task-specific industries. Even so, by the time the research team met Randy in January 2000, he was 40 years old and had developed appreciable expertise in the construction field. He also had contributed notably to his African cultural community in Milwaukee and the surrounding area.

Before coming to the United States, Randy had earned a bachelor of science degree with honors in plant biology in his African homeland. Two theses written in English were required for his degree, and he had taught mathematics in English during his post-BS national service year. Both accomplishments were evidence of considerable English proficiency, yet Randy's construction job foreman in Milwaukee said initially, "I have trouble understanding Randy, trouble with language."

Randy had first come to the United States to visit his brother and then stayed, partly because of the political unrest in his home country and partly for the greater professional opportunity he perceived in the United States. He first tried to get a research job in his field of botany but was not able to obtain one. He thought the reason was the policy challenges endemic to U.S. education equivalency-translation services, which often do not translate equivalently:

> I'd have liked to have pursued a master's degree or a Ph.D. America is not hospitable to foreigners. Even if you graduate from college, it's hard for everyone to find a job. The big problem with foreign

education was looking for a job. Employers [in Wisconsin] recognize foreign education but find it difficult to hire you. They prefer U.S.-based college. They hire you because of the ties.

This statement on the website of one translation service seems to confirm Randy's concern about grade translation: *"Due to the differences between U.S. and foreign education systems, the evaluations do not necessarily equal the same number of credits, years of study, grades and degrees/titles granted in the original country"* (Academic Evaluation Services, Inc. 2020).

Confronted by grade translation challenges and absence of network ties, Randy initially settled for work in maintenance management and, for the next nine and a half years, held the position of senior maintenance technician, where he did "electrical work, carpentry, and all kinds of maintenance" in various settings, most recently in a furniture and appliance store. Considering his family's high-status background in Africa, the occupational barriers in the United States were humbling and frustrating. Jones-Correa (1998) highlighted a similar phenomenon in his discussion of the social dynamics of immigrants accepting host country positions that are lower in status than the positions they held in their country of origin. In fact, the immigrants and refugees in the research studies represented in this book all experienced a similar disjuncture between their homeland status and their immigrant status.

Never one to give up, Randy enrolled in a construction-oriented workforce program in Milwaukee in January 2000, noting that his sole goal was to get a job, which he did very quickly. His more general goals were oriented both to professional development and to family well-being: "Better condition of life—own a house, be my own boss. I want the kids to have the best education, live an upright life, and make good decisions."

For the past 20 years, the construction industry in Milwaukee has been up and down. Recently, construction employment began to slow in 2018 and was projected to slow further in the 2020s (Wisconsin Department of Revenue 2019). In the Milwaukee of 2000, however, the construction market was considered good because the industry had a shortage of trained workers. There were also barriers to construction work for some individuals. An employment specialist at Randy's workforce program said that "the construction industry relies heavily on social networks for recruiting employees, the 'good old boy network,' and was systematically racist in its employment practices." An African American woman in Randy's program who was employed as a material handler and trying for an apprenticeship in sheet metal also mentioned racism: "The boss told me I might be laid off. That's messing with my head. They don't want to see people of color in the trades. A lot of racism. I will pass that test, no matter what." In the early 2000s, racism and racial incidents associated with the construction industry also occurred in other cities (Iversen and Armstrong 2006).

In Milwaukee, Randy was encouraged to make use of the workforce program's learner center to seek an apprenticeship, which he did. The technical development possible there was noteworthy, the program head said:

> The learner center lab is staffed by a local technical college teacher who is also funded by the college. They do GED training and pre-apprenticeship training. It's self-paced. The teacher is there for advice, direction, and practice. They deal with basic math, reading, writing, algebra, geometry, spatial relations, and mechanical reasoning, all required for the pre-apprenticeship test. The apprenticeship test is a seven-part test in the same categories. To take the test an individual must (1) have a driver's license, (2) have a car, (3) have a GED or high school diploma, and (4) must take the seven-part test. Not all parts apply to all trades.

Randy signed up to take Joint Apprenticeship and Training for the Electrical Industry. Even though an apprenticeship would be financially difficult, for him as for other lower earners, he was confident that his solid educational history in his home country would enable him to pass:

> I signed up in January to take the test in March. March 8 test is for all January applicants. You can only apply the third Monday of the month. The application process is as follows: (1) you sign up for the test, (2) you take the test at the JAT office [some distance from Randy's home], (3) you have interviews, (4) if accepted, after the test and the interviews, you work at an electrical firm for three days a week and have paid school two days a week. They pay for both, plus benefits. But I'll be making less money than now. [Randy was making $16.40 an hour—about $25 in 2021 dollars—at his construction job.] In the first year of apprenticeship, I would make $9.71 an hour [$15 in 2021 dollars]. Every thousand hours, which is about six months of full-time work, I would earn more. As a journeyman in four to five years, I would make a little over $24 [in 2004 dollars; $40 in 2021 dollars]. I can't understand why they wouldn't accept me.

But Randy had virtually no knowledge about test taking in the United States, and so he came close but did not pass the test. He had answered the hard questions first, leaving the easy questions until last, but ran out of time and was unable to complete the test. He scored a 4 on the test, but a 5 was required for apprenticeship eligibility. He felt he would easily have passed if he'd read the whole test first, but he didn't know that was the better strategy. It seems that practice in U.S. test-taking strategies, particularly for immigrants, might be a very useful part of workforce training, especially in places like Milwaukee where city contracts require contractors to hire a certain percentage of "disadvantaged workers."

Although Randy was eligible to repeat the test, he was also very concerned about the low apprenticeship wages, which were clearly oriented to young single men for the most part, rather than to older persons with work experience and family responsibilities. Randy's long-term professional goals were also a constraint. He wanted to get master's and Ph.D. degrees, or possibly a law degree, but if he went to school full-time, he would not be able to support his children. As a result, Randy opted out of further apprenticeship training. A workforce program specialist said that out of about 220 individuals in its short, one-week construction training program and its longer-term learner center program, only around 10 or 15 had gone on for apprenticeships. The opportunity cost of apprenticeship training was obviously too high for most, as Randy's situation exemplifies. Nevertheless, the workforce program did enable Randy to obtain a laborer position in a unionized construction company that offered him a better schedule than his previous maintenance work had, even if slightly less annual income: $32,800 ($51,000 in 2021 dollars) versus $37,000 ($57,000 in 2021 dollars), which had included $10,000 in overtime.

Randy was considered a stellar example of a construction trainee by both the workforce program's employment specialist and jobsite supervisor. Randy survived numerous company layoffs and learned new competencies, as we observed, largely on his own without complaint or sense of entitlement:

> But you know when you take a job you don't get to choose what you do. If you don't want to do something or if you don't know how to do it, you just figure it out. If you can't figure it out, you ask questions. Like today, I had to tear down this wall and a ceiling. I had to build a kind of bridge [a scaffold] to get the job done. I had to use a jackhammer to tear everything down. It was hard. I had to figure out how to do it. I had never done that before. Now I know how and the next time it will be easier. I don't understand why people get a job and think they are not supposed to work. Work is hard, but that is how it is supposed to be.

After Randy spent about six months on a job demolishing a downtown department store and contending with asbestos-filled air without a safety mask or guidance, his supervisor invited him to do office work instead of manual work. This involved "daily logs and inventories and paperwork for all kinds of things," according to Randy, though neither his job title nor his wages changed as a result: "Paperwork is a privilege, but I don't get extra money for it." Randy did get regular raises, which would top out at $21.10 an hour ($32 in 2021 dollars), but the important change was eligibility for union health insurance coverage.

Nevertheless, despite the benefits and learning new competencies in the union construction company, Randy continued to have professional goals: "I want a career, not just a job. I want a career, like law. I was a science major but I was good at social science, too. My boss is mad at me when I talk about law." Randy's boss actually encouraged him to pursue civil engineering and the workforce program specialist pressed Randy toward the path of electrical apprenticeship. Randy remained torn about his work in the future:

My original aim in the United States was to go to medical school. But it was going to take too long. Since I got this job, I've thought about civil engineering. But any studies I do, my family will suffer. Even if my wife works, she can't earn enough to carry us. If I go to school for four years, which would be the minimum for civil engineering, that would be a lot of years. Local University gave me law school admission a year ago—I went to some seminars. I'm thinking about doing that. It's shorter than an apprenticeship.

Without knowledgeable counseling about professional career opportunities for immigrants, many of whom, like Randy, leave their home countries without valuable papers such as graduation certificates and university transcripts, Randy concluded that he could not commit to pursuing his true goals. Instead, he decided to try to advance into a higher position in the construction industry.

Consequently, Randy ended up accepting his boss's invitation to join him at the boss's new construction company, where he earned a higher wage and felt that his work capabilities were appreciated and valued. His union membership carried over, and so his health benefits continued. But when the research team tried to contact Randy and his family in April 2003, we were unable to locate them. We learned from a former staff member of Randy's workforce program, which had closed down, that the boss's construction company had also closed down in the aftermath of the 2001 recession. Possibly the family returned to Africa or moved to somewhere else in Wisconsin, both of which they had talked about doing earlier. In the absence of knowledgeable career counseling, it is unlikely that Randy was in school pursuing law or medicine. And if he remained in construction, where he was very competent but not following his desired career path, he was likely not making much progress in wages or capabilities because of the declining state of the industry.

Clearly, if a worker survives the union apprenticeship regimen, a vertical employment ladder is still available in the construction industry. But if racism, lack of belonging to a network, and lack of money preclude that path, employment security in today's construction industry is tenuous and unpredictable, as Randy's, Joseph's, and many others' experiences demonstrate (Iversen and Armstrong 2006). Randy's construction program mentor contended that "if Randy can't make it, nobody can." As his story shows, the larger, more precarious environment of the construction industry is likely to take a toll on all construction workers, even those as competent as Randy.

The toll on Randy, however, was mediated by his passion for African music and dance, which he taught in his children's elementary school as a community service. The entire school community applauded this enrichment and wanted him to do more of it. If a program sustained by foundation or community funding, such as compensated civil labor, were instituted (see Chapter 7), allowing Randy to be paid for three-quarters-time work at construction and one-quarter-time at the school, his African music and dance teaching would benefit the children and the community and Randy might more easily weather the ups and downs of the construction industry.

Kevin, Printing Industry Jobs, Early 2000s, Milwaukee

The final story about how today's manufacturing, construction, and printing industry jobs affect real opportunity is that of Kevin, a 29-year-old African American man living in Milwaukee with his fiancée and their three children, ages three to six. Kevin's story centers on the multiyear pathway to promotion in the printing industry, influenced by the industrywide decline in occupations and major technological changes during the 2000s (Stowe 2015). His story also illustrates how other aspects of the labor market intersected and confounded his printing career goals: in particular, the rise of the dual-earner family and workplace policies that were inhospitable to families.

Many tasks done today by individuals at their computers used to be done by printing professionals and businesses. The printing industry for which Kevin was trained and that he entered in the early 2000s illustrates the beginning of the downward trend. At that time, the printing industry had about 710,000 wage and salary jobs, in addition to 33,000 self-employed workers. But the industry and its related support establishments as a whole were projected to grow only 3.3% over the next ten years (to 2012) as compared with a projected 16% growth of the economy as a whole (MyPlan.com 2004). A printing industry workforce program administrator explained that only 20% of the industry was unionized in the mid-1990s, down from a much larger percentage in prior decades. If Kevin had elected to remain in the industry through the two economic recessions between 2000 and 2010, he would have experienced the mid-2000s as the high-water mark of the industry, not seen since then (Vruno 2016). Job descriptions in 2016 were supportive of this analysis, as wages for many printing positions had decreased from an average of $16 to $17 an hour in 2010 (BLS 2011) to around $10 to $13 an hour in 2016, and projections for all but the largest establishments suggested that wages would remain near the 2010 level at least into 2020 (BLS 2020b).

Back in 1999, though, the eight-week, full-time printing workforce program, the Printing Project, that placed Kevin in the industry gave him a second chance—after prison and two postprison years of low-wage, dead-end jobs—to develop career-relevant capabilities that would continue to benefit him in later pursuits. At the same time, other labor market struggles persisted, affecting Kevin's career success, as his story will show.

Kevin was initially skeptical about training programs. He'd previously completed a plumbing apprenticeship, after which, as with Joseph's construction apprenticeship experience, he did not receive the tools he needed to find a job or learn about a network of potential employers:

> I was in a plumbing course before the Printing Project. It was different from this one. You had to go to look for a job yourself. If there had been more help job searching—like this program [the Printing Project]—it would have been a nice program. At the time, I didn't know what I was looking for. I didn't have my driver's license. I was a felon, and that was looked at negatively. I was into the program, the classes, and figured they'd help me find a job. We were a team. I was thrown for a loop when they didn't. I never went for the final aptitude test at the local union. We were supposed to take it together. But the teacher left. If people would have sent us to meet Bob, Joe, Lou, it would have helped. Like the Printing Project program did.

Kevin also felt that programs such as the Printing Project should be more widely publicized in the community, noting that "when I grew up, for Blacks and Latinos, there were only two things pumped, college and armed forces." Kevin suggested that a broader outreach effort should be made and notices posted in many places:

> KEVIN: High schools, newspaper, community center, like the center near here. Post it up. People don't get good information; we only got good information when we were in prison. Visit halfway

houses. Put it on TV. The only ads on TV are for military or college. This limits a person's choices. They don't hear about apprenticeships.

INTERVIEWER: Would you have done an apprenticeship if you'd known about it?

KEVIN: I probably would have done it. I don't mind going to school, but I'm not a college-bound type of person. I tried it, but I was discouraged. If you're not good at school, then what?! You don't feel like there are any options.

The focus of Kevin's eight-week printing program in 1999 was on printing as a career—ironically on the eve of the sustained industry downturn in both number of jobs and available firms. The Printing Project manager characterized the printing industry's position in 2000 as caught between the old and the new, emphasizing the industry change, such as more racially diverse workers and many more two-parent working families, accompanied by uncertainty about what lay ahead:

Printing establishments want to replace retirees with individuals who come all the time, no matter what, just like the retirees did—for example, come when baby is born—but those patterns are gone. This was considered a success—but at what price? Children didn't know their fathers. Employers want to reinvent a glory day that doesn't exist anymore.

Even so, the Printing Project's network and prior arrangement with an employer enabled Kevin to begin work after the eight-week program in April 1999 as a floor person in Elite Bindery's pressroom, where he earned $9.76 an hour ($15 in 2021 dollars) with full nonwage benefits. The Printing Project staff, however, warned Kevin that advancement was unlikely at that facility. After five months there, Kevin felt the need to look beyond Elite Bindery for an establishment that would help him advance his career. Even though printing employers expect employees to stay with one employer, Printing Project staff connected Kevin with Printing & Bindery in September 1999, which was more of a full-service printing company. Although Printing & Bindery was a lateral move in terms of wages, Kevin saw it as a union position with room for advancement, including further education:

There's room to move around. You're not stuck in tunnels. I could even move to an advertising agency to check colors, do desktop publishing. It's not a dead end. At a bindery you can only do so much—there's a fixed number of machines. Now I also go to school through my worksite. I work on different machines. It pays about the same, but I can do a lot more. The road to a higher position is floor person (my job now), jogger, roll tender, compensator, second pressman, first pressman, and foreman.

A visit to Kevin's s jobsite in early 2000 began at the paper-rolling point in the process of publications. Kevin described this as "not the first step, but the step at which you can see the paper being printed with a variety of colors." As a floor person, Kevin picked up stray rags and paper littered on the floor and put them in their proper place, noting that "they are getting the magazines ready to be shipped. Mostly women work in here, where it isn't so heavy or hard to work. Only two women work in the area where I do. Here, I'll show you how this works. The machine starts right here. These are the containers of ink. They are measured out here. We have to watch them to see when they are low. Sometimes the paper comes out without ink, then we have to throw it all out."

Kevin's attention to detail drew this comment from one of the supervisors: "We'd like to clone him!" Hearing about the "clone" comment, Kevin said, "Yeah, a lot of people don't take their work too seriously, so they're glad when somebody does. Someday I want to own my own business, and I think about having people work for me. I want someone who will show up and not just always call in, you know what I mean?"

Six months later, Kevin was promoted to jogger at Printing & Bindery, which paid $10.61 an hour plus a 90-cent bonus for working the third shift for a total of $11.51 an hour ($18 in 2021 dollars). The position description for jogger specified the tasks of jogging as working with a vibrating machine that evens up stacks of printed materials, folder tending, and make-ready assistance. All are necessary for the quality operation of web offset printing. Kevin chose to work third shift there (11:00 P.M. to 8:00 A.M.) because he was in a dual-earner family in which a parent needed to be available at home at all times: "Third shift works good with my family—that's why I work it. I get tired of it sometimes, but third shift saves me and Lynn a lot of stress. If kids need to go to the dentist, be picked up at school, are sick, we don't have to worry about getting them, taking off from work. I may be tired at night when I go to work, but not often."

Kevin's supervisor even commented on Kevin's heavy load of work and family responsibilities: "I do not know when he sleeps." The comment is reminiscent of Arlie Hochschild's (1997) revelations about the "double shifts" that resulted from the increase in dual-earner families. Kevin was fortunate in that any fatigue he may have felt did not result in workplace injury—at least not yet.

Kevin also valued being part of a team at Printing & Bindery. There were many learning opportunities and there was a supportive environment.

> KEVIN: The workforce network that my printing program was affiliated with made it easier. In my new position as jogger—I'm motivated at work. You work as a team on the press: two joggers, a compensator, roll tender, first and second pressmen. We work together to keep the press running or get it started back running. The press I'm on, these are people I don't mind working with.
>
> INTERVIEWER: What makes them "people you don't mind working with"?
>
> KEVIN: Two reasons. One, they're all older, some 20 or 30 years or so. I love that. I like to work with older people. I'm 29; the youngest is 34 and the oldest is 52. They have more experience. I respect them more—they put in the work. Two, they're more serious. They laugh and joke, but they know a lot. I learn from them. I hope we stay a team.

In fact, Printing & Bindery was ahead of many other printing establishments in its emphasis on adaptability, innovation, and improvement, characteristics seen today as critical for printing industry survival (Lynn 2012). To that end, Kevin attended three-hour printing classes for jogger and press operator at the Printing Project after his shift, which meant working for 12 hours straight, from 11:00 P.M. to 11:00 A.M. After he completed his press operator class, he hoped to take computer classes. The project manager reported that "Kevin did really well in the operator class," and Kevin seemed to view the union-related advancement training policy as his golden opportunity:

> You can really get ahead in this business. There is a lot of opportunity to do that. You can just keep moving up by taking classes. I don't know if I want to stay in it, but you learn a lot of things that will help. The classes are easy. Except going there after work. I take it upon myself to train, nobody is holding me back. The Printing Project offers more education. I'm getting more knowledge of the printing industry. I'll be ready for the next position.

Although the path to advancement was visible, it was also extremely slow. Kevin knew that his ability to advance was contingent on open slots and that it could be up to five years before he achieved a higher-paying position such as pressman or foreman: "I'm something like number 27 now on the list for the next promotion. It will probably take three to four years until the next position, five at most."

By May 2001, Kevin still worked at Printing & Bindery and his wage had increased to $11.19 an hour plus the 90-cent bonus for working third shift, totaling $12.09 ($26 in 2021 dollars). Kevin had filed his income taxes incorrectly eight years earlier, however, and just learned in 2001 that he owed IRS $9,000 (just over $19,000 in 2021 dollars). The original sum, which came from an earlier training debt, had accrued interest while he was in prison, unbeknownst to him. In 2001, the IRS was garnisheeing his paychecks 15%, which "leaves me with nothing," he said. "Here I am trying to get it right, and I'm in another hole that I've got to fill up." To remedy this, the previous week Kevin worked 24 overtime hours, which was "a hardship on my family. Lynn needed a break; My kids needed to see me." Fortunately, a few months later the Printing Project manager intervened and was able to help Kevin eliminate the tax debt. According to her, "The IRS eventually just dropped the whole thing because he had been in prison at the time."

Eventually Kevin found the advancement pace too slow. The pace was limited both by union negotiations and by widespread speculation that Printing & Bindery would not stay in business. In spring 2002 Kevin said that he had been fired from Printing & Bindery the previous spring when he took time off to help his ill father in another state. Kevin believed that his layoff was due more to the 2001 recession and that terminating him for family reasons was "a convenient way to bolster company finances." Considering that his leave would have been covered under the Family and Medical Leave Act of 1993, Kevin's analysis may have been correct. In fact, Printing & Bindery declared bankruptcy in 2008 and by 2010 had been acquired by one of the largest printing firms in Wisconsin, consistent with industry practices at that time. Kevin's original printing firm, Elite Bindery, also seems to have been acquired, but no details were available.

Although Kevin found work at Oil Company after his Printing & Bindery layoff, and although he was interested in printing as an ongoing career, his passion lay in his long-standing and deep desire to help the African American community by establishing a club: "My dream, since high school, is to own a club with music and people—maybe a hip-hop club where nice people can come to talk and dance. In Milwaukee, we don't have clubs for Blacks, especially ones that are hip-hop oriented. Or if we do, they're deep in the urban community where there's violence." Seeing that dream far in the future since he had no business knowledge or license at that time, Kevin devised another plan that would bring in additional income and combine the printing and the business worlds: creating personalized calendars. He bought a digital camera and was "learning how to use it to make cards and personalized letters and calendars. I want to see how that goes as a business. I'm learning on my friend's computer."

As the 2000s wore on, desktop publishing and personalized customer service became increasingly critical to the printing industry's future survival (Romano 2019). In fact, in spring 2002 Kevin started an internet-based international import-export trade business that, by 2019, seventeen years later, had hundreds of international partners. Although Kevin had left the printing industry, his original Printing Project program staff directed him to an entrepreneur center that helped him with a start-up format for self-employment. Together with his printing and publishing expertise, the entrepreneurial training notably contributed to his ability to start his "wholesale/subwholesale" trade company. He describes the purpose of the company is "to connect buyers and suppliers and help guide them through the import-export process, as stress free as possible. We also introduce products to new global markets." While he has not yet realized his dream of a club for African American music and people, the company *is* his own and it seems to afford real opportunity.

What Do We Learn from Tisha, Joseph, Randy, and Kevin?

The stories of Tisha, Joseph, Randy, and Kevin constitute typical examples of how old avenues to upward mobility for lower-educated, less-trained individuals in the fields of manufacturing, construction, and printing are no longer functional in today's society. Their stories also show how workers, their families, and their communities are hurt when the labor market dominates workers' time and energy. For example, both Tisha and Randy were invited to give inspirational talks to participants in their workforce programs, an activity they relished and valued. But the time constraints of their labor market jobs prevented them from doing so very often. Even more, Randy and his children also performed traditional tribal dances at their African-country cultural group gatherings, at state fairs, and at the children's school. Their performances were very popular cultural events for both students and teachers, as reported by one of the children's teachers. Randy's on-site construction job did not allow him time to engage in these family and community events, and so he was very glad that his construction office job allowed him time for cultural activities that he felt contributed to the development and education of his children and the broader community.

Each of the stories also shows that workforce development programs' sole focus on labor market industries and jobs results in employment that is often highly vulnerable to economic changes. This leaves workers such as Tisha, Joseph, Randy, Kevin, and millions like them across the United States stuck in insecure and financially inadequate employment conditions. In that each of the four workers had a "heart-string" activity or career direction that was not being realized, greater policy support for compensated work activity at the community level, even if concurrent with labor market work, could make workers' dreams and productivity goals much more possible to realize. Likewise, as these four workers and millions of others across the country struggle to compensate for wages that are too low (Kalleberg 2018), their stories may convince policymakers that eligibility levels for work supports remain overly restrictive and inadequate. Finally, the stories of these workers suggest that traditional labor market work could be fruitfully combined with work that individuals also wished to do if a system of compensated civil labor were in place (see Chapter 7).

3

The Big Shift from Manufacturing Jobs to Service Jobs

Clerical Work, 1980s to Today

B y the 1980s, service industry[1] jobs already accounted for two-thirds of the jobs in the United States (Covert 2015). Having examined what workers do in manufacturing, construction, and printing industry jobs and how they experience their work in the previous chapter, we now take a look at workers' opportunities and challenges in four main types of service-producing jobs: clerical work (this chapter); healthcare (Chapter 4); food services, food stores, and retail sales (Chapter 5); and real estate, architecture, and automotive service (Chapter 6). Through interviews and analyses, these four chapters will explore what workers' service jobs have really been like since the 1980s.

Overall, workers in these service sectors describe their work lives in various ways, as good, bad, and precarious, regardless of their specific jobs, wage levels, decades of service, and geographical locations. Notably, these workers provide services that the broader population makes regular use of and would have difficulty living without. Yet most remain underpaid and generally find themselves at a dead end with little to no real future advancement opportunity. In many instances, though, valuing and believing that the services they provide are helpful to others also helps them cope with

---

1. Service industries overall include utilities; wholesale trade; retail trade; transportation and warehousing; information; finance, insurance, real estate, and rental and leasing; professional and business services; educational services; healthcare and social assistance; arts, entertainment, recreation, accommodation, and food services; and other services except government. (Bureau of Economic Analysis 2018).

their job or workplace struggles. Confirming interactions during the workday with peers, supervisors, and clients or customers may enhance the service worker's sense of self-worth, which can result in either putting up with the bad aspects of their job or leaving that job in hopes of finding a better job (Dutton, Debebe, and Wrzesniewski 2016). Neither alternative promises automatic satisfaction, particularly during times of economic downturn during which layoffs from lower-wage jobs become more frequent and wages in the new job are lower (Vroman 2005).

Clerical Work in the 1980s and 1990s

In 1870, only 1 of every 100 nonagricultural workers in the United States held a clerical job. But by 1980, 51% of women were in paid work, 1 in 5 nonagricultural workers were in a clerical occupation (Rotella 2002), and 8 in 10 clerical workers were women (England and Boyer 2009, 325). Some of the growth in women's employment during the 1980s and beyond came from the rise of dual-earner families, especially as the formerly high wages in manufacturing jobs for men stagnated or dropped and layoffs became more frequent.

The occupational category of clerical jobs is extremely diverse. Traditional office occupations categorized as clerical work include secretaries, typists, stenographers, file clerks, office machine operators, cashiers, and receptionists (Hunt and Hunt 1986, 1). They are also the most common positions held by clerical workers whose stories appear in this book. The big four clerical occupations—secretaries, bookkeepers, cashiers, and typists—accounted for almost half of all clerical employment in 1980 (Hunt and Hunt 1986, 3), and clerical workers were largely concentrated in the service sector. One contributing factor to the steady rise in clerical workers is thought to be the increasing number of women in the labor force by the 1980s. Female college graduates in particular, who were prepared to hold more advanced clerical positions, could apply some of their educational knowledge to learning microcomputing, as they had fewer alternative employment options than men did at that time (Rotella 2002).

At the same time, the Bureau of Labor Statistics and other governmental projection groups predicted that staffing ratios for clerical jobs would fall from 1990 onward as a result of office automation (Hunt and Hunt 1986, 5), which also became known as the "computer revolution." In fact, England and Boyer (2009) found Hunt and Hunt's prediction to be accurate—that, beginning in the 1980s, "the invention and diffusion of computer-related innovations facilitated the development of small, inexpensive data-processing systems and put automation within the budgets of even the smallest firms" (329), thus, by the 1990s, the growth in clerical work had stagnated (330).

Regarding the clerical workers showcased in this book, in the early 1980s, the immediate goal for the Teen Study teenagers, all of whom were African American and most of whom came from poor or relatively poor families but managed to graduate from high school, was to make money. Most felt that the convenient route to making money was some type of clerical job. Yet, in 1989 and 1990, when the women in the Teen Study Follow-Up were in their early to mid-twenties, most said they regretted not having gone straight to college. Those who had actually started college but got derailed by financial or family problems also wished they had been able to complete a college degree, whether a two- or a four-year program.

Roselyn

In the mid-1980s, 20-year-old Roselyn took a job as document control clerk and inventory management specialist in a military facility, even though she "did military on the spur of the moment." By the Teen Study Follow-Up in 1989–1990, Roselyn had risen in the ranks and supervised three persons in her office. Earlier, Roselyn had spent two years in community college studying data processing, one year of which was her senior year in high school. She had earned her data certificate and had worked at a department store during those years. Unlike most of her peers, Roselyn felt that working while in high school "would have taken away from my education." In the early 1980s, Roselyn had expected to "finish high school and college and go on to my master's" by 1990, but she had not done so. She felt her capabilities increased, however, during military training.

Roselyn's first post–high school job was as an "off and on" cashier for a major department store. The company viewed her work schedule as flexible, but for Roselyn the flexibility made her job feel insecure and unpredictable, a work situation McCall (2000) has identified as common. In 1990, Roselyn expressed regret that she had not pursued a four-year degree earlier, which she attributed in part to her parents' inability to afford college. She planned to enter a college near her military base in four months, however, where her basic training would count toward a bachelor's degree in data processing. The military would pay 75% and she would pay the remaining 25%. She described the content of her military job as "computer work, reverse posting, trouble-shooting, and error correcting." Roselyn earned about $18,000 a year in 1990 ($37,000 in 2021 dollars) and had a full range of nonwage benefits. She felt she could train for work in another field, which she considered a form of opportunity, but she liked the content of her military job. Her only wish was to be able to work part-time while she attended school, but the military does not allow that. Her goal was to get a bachelor's degree by the mid-1990s and attain a higher rank. Regarding opportunity, from

Roselyn's perspective, the military offered what is today called the old employment contract (Kochan and Dyer 2017): job security, regular advancement options, and pension and retirement packages.

Others in the Teen Study who pursued clerical jobs in the early 1980s related experiences similar to those Roselyn had described. Despite the contention in decades to come that postsecondary education would be necessary for workers to advance, by the late 1980s, clerical workers had found that post–high school training led only to moderate future opportunity. The work that many spoke of really wanting to do was in the caring labor category. But even when such women pursued training in the healthcare field, their jobs were generally clerical with little opportunity for advancement.

Kenya

For example, twenty-three-year-old Kenya initially saw hospital clerical work as a way to manage her prior education debt. After high school, Kenya had attended college outside Pennsylvania, but after three semesters she returned to a community college in the Philadelphia area. She originally studied biology and premed but switched to liberal arts at the community college. After a semester there, she enrolled in a for-profit training program, where she studied medical terminology for nine months and earned a certificate in 1988. By then, Kenya had gone into considerable debt, a situation eased somewhat by her job as a medical records file clerk at a local hospital that she had held for 16 months by the time of the Teen Study Follow-Up interview in 1989. Her job called for competencies she felt she had learned in high school, but it seemed likely that her college experience and specific medical training had provided her with additional credentials for her job: "I chart requests for doctors, do specials, keep records, phone occasionally, and use the computer. I needed specific medical terminology training, which I got in high school."

Kenya earned $17,212 in 1989 ($37,000 in 2021 dollars) but did not feel her file clerk position offered future opportunity because "there are not too frequent openings." She also acknowledged that her goals and expectations for jobs in the future had changed "because I was wanting to work with people. In school, I worked at [X] Hospital as an aide; I loved it. Work experience resulted in my goal change and the change in direction." Kenya hoped to be in a technical position by the mid-1990s, but she was realistic about the challenges involved in advancing her career:

> I'd like to be a coder-technician. The hospital offers classes and pays
> for them. I'd have to do two years of an RT [registered technician]
> degree first, and I'd hope to earn $35,000 to $40,000 [$65,000 in

2021 dollars]. I hope I won't lose my interest. My outlook is different now; I'm more dedicated. Maturity. It's not easy in the real world, there's no way around it.

Vanessa

Twenty-five-year-old Vanessa, also in the Teen Study Follow-Up, told a related story. She attended college outside Philadelphia for three semesters and studied liberal arts toward a nursing degree. Despite a generous Pell grant, her loan was only one-third paid off. She then returned to Philadelphia to attend the same medical technology school that Kenya had attended and studied "medical office assistant, anesthesia, office administration [business], medical terminology, and medications." Previously, Vanessa had expected to have a "master's in nursing by now" (1989) and still had that goal. But she was pursuing it with a different time frame and balance between work and school in mind: "It was too hard, too stressful, to be working and go to school. I'd like to get back to college—I hope in a couple of years."

In the meantime, Vanessa had been working in the billing section of an orthopedics department at a suburban hospital for the previous 15 months: "I began in the filing department and then applied internally to the orthopedic department. I post charges on the computer and handle HMO bills and phone calls. They trained me on the computer on the job." Vanessa was working full-time and earning $15,210 a year ($32,600 in 2021 dollars). She felt there were opportunities for advancement in "different areas in the department I can move around to and do different things, versus my previous job in which I couldn't move. Plus computer." Although her original goal was to have a career in nursing, she had recently changed her goal after learning about several hospital positions: "Since I've been around doctors, I'm not sure of nursing. I'd like to do a higher-level, something challenging—most likely, maternity nurse. To do this, I'd need to go back to school to get my BA." As to reaching that goal, Vanessa felt that "money is the worst, the most likely thing that would get in the way of me actualizing my goal."

Kenya's and Vanessa's experiences both show how the need to pay off education debt was a driving force determining career direction in the early 1990s. Their experiences also show that working for a hospital in 1990, particularly a university-affiliated hospital, was one of two remaining bastions where the old employment contract held fast. University-based hospitals continued to provide and financially support additional education for employees through the 1990s, but other hospitals reduced or eliminated such support practices in the 2000s, as will be shown in Chapter 4. Government was the other bastion of labor market stability and security, as Fatima's experience illustrates.

Fatima

Twenty-four-year-old Fatima, another Teen Study Follow-Up participant, had attended a vocational high school and taken typing for a few weeks at night but had not completed the course, though by the late 1980s she wished she had. After receiving her high school diploma, she held a couple of cashier jobs in various types of small stores. She was paid the minimum wage at the time, $3.25 an hour (almost $9 in 2021 dollars), until she landed a seasonal position as a tax examiner for the federal government in 1988. She still held that position 15 months later, although she had been furloughed for three months during 1989. Fatima described her job tasks as follows: "I examine taxes, adjust taxes and talk with taxpayers, and work with computers. I need better typing skills." She got the specific training she needed on the job, although training at federal agencies today is just as likely as training at companies to be off site and conducted on the employee's time. In the late 1980s, however, Fatima's arrangement with the federal government was that "the job is seasonal for 12 months and then I'll get a permanent position." In other words, she worked part of the year at $6.98 an hour ($14.50 in 2021 dollars) and expected to earn $7.81 ($15.50 in 2021 dollars) in January 1990, but she needed to accrue 12 months of work before she was hired permanently. She felt that "having gotten my foot into the IRS (Internal Revenue Service), I've exceeded my earlier expectation for myself. I expect raises in the next couple of years to enable me to earn about $16,000 a year" ($36,000 in 2021 dollars). How did Fatima get hired by the IRS with just a high-school diploma? Her social network (Granovetter 1973, 1983) certainly helped, as Fatima's mother had worked there for the previous five years. In five years, Fatima hoped to still be working for the IRS and she "might try for the next position—to be a lead. I'd learn the skills that are necessary on the job because they do on-job training." The reality, however, was that the IRS had likely moved its training completely off site by that time, which is a pattern that continues today.

Helena

Twenty-four-year-old Helena's job pathway was enabled by a government stay-in-school program. As she reported in the Teen Study Follow-Up interview, she'd had a rough transition to high school and repeated ninth grade. But after graduating in the early 1980s, she studied accounting for a period and took some short-term word-processing classes. She described her job in 1989, which she had held for nearly five years, as follows:

> Clerk for the Department of Defense Personnel in an office where I do typing, filing, word processing, and insurance. I began as in-school

whereby I could keep the job as long as I go to school. It was a stay-in-school program. I got the job when I put in an application at City Hall for a summer program.

Helena earned $650 every two weeks and worked 30 hours of overtime bi-weekly, so her total annual income in 1989 was $19,400 ($41,500 in 2021 dollars). At the same time, her actual work hours did not qualify her for benefits and, because of that, she saw little opportunity ahead since "our level is too low." Work arrangements like hers became a common problem in businesses starting in the 1990s, seemingly foreshadowed in the late 1980s by practices in the government. Constructing an annual income with limited work hours plus compensation for overtime left Helena ineligible for benefits—the "risk shift" from employer to employee that Hacker (2008) documented two decades later. Still, Helena's goal by the mid-1990s, especially if she could find a helpful social network connection, was to "still be doing office work but with some traveling to outside plants. This would be a higher General Schedule [GS] level job. To do this job, it depends on the field and who you know."

As for future opportunity in clerical work for Roselyn, Kenya, Vanessa, Fatima, and Helena, although the 1990s began with a recession, the remainder of the decade saw considerable economic growth. Technological advances, demand for more services, and the 1996 welfare reform legislation drove up employment in the service-producing sector (Hatch and Clinton 2000, 3). Many clerical positions were computerized, especially as computers became less costly, which left clerical workers without computer training behind and which likely became the plight of many clerical workers in the Teen Follow-Up Study. In addition, clerical positions that were not heavily computerized morphed into customer service positions, frequently in insurance companies, fed by a growing population of welfare and workforce program trainees after 1996. Examples next from the Ethnographic Study in the early 2000s and the Family Study from 2008 to 2015 or so illustrate these major changes in the clerical field, including a sizable increase in businesses' use of temporary workers to offset recession-based downturns.

Clerical Work in the 2000s

Wendy: Clerical and Customer Service Call Center Work, 2001 to 2003, Philadelphia Area

Before entering the clerical field in 2001, Wendy, a 32-year-old Latina who participated in the Ethnographic Study and had a 14-year-old son, had worked for more than 12 years as a pharmacy technician. There, she experienced an abusive boss, had no opportunity for promotion, and received only minimal raises.

> I loved the job but you never moved up in that company, you just stayed in the same title, which I don't think is fair because I was doing everything there. I ordered medication, I pulled prescriptions, I took prescriptions on the phone from doctors, I would call insurance agencies when the members were not active in the system. I did everything you can imagine [but] he didn't appreciate it. One of the other girls worked there for 20 years and never got the title of manager or anything. How can you do that? A girl gives you 20 years of her life and she was just a pharmacy tech. . . . I didn't have a future there; it was a dead end. That is one of the reasons I had to get out of there. It was ridiculous and he was abusive. [That] was another reason I didn't like it. He would curse at us, which is something that we never knew was harassment, and he could have had a real lawsuit had we investigated it. He would call us the B word and he would make us feel like we were worthless.

After being laid off briefly, Wendy saw a flyer at the unemployment office about a six-week customer service training program that advertised it developed "committed, professional employees for careers in banking, insurance, retail, call centers, hospitality, and travel," and she eagerly enrolled. The program emphasized communication capabilities, including defusing angry callers. It also brought in customer service representatives from the field to speak about what employers expected from employees, which Wendy felt "added authenticity to the program." But the program did not offer phone or computer training, which eventually became problematic for Wendy.

Wendy's first postprogram job as a representative in provider services in the 300-employee Medical Billing Company in June–July 2001 interested her because "I like the medical field for some reason." Wendy was paid $9.50 an hour ($14.50 in 2021 dollars) with the opportunity for a $1 raise after three months of employment, although the company did not offer any health insurance benefits. She found the environment fast-paced but supportive. The company's location in a suburb outside Philadelphia was emblematic of the "increasing relocation of routinized functions, or even all functions, out of central cities." This relocation of companies into the suburbs decreased local clerical job opportunities and produced lengthy reverse commutes for those living in city centers (England and Boyer 2009, 331), affecting urban African American and Latina women especially (McLafferty and Preston 1992). Wendy's reverse commute, which took more than an hour each way, became exhausting and expensive, as she explained:

I didn't like traveling all the way out there. I would get home so late, it was too much. It takes about an hour to get there, and if you miss the train either way you have to wait almost a whole hour [until the next one comes]. And I had to take the Amtrak train. Those Trans-Passes are very costly, about $30 a week. It was almost like it was not worth it to travel that far. I would come home at 7:00 P.M. and it was getting to be ridiculous. I said, "I cannot see myself traveling this far; I cannot do this."

Thus, tiring of the toll the commute took on her and her parenting, Wendy left Medical Billing Company for the position of member services representative at the city-based, five-thousand-employee Medical Insurance Company, which, she reported, was "closer to home. I can catch the [subway] and I get home in about 15 minutes. I walk right there to the station and it is close to home." Her wage was higher than in her previous job, at $12.31 an hour ($19 in 2021 dollars), and she received full health and dental benefits. She received additional training but gradually experienced the high pace at the company as impersonal, bureaucratic, and stressful. Taylorist (Taylor 2014 [1911]) "scientific" supervisory practices such as taping and grading time spent on every phone call to evaluate employee performance, an intrusive level of direct surveillance, and her supervisor's refusal to help her with caller issues not covered in training, such as COBRA coverage for a newborn baby, cumulatively wore on Wendy, even though her review grades were excellent. After numerous experiences like these, Wendy's headaches and a gastrointestinal condition that she had suffered for years under her old pharmacy boss resumed, and she began to consider leaving Medical Insurance Company:

> I leave there every day with such a headache. I can see why they hire so many people because they all leave; it's too stressful. I just can't be coming home all stressed and depressed like this, I cannot come home so tired. I'd rather deal with a job that will pay me less and where I can be happy and supported. I was in a job with an abusive boss for 12 years and I don't need this.

These experiences also convinced Wendy that customer service work was not the career she had imagined, and so, after resigning from Medical Insurance Company, she located a position at Independent Pharmacy in her neighborhood. As is more typical with job changes than was the case when Wendy moved to Medical Insurance Company, her wage in the new pharmacy was lower, at $10 an hour ($14.50 in 2021 dollars). Health insurance would be available in three months, but only for her and not for other members of her family. Less than a month after being hired, her wage was increased to $13 an hour ($20 in 2021 dollars) after a coworker left. In addition to the content of the job, Wendy noted how important the positive work atmosphere was:

> This job is good, I like it, the people are so nice. My boss, he is such a sweetheart. You can ask him anything and it doesn't bother him. The people I work with are really nice. There is another girl and then my friend, but she only works Tuesdays and Fridays, so there's three of us. It's a pretty busy store, [but] it is nice; everybody helps out and everybody works together. People get their medications and they're happy because we are quick. It works out pretty good.

Even so, the work Wendy found most satisfying involved listening and talking with youth, which she did regularly, but informally, at her church. She considered counseling as a career change but felt it would entail too much schooling. If her youth engagement activity could have been compensated as civil labor, she might have been able to do more of it part-time and remain at her satisfying pharmacy job part-time as well.

Loretta: Clerical and Customer Service Work, 1999 to 2001, St. Louis

Latina and part of the Ethnographic Study, Loretta had experiences in the clerical field in St. Louis that were similar to Wendy's in Philadelphia. Loretta, 27 years old in 2001, had graduated from high school with honors in the early 1990s. For three years after graduation, she worked part-time jobs "here and there" and completed 11 credit hours at a local community college, where she took medical records training. In 1994, she obtained a summer position in the medical records department of a home health provider and was paid $7 an hour ($12.50 in 2021 dollars). After a temporary move out of state, Loretta returned to St. Louis and enrolled in a one-month workforce program called Health Program with the goal of being trained as a medical assistant. For the next two years, Loretta held and lost various jobs, mainly because of lateness she attributed to childcare problems for her seven- and three-year-old children and low wages in jobs she had attained. McLafferty and Preston (1992) similarly found that long commuting times and less localized labor markets were particular challenges for lower-earning Latina workers, illustrating the intersection of gender- and race-based segmentation across the occupation spectrum. Even so, Loretta worked relatively steadily in filing and simple clerical tasks for two healthcare temporary agencies. In spring 2001, she participated in a new workforce training program, Customer Service Program, and learned that she was a very slow typist. She also acknowledged that computerized testing in training situations made her nervous.

Throughout the Ethnographic Study we learned that many respondents and their program trainers felt that test anxiety severely curtailed their progress. We also learned from repeated administration of the CES-D scale (Center for Epidemiological Studies Depression Scale) (Radloff 1977) to all study participants that Loretta scored high on depressive symptomatology. The CES-D scale has been shown to be equally reliable for African Americans, Mexican Americans, and whites (Roberts 1980). An important result of the training program was it helped Loretta locate helpful and affordable counseling.

The final job the training program helped Loretta locate was a telemarketing position at Business Company. The company's workplace practices were some of the worst we saw during the many hours we spent at the 74 sites that the Ethnographic Study participants worked at between 2000 and 2005. For example, when Business Company workers went on break, they sometimes found themselves without a desk to return to, a kind of musical chairs scenario in which there were never enough desks for all the employees. As is not surprising, being left without a place to work translated into problems meeting the company's stringent telemarketing quotas and being sent home for lack of productivity, as the following conversation illustrates:

INTERVIEWER: If you have to spend a lot of time looking for a seat, how does that affect your productivity?

LORETTA: Yes, ma'am, and your concentration, don't leave that out. It was just so odd because I have never experienced such chaos in my life at a workplace.

INTERVIEWER: The folks at Customer Service Program didn't have very much good to say about this particular office of Business Company.

LORETTA: I mean for them to be a major business, they run number one in sales, because the only thing they think about is they want you to sell, sell, sell. If you don't sell you go home. Like, OK, I get there at nine o'clock. If I don't make a sale within my first 10 calls, I go home.

In addition, call centers like Loretta's were particularly prone to moving their clerical divisions out of center cities into far-flung suburbs, which meant that inconsistent transportation reliability added external strain to Loretta's internal office struggles (England and Boyer 2009).

Loretta's deepest wish was to participate in her children's activities and explore their interests, such as scouts with her son and beauty pageants with her daughter, and also to encourage their continual learning by accompanying them on library and nature outings. Loretta said she would have been even more active at her children's school if she hadn't had such an erratic and demanding work schedule. For example, if she were able to work half- or three-quarter-time at her job, she could devote more time to helping out at school. In fact, many schools like the ones Loretta's children attended might experience greater parental involvement if involvement took the form of compensated civil labor (see Chapter 7).

Isabell: Tech Work, 1999 to 2001, Seattle

At the Seattle site of the Ethnographic Study, 31-year-old Latina Isabell reported experiences similar to Wendy's and Loretta's at a new internet business called Tech Company. Coming from a city-sponsored training program called Business Skills Project, Isabell had interned at Tech Company and landed a tier 1 customer service representative position there five weeks later at an hourly wage of $11 ($17 in 2021 dollars). But the pace and near-superhuman expectations took a toll on Isabell. First, there was no such thing as a predictable schedule or product, which made meeting her four- and two-year-old children's needs at home very challenging. Second, employees were expected to devote their full energy to Tech Company. Thus, the company generally hired young, single individuals without families, which was not Isabell's situation, as she explained: "I am the only one in the group who has children. No one understands what I go through—when a kid fell down the stairs or I tripped on the way to the car. It gets a little frustrating sometimes. I don't go home to my cat like they do."

Isabell's duties as a customer service representative involved researching answers to customers' questions; reassuring customers even when their calls took time away from her lunch hour; and corresponding quickly and definitively via phone and email with customers and her supervisors. She was expected to average at least seven phone calls per hour over a four-hour shift and a similar number of highly complicated email contacts per hour for the other four hours. Despite these multiple duties, Isabell managed to make more phone contacts than anybody in her group and was eager for guidance on how to improve areas in which she struggled, such as composing emails. Isabell also tried to stay abreast of constantly changing company tools and information, an effort that required her to study during her "free" time. Isabell's description of her job after these first months of long, harried hours illustrates the strain of working in situations that foster a work-family imbalance: "It's my hardest job ever—a challenge—but I like it. I've got to make them more family oriented, though."

Like Wendy and Loretta, Isabell perceived an absence of reciprocity in her relationship with her employer, a situation that became much more prevalent in businesses in the 2000s, as noted in Chapter 1. The old employment contract for clerical workers that Roselyn and the others had known in the 1980s was no longer in place (Kochan and Dyer 2017). Isabell was asked to stretch her capacities but did not see Tech Company willing to stretch theirs. Isabell's wish, like Loretta's, was for more time to contribute to her children's schools and family activities.

Ayesha, Clerical Work in a Financial Services Company, 2001 to 2003, Philadelphia

In contrast to the experiences that Wendy, Loretta, and Isabell related in the 2000s, Ayesha's story of clerical work was the sole example of opportunities that were available in a well-run business in the early 2000s. In fact, Ayesha's was the *only* establishment out of 74 in the Ethnographic Study that offered an official flexible time policy to all employees. Her company's flextime policy allowed workers to take time away from work for personal needs and make up the time later, with no wage loss. This rather unique official policy was particularly important for Ayesha because her three school-age children had numerous developmental and behavioral problems and needs that their schools often called on her to mediate.

African American and in her mid-40s in 2001, Ayesha was a parent and grandparent whose recent on-job injury had forced her to seek a new career path. Her initial career as a certified nursing assistant (CNA) in a Philadelphia nursing home had been very successful. But after more than 10 years there, Ayesha described the physical strain of handling 16 to 18 patients a night: "That means what? Four, maybe six changes per person. Showers. Feeding. Getting them ready for bed. That took a lot of lifting because a lot of my patients were not able to lift themselves. They tore me up." The level of lifting required eventually led to a serious back and shoulder injury. Ayesha's diligence in protecting a patient when she transferred the patient from wheelchair to bed compromised Ayesha's own safety: "When she fell on me, I took the weight of her in my lower back and my shoulders because I wouldn't let her hit the floor." (We see additional examples of healthcare job-related injuries in Chapter 4.)

Ayesha's serious injury resulted in her leaving the healthcare field. She subsequently enrolled in Career CBO, a nonprofit, community-based affiliate of a Philadelphia-based workforce development network. According to the Career CBO brochure, welfare-to-work and workforce development services were focused on "women on welfare looking for a way out; laid-off workers who need to update their skills; out-of-school youths looking for direction; and people trying to extricate themselves from low-paying, dead-end jobs." Although Ayesha was receiving unemployment insurance rather than welfare cash assistance, job placement at Career CBO was influenced by the 1996 welfare reform legislation mandate of "work first," meaning the program participants would be strongly urged to take any job offered. Ayesha's successful employment history had given her the confidence to hold out for a job with promise, rather than the restaurant waitress job Career CBO offered.

One of Ayesha's frustrations was that Career CBO provided minimal computer training for two or fewer hours a day, offering nothing more complex than data entry and Microsoft Word. The computer instructor at Career CBO echoed Ayesha's assessment that her computer training was not sufficient for a jobseeker to secure a position in an office environment: "The early computer training was too basic. We spent a lot of time on soft skills. They might only have learned how to save a file on the desktop, delete a file, and edit a document."

Fortunately, Ayesha received additional computer training on the job that she held out for. Early in 2001 she was placed at Financial Services Company in a temporary position, a common method of hiring employees in the 2000s (Osterman 1999) that cushioned companies, but not employees, from labor market flux. Ayesha's initial wage was $8.25 an hour ($12.50 in 2021 dollars) plus benefits. Three months later, she was hired permanently as an assistant associate in bill distribution. Her wage increased to $10.50 an hour ($15.71 in 2021 dollars) plus paid vacation and benefits. Ayesha described her position's multiple tasks and how her earlier work as a certified nursing assistant benefited her in her new domain:

> I distribute bills, too, and I take in checks. I take in checks and send out mail. I deal with incoming files, outgoing files, updating the PC with data on new clients that we were receiving. Sending files off site, which is a whole lot of work because so far I have sent away 189 boxes, which is about 20 to 30 files per box. So, I am in the process of cleaning the place back up. Bills are a process that we do every month and that's sixteen thousand or more per month and they are coming in tomorrow morning. I just got an update. And I don't have nobody riding my back. Basically, I am in charge of the file room. I'm in charge of distributing the bills every month. I have a lot of responsibility dealing with this job and the different aspects of it, the way I had it when I was a CNA.

There was always more work than could be completed in a day, so Ayesha's supervisor encouraged her to work overtime, which she did and which was fully compensated. But, because overtime was included in her official paycheck, Ayesha suddenly did not qualify for food stamps (later, SNAP) or other work subsidies, even though her annual income was only $22,000 ($32,914 in 2021 dollars), which placed her at 106% of the federal poverty level for her family of five.

On-the-job advancement training was available for employees at Ayesha's level, which was another unusual aspect of her company as, from the early 2000s onward, most companies offered on-job training only to higher-level employees. For Ayesha, classes and subjects such as computer technology and customer service were offered on company time. Lunchtime sessions on women's health issues and other lifestyle topics also were offered to all employees. Ayesha took full advantage of these opportunities and planned to take advantage of the firm's tuition benefit (80%) toward the goal of being an underwriter and eventual case manager as soon as she could afford her 20% contribution.

Ultimately, Career CBO's relationship with a good temporary employment service agency, and Ayesha's insistence on finding a job that would use her competencies and experience, resulted in success for Ayesha. The company's official flextime policy also contributed significantly to her ability to be a working single mother with three children and a grandchild at home. Still, since the need for computer capability manifested quickly after 2000 as more and more businesses upgraded and extended their technological requirements, if Ayesha had entered her clerical position with more computer knowledge, her base income might have been higher. By 2003, Career CBO offered enrollees the opportunity to develop computer capabilities in a computer laboratory three days a week for the entire afternoon.

Clerical Work Later in the 2010s

The Great Recession, officially 2007 to 2009, the second and much more devastating recession in the first decade of the 2000s with its aftermath still evident in 2020 when the COVID-19 pandemic hit, spread lower earners' persistent concerns about financial stability and mobility into the daily lives of workers in middle-earning clerical positions. In the Family Study, middle income was defined as 75% to 125% of the median family income, which translated roughly to around $45,000 to $75,000 a year in 2010 (Gauthier 2015). In addition to talking about their jobs, participants in this study talked about what the American Dream meant to them. Virtually all mentioned financial security: "getting what you want and what you need." Most also mentioned that the avenues to future opportunity were shrinking. Shannon's and Susan's stories about clerical work during and after the Great

Recession provide contrasting yet similar views on the spread of financial instability to middle earners.

Shannon: Clerical Work, 2008 to 2013, Philadelphia Suburb

Later in the first decade of the 2000s and into the second decade, Shannon, a white, 42-year-old married woman with two early-teenage daughters, worked as a legal administrator in a law firm, which she characterized as "advanced clerical." The job was emblematic of how the new flexibility in employment relations can engender in workers at once a sense of freedom and insecurity, as Kalleberg (2012, 2018) and McCall (2000) have suggested. Shannon described both the struggles and satisfactions of her job during the first Family Study meeting in 2008:

> I had a real, real stressful job doing odd enforcement jobs for the county court system before I took on this position and I actually took a huge cut in pay to take less stress. I was offered flexibility and access to work from home, although they're in addition to your normal work times. So, I kind of felt a bit tricked into taking a position that I thought was one thing and actually turned out to be another. However, after some kicking and screaming, I kind of got that straightened out with my boss and was like, "No, you can't have it both ways. I can't be salaried when it comes to paying me overtime, but not salaried when you're deducting my time because I had to stay home when the kids were sick." So, after a year I got that straightened out. I guess a lot of people have the same issues. I feel like I wear too many hats to be very efficient in any one of those particular areas. I definitely do too many different jobs, and I've talked to my boss about she should be hiring some clerical staff. Really, I'm not clerical staff; however, I do know how to type, I do know how to answer the phone, yes, so do most people. You're paying me an awful lot of money to sit there and answer your phones. There are some days that's all I do, because the phones are going crazy and I can't do anything else. I took the job because it was less stressful than my last job, and it turned out to be stressful. Different type of stress, but still in a negative way. [When I left the county job,] I took a step back careerwise to kind of regroup and maybe in the future take some smaller steps forward.

In 2008, Shannon's declared goal was to be a lawyer even though she knew that the road to a law degree was intense and time-consuming because programs expected students to attend classes full time. Notably, Shannon did not talk about the law content of her current job—only about the administrative and secretarial aspects, which she seemed to consider demeaning. She was attending a local college part-time to obtain a bachelor's degree but had trouble finding time to study with a full-time job and family responsibilities. Difficulty juggling full-time work, family, and school responsibilities was a common plight among women across the United States, whether we talked with them in the 1980s, the 1990s, or the 2000s.

A year later, in 2009, Shannon reported that she had returned to a county court job as "a supervisor in an accounting office" that she had held before the law firm job. She was "very excited to be back, so things are looking up on the employment front." She liked having a staff (of 22) in her county position, which gave her the autonomy and authority that she missed in the law firm position. During the year of changes, Shannon also decided against pursuing law as a career. Technically Shannon's current position was that of court unit supervisor, as she explained:

You know you see on TV there's people that sit in front of the judge and give him the files and they might answer the judge's questions either procedurally or for the record or this or that or whatever. My staff is the ones that sit in front of the judges that have all those files, that answer all the questions, and actually write the order up as the judge talks about it, so they don't use stenographers in my county. It's my staff that records it here, so it's kind of high pressure.

"It didn't hurt," Shannon said, "that going back to my old position was about a $10,000 pay increase, which is starting to feel like a lot of financial easing." At the same time, when Shannon left the county court position earlier, she had taken her savings program funds ($37,000). Now that she had returned, she was required to pay it back before she could begin to rebuild seniority equity: "They take an additional almost $300 per paycheck to buy back the seniority, plus the 10% [$3,700] to begin with." Being able to rebuild the savings program was one of the compelling reasons Shannon returned to the county position, especially since her husband's job did not offer a pension or savings program.

Because of her move back to a position with county government and her husband's attainment of additional truck-driving certificates, which he felt made him more marketable, neither was worried about layoff in 2009, despite being in the middle of the Great Recession and seeing several neighbors lose their jobs and homes to foreclosure. Both felt that companies were using the recession "as a way to decrease their workforce," which Maciag (2017) reported was particularly taking place in state and local governments.

In 2009, Shannon was still pursuing her bachelor's degree in business and hoped to continue for an MBA. Nevertheless, she indicated that she wouldn't need an advanced degree to move up at work: "I don't think it would help me or hinder me either way at work." More to the point, she was happy to be at her current level, saying, "It would be fine if I moved up in the future, but I like what I do. I'd like to stay right where I am."

Shannon's sentiments were in line with the preference for job security and stability that many women expressed in interviews over the years. The double shift of work and family responsibilities that women have often assumed (Hochschild 1997) has often made the prospect of new job duties, a new supervisor, and possibly a new work location seem overwhelming, especially to workers who presently like their current job and supervisor. The many concerns and responsibilities Shannon and other women factor into their decision-making about jobs, rather than having promotion as their highest priority, was very surprising to employers and workforce trainers across our research (Iversen and Armstrong 2006).

Part of Shannon's hesitation about taking a higher position also resulted from the stress she felt at work, which was exacerbated by the ways that technological advancements actually enabled employers to intrude productivity expectations into employees' family lives:

> I don't really feel like I'm living the American Dream because work kind of overspills into family time. There are a lot of times I'll bring some work home, even though my work is flexible, like employee schedules, stuff I can do here. Those things infringe on my family time. With the onset of computers and programing and emails and all those things to make you work faster, that were intended to shorten the workday, it actually made it more stressful—like you're now expected to do more in less time. Where maybe you took three people to do that job, now you've got the one person doing that job. The company's saving money but you're not getting paid more. . . . I think it's very far and few between who can see the American Dream.

Four years later, in 2013, Shannon was still working at her court position. She was facing her older daughter's upcoming college costs but had not received any raises at her job. Her daughter Rebecca said, "My mom works really hard at her job. It's very stressful." In discussing her own student work at the mall, Rebecca commented that "My mom works there, too, part-time." This suggests that Shannon's need to repay the court the $37,000 in her prior savings funds plus Rebecca's college costs would keep the family in tight financial straits for some years ahead.

Susan: Lower-Level Clerical Work, 2008–2013, Philadelphia Suburb

Susan's work experiences in a lower-wage clerical job were very different from Shannon's in higher-end clerical work, particularly in terms of pay and job tasks. To some extent, the difference was a function of differences in the two women's degree of educational attainment, but to a greater extent it was a function of differences in the worksites themselves. While Shannon worked in county government, Susan worked in the public schools.

In 2008, Susan, 49 years old, white, and married with two early-teenage children, had just completed her associate degree at a local community college and was working in the local high school. She'd begun working in the school district about eight years earlier, having been an at-home parent for about 10 years to care for her son, now a teenager, who had been diagnosed with autism. In 2008, as a participant in the Family Study, Susan reflected on her reentry into the labor market and entry into school district employment:

I work for the local school district as a secretary at the high school. I started at the school district, basically as a teaching assistant, seven years ago. I went back to work for benefits—health benefits. I make little money but have big benefits. My husband makes the money and I bring home benefits.

Specifically, Susan's first job in the district was a nine-month position as an English-as-a-second-language assistant, which she loved: "Couldn't believe they paid me to do that job. That was the greatest job in the world." She laughed ruefully, however, about her nine-month salary of $7,800 ($11,600 in 2021 dollars] when she left the position after working there for three years. She particularly loved working directly with the students, helping them adjust to the new language and school system. She also found that the nine-month position worked well with her parental responsibilities.

Earlier, in 2004, Susan had moved into a 12-month, full-time clerical position in the high school's audiovisual (AV) center as a secretary at the "whopping salary," she said, tongue in cheek, of $18,000 ($25,000 in 2021 dollars). The position clearly had been influenced by technological changes, as Susan explained:

Running the old AV crew, that we now call the media crew. For the teachers that don't have technology in their classroom, I organize the deliveries of that equipment to the classrooms and then have the kids bring it back at the end of the day. We also do things like sound and audiovisual equipment or computers connected to projectors for conferencing and things like that. In addition, I do all lost student IDs. The school is very large—several thousand students. They need their IDs to go to the bathroom. Their bus passes, they need them to get their lunch. Even if they're not free and reduced federal lunch programs, they still have to swipe their cards. So, those kids need them for everything. So, after the photographer comes in, if they're lost or stolen or whatever, they need a replacement and I print them a new one. I also do the IDs for all the staff and employees at the high school as well as the administration for the entire district. I like the students. That's the best part of the job.

Her main job in the summer during those years was to clean and inventory old computers coming into the district. In fact, the summer position turned out to involve heavy-duty maintenance work. So, in summer 2008, Susan worked as a temporary substitute for a secretary on medical leave, hoping it would help her move higher in the school system's formal clerical path:

I've applied for another position in the school that's one classification higher, but it's minimal in the amount of pay increase. I'm seeing my position as a floating secretary as a steppingstone because I want to get into being a center secretary or a school secretary at one of the elementary schools, and it may be a steppingstone into one of those other positions. As a floater, I float from one center to the other, one school to the other, inside the high school, helping that secretary. I was working with the AV crew. Loved the job, between September and May when the kids were there with you. After they left for the summer, I'm not too crazy about the job. My boss is extremely difficult, extremely difficult. He wanted me to basically perform as a maintenance worker, unloading trucks, helping move 300 computers into the high school. Laser printers are huge. It's not the job of a secretary to carry a 30-pound, 50-pound printer. I can't wrestle them. Let alone some of the servers, which are basically computers with hard drives in them, and they can go 100, 150, 200 pounds. Like I can really lift that up? But the district only hired one summer help person instead of the usual two. And, in the spring, I was elected president of my union association, so I couldn't very well be president of the union, trying to set the example for the other women in the school district, knowing I was doing something that a secretary shouldn't be doing. So, that was part of the reason for looking for other jobs in the high school and to move away from that boss.

Much of Susan's 2008 interview pertained to the family's difficult financial situation during the Great Recession. In 2009, Susan and her husband, a truck driver and crane operator, were both trying to find second jobs. Susan's husband was looking into a supermarket job and Susan hoped to get a job in daycare in the township's department of recreation. Despite her hopes for mobility opportunity in the clerical arena, Susan indicated that she worked for the school district "for the insurance," a common thread among all the study participants who worked for this local school district. School district wages were quite low, but the benefits were quite high—by some estimates, worth $5,000 to $10,000. *If* one needed the largesse of the benefits, the terms of employment may have worked out on balance. But the school district employees interviewed universally wished for higher regular incomes unless their family had extremely high medical needs.

Notably, although the suburban area where Susan lived tended to be relatively conservative, Susan had quite progressive ideas about government benefits. She regretted that the family assets, minimal as they were, prevented them from accessing SNAP benefits during the hard recession years. Asked whether raising the allowable asset levels to qualify for SNAP benefits might help, Susan jumped on the idea:

> Wow! Wow! I never thought . . . that would . . . Wow! Being able to get food stamps with $2,000 in the bank, I didn't think that was possible. Sure, in some ways I'm very much a socialist that I'd be willing to pay a little bit more in taxes to get free education and free healthcare, and I don't know if it's because now I'm a mature adult with children and realize that these are the two biggest chunks of money next to a mortgage. If the government could offer me healthcare the way I'm getting healthcare now [by working at a low-wage job before passage of the Affordable Care Act], the same quality, the same type of healthcare, for free, I'd go for it. Could I get my kids into state college for free—definitely!

Susan sagely reassessed the economic situation in 2013. "I still think that we're at the tail end of the recession," she said. The family was not struggling as much financially as they had in 2009, but "it's still tight." They experienced some serious medical situations, for which they were insured, and both children, including the son with autism, had made significant academic advances. Susan described her current job with the school district as the "secretary in the freshman academy, which averages around 900 freshmen. Four years ago, I had just made the leap from secretary to floater secretary. Now I'm a center secretary, a little bit more prestigious but a lot more stress." The new job also provided only a little more money, per the union contract: "This new contract that will start July 1, 2014, I got a $500 a year raise [$560 in 2021 dollars], which basically works out to about three percent. My husband had a two-year freeze right before that. So, for the past three years, we've basically lived on the same money." Thus, Susan's mobility opportunity was not accompanied by greater financial gain.

At the same time, Susan repeated what she had said four years earlier about working for benefits rather than wages, even though she did achieve her goal of moving up a little. Reflecting a growing national concern, she also reiterated the apprehension she'd had in 2009 about possible layoffs:

As much as I'd like to say I have job security, it's always a possibility. It's been a possibility. There's been talk about it. Ten years ago, the school district tried to lay off the white-collar secretarial staff, which resulted in huge, huge rebuttal from the public and, more importantly, the principals. Like if you take away our support staff, how are we supposed to run the schools? Well, this bout in the past two years was more about cutting arts and music within the district, which made the local news. So, it was a definite possibility even though I knew that they weren't gonna directly attack the support staff. Let's face it, in this economy, it's always there, always there.

What's the Future for Clerical Workers in the 2020s and Beyond?

The median pay for secretaries and administrative assistants in 2019 was $19.16 an hour (BLS 2020i, which amounted to $39,853 annually if a person worked 40 hours a week and 52 weeks a year. In fact, an annual pay of $39,853 reached 236% of the 2019 poverty level, which is considered basic sufficiency, for a family size of two (U.S. Department of Health and Human Services 2019). However, because clerical pay also varies from state to state and locale to locale, the median pay for clerical assistance will be minimally to moderately sufficient in some areas and insufficient in others.

A broader look at pay shows that as of January 5, 2021 (National Conference of State Legislatures 2021), the minimum wage in 16 states and Puerto Rico has remained at the federal minimum wage level of $7.25 an hour since 2009. Five states have no required minimum wage laws, which means that the federal level applies, and 29 states and the District of Columbia, Guam, and the U.S. Virgin Islands have increased their minimum wage beyond the $7.25 minimum over the past 10 years. In terms of wage policy, then, pressuring state legislatures to increase the state minimum wage may be more successful than focusing on federal wage action.

In 2020, a high school education was still sufficient for lower-level clerical jobs. But the narratives of some clerical workers in this chapter foreshadow the trend toward requiring postsecondary degrees and advanced computer capabilities in order to obtain higher-level, higher-paying clerical jobs such as administrative assistant. Although several women interviewed had completed one to three years of college, none held a four-year college degree, and only one had earned an associate degree. With the higher cost of a college education by the 2020s, further schooling—particularly obtaining a four-year degree—seems particularly challenging considering that the women here, in each of the decades since 1980, spoke of family financial strain. Some researchers (Covert 2015; England and Boyer 2009) predict that in the 2020s jobs in the clerical fields will polarize further than they already have. Workers without four-year college degrees will fall further to the bottom, doing call center, cashier, and lower-level secretarial work like filing and some stenographic tasks, and those with a four-year college degree will be pushed toward the top with their knowledge and capabilities related to computers, data analytics, budgets, finance, and other complex tasks. Wage levels will decrease and increase accordingly. Since most clerical jobs are held by women, and increasingly by women of color or women without postsecondary education (Autor 2015), the field would seem to be siphoning nonwhite and less-educated female workers into positions that have little future opportunity. For workers who are moderately educated and are single parents, or have the extra transportation and access challenges experienced by the Latina and African American workers in the four studies, clerical work may not be a viable choice. The heavy task, schedule, and transportation demands evidenced in most of the clerical jobs examined in this chapter suggest caution in viewing such jobs as likely to provide real opportunity. We look next at what the healthcare field has offered since 1980 and what its status is now in the 2020s.

4

In Sickness and in Health

Healthcare Training and Jobs, 1980s to Today

Workers in the 2000s became increasingly sought-after by employers in the growing field of healthcare. The field's growth was partly due to demographic changes that began in the 1950s with the general aging of the U.S. population, which was then boosted by the baby boomer group, born between 1946 and 1964. The boomers began to turn 65 in 2001 and, by 2020, the youngest among them were around age 56. Older persons are the largest users of healthcare services, especially toward the end of their lives, which contributes to a growing need for healthcare services and an increase in related jobs. Life-sustaining technological advances, such as organ transplants and cancer treatments that extend lives have made for even broader employment possibilities in the healthcare field.

The demographic changes in the field also coincide with women's greater participation in the labor force. The number of women in the labor market between 1948 and 2015 more than quadrupled, from about 17 million to more than 76 million. By early 2020, women's share of the labor force rose to 57.3% from 28.6% in 1948, while men's share fell to 68.5%, 18.1 points below its peak of 86.6% in 1948 (BLS 2020g, h).

Other changes in the field also affected the nature of healthcare jobs. For example, although women whose narratives appear in this chapter expected the healthcare field to be fertile for employment, cost containment and efficiency efforts kept hospital-based staff-to-patient ratios high and hiring low. Punishing debt and growth in for-profit healthcare training institutions that promised but did not come through with jobs, temporary contract positions without benefits, and an increase in the credentials required for employment, whether or not actually needed for the job, meant that many women were stuck at lower levels of pay than they had expected. In addition, many of the women worked in a medical assistant or clerical capacity rather than in direct healthcare, which also resulted in lower wages than expected. Even so, during the four decades addressed in this book, occupations in healthcare were often a job seeker's preferred choice.

Working in Healthcare in the 1980s and 1990s

Healthcare is another occupational area that exemplifies some of the compounding changes in the labor market over the past several decades. Keeping the same job for life, a reality for many workers in decades past, became less and less common in the 1980s and 1990s. Many workers now had mixed job histories in both clerical and medical areas. Some were dealing with geographic distance from their jobs and single-parent family challenges, and others were experiencing "creeping credentialism." Creeping credentialism refers to employer practices of increasing education and skill requirements when hiring employees, even if the actual job or position does not require such increases. This selective practice was particularly evident in the healthcare training-focused welfare-to-work programs in the mid-1990s, as healthcare employers began to require new hires to hold high school diplomas or have passed GED tests. But welfare-to-work training programs were funded only to provide job skill training, not remedial high school education, which meant the programs were potentially discriminatory, even if the discrimination was unintended (Gaddis 2014).

Several women who participated in the Teen Study in the early 1980s held clerical jobs in medical settings at the Teen Study Follow-Up in 1989–1990. Few of these women, however, expressed passionate interest in health issues per se. They were primarily interested in the clerical aspects of their jobs, having had general clerical training in high school and medical terminology training after high school. In 1990, they held positions such as medical records file clerk and supervisor of field representatives for a medical record copying company. In 1989 and 1990, when the women were in their mid-20s, most said that, although their earlier occupational goals were nursing, pediatric registered nurse (RN), and the like, the educational path to those goals was too long or they found, by working or volunteering in a medical setting, that they did not really like the field. Even for those who felt they wanted a higher degree in nursing, such as RN or even bachelor-level nurse, that goal presented both financial and time challenges, as some women's stories will show. Other women strongly wanted active healthcare careers, as Laquita explained.

Laquita: Care Manager Work in a Geriatric Center, 1989–1990, Philadelphia

In January 1990, Laquita was a 24-year-old African American participant in the Teen Study Follow-Up who worked as a care manager in a Philadelphia geriatric center. In the earlier Teen Study in 1983, her goal had been to be a nurse. After graduating from high school, Laquita enrolled in an eight-month keypunch training program followed by a semester of community college, where she studied general mathematics and English. She paid for both programs herself. Her goal then was to enroll in a three-year RN program, but instead she held clerical jobs for the next couple of years. In 1987, she learned about a one-year licensed practical nurse (LPN) program sponsored by the Philadelphia Public School District and quickly enrolled. In the program, she took courses in mathematics, science, psychology, nutrition, and pharmacology, but no computer training was offered. The program cost $4,000 and, by 1990, she had not yet paid off her loan. She completed the training, however, and received her LPN certification, one step beyond the more common and lower-paid CNA certification. Laquita had thought she would have achieved her RN degree by 1990. Even so, she said, "I've gotten less education than I expected, but I did it [financed it] myself and feel pride about that."

Even after completing her LPN certification, Laquita was able to find only a part-time position in 1988 with a temporary nursing agency, from 7:00 A.M. to noon for $11.50 an hour ($26 in 2021 dollars). Temporary positions in healthcare had become quite common in the 1980s as the population of older persons increased, which then necessitated more nursing-related staff than was the case in prior decades. Laquita's position with a temporary agency, though, meant no job security, no nonwage benefits, no consistent hours, and no advancement opportunity.

After a few months doing temporary work, Laquita was hired full-time by a private nonprofit geriatric center as a care manager. She had held that position for 14 months at the time of our 1990 interview. She described her work duties as follows:

> I'm in charge of floor, in charge of the nursing assistants, and in charge of a 32-bed unit of intermediate patients on Medicare. The training I had I got on my own in an earlier training program. My job doesn't offer advancement opportunity. To get that, I'd need more training. I'd need to be an RN to be head of the nursing staff.

Although Laquita's geriatric center wage was similar to her wage from the nursing temporary agency, the center offered several nonwage benefits, including partial payment of tuition toward RN certification, which could help her reach her career goal. The benefits were particularly important since Laquita was still paying off the cost of her LPN program. She liked her work schedule, saying, "This is my first job that I don't work on weekends."

But she knew she needed more education to advance. Her stated intention was to proceed with her RN goal, which could help her move from her current position to a hospital position that was more focused on providing medical care. Thus, she hoped soon to attend a one-year RN program for LPNs with a good record at a local community college:

> I want to go back next year for RN. Community College has a one-year RN course for LPNs if you have a good record. They have a waiting list. Agencies will pay more for RN. Education is really important for getting a healthcare job. A high school diploma is not enough. The big problem, though, is you give money to trade schools and they don't help you apply for or get a job. They're a scam. I wish I'd heard of the LPN school earlier. I heard it from my mother; it's under the school system. I didn't hear until I was 22. The neighborhood paper had a flyer on the blackboard and on poles; also word of mouth.

Laquita's concern, however, was the waiting list for the program and her debt. The larger policy question here was whether Laquita could apply for a student loan, or even utilize her job's tuition benefit, since she still owed money from an earlier loan. It might depend on whether hers was a federal or private loan.

Overall, Laquita was fortunate to ride the tide of the growing geriatric population in the United States in the late 1980s and early 1990s, which translated into higher wages than had been available to her in earlier non-healthcare jobs. Still, to earn more than her early 1990s wage, which at $11.36 an hour ($32 in 2021 dollars) amounted to $22,700 a year if she worked full-time ($44,000 in 2021 dollars), she would need to obtain her RN credential. For added context, Laquita's yearly income in 1990 of $22,700 put her well above the 1990 federal poverty level of $6,800 for one person, but if she were in a three-person family of one adult and two children, her annual income would be below 200% of the poverty level.

In the 1990s, however, certain positions in the healthcare field became populated heavily by women attending welfare-to-work healthcare training programs. The programs specialized in filling the demand for low-level positions, especially in-home elder care and care for persons with disabilities. Basic nursing aide jobs also were common during this period, with CNA certification as the ultimate goal.

Welfare-to-Work Healthcare Training in the Mid-1990s

The passage of welfare reform legislation in the mid-1990s (the Personal Responsibility and Work Opportunity Reconciliation Act of 1996) and its implementation program, TANF, required public assistance recipients to either find a labor market job or participate in work-related training in order to receive cash assistance. As a result, healthcare and related organizations jumped on the healthcare training bandwagon to try to build up their healthcare staff in the face of a growing aging population and reduced or nonexistent funding for professional training for nursing staff. At the same time, healthcare costs were rising exponentially and hospitals and nursing homes could not keep up with the high wages of professionally trained healthcare personnel such as RNs and even LPNs. These three factors—changes in federal policy, healthcare system financing, and the requirement for cash assistance recipients to get jobs—created a perfect storm of system need, employer need, and job seeker need.

Faith: Healthcare Training, Later 1990s, Philadelphia

Twenty-year-old Faith, a white participant in a hospital-based Welfare-to-Work Study in Philadelphia in the later 1990s, emphasized that "school was always tough for me," partly when the content became more difficult and partly because of peer pressure, which she defined as "sex, drugs, everything, such as skipping school" when she entered high school in ninth grade. She dropped out of school in 10th grade and lived with her boyfriend, soon becoming pregnant. This resulted in a turnaround of taking responsibility for herself and her child. She enrolled in a nurse training program in which she earned her CNA certification and then was motivated to pursue her GED degree: "I'm-a keep moving on and try to better myself so my son's life can be better than what mine was."

When Faith entered the TANF-sponsored healthcare training program at Hospital-PA, the program required her to be available five days a week, full time. But she had a hard time complying with the full-time attendance requirement. As Faith noted, "I had to go back and forth to court to get a restraining order on my son's father." In contrast, some scholars have contended that the full-time requirement is based on the persistent belief that women who receive welfare are lazy and need to be officially pushed to participate (Mead 1992; Murray 1984). This assumption fails to take into account the ways in which suddenly sick children, family members' needs (including a woman's own), and challenging relational problems such as filing for divorce or a restraining order can interfere with full-time attendance.

Similar constraints were imposed on programs' training purposes, as a Hospital-PA program staff person explained: "Every Monday morning, programs must take their students' time sheets to the central welfare office for validation, and every Friday programs must return to the central office to get their students' paychecks." Complying with these regulations took time away from the healthcare training content. The regulations also stipulated that if an attendee was not present on Monday morning, she would forfeit her weekly cash assistance unless she had a compelling reason for nonattendance.

Faith reported that another challenge in meeting program requirements was being asked to leave a message on an answering machine, which could be daunting. She said, "I want to talk to her directly. I don't like talking to answering machines. Me and answering machines do not get along." The same complaint was voiced by participants in other welfare and workforce training programs across the United States (Iversen and Armstrong 2006).

Ultimately, although Faith had gained nurse aide expertise from an earlier program and had passed her CNA certification examination, by the mid-1990s healthcare facilities increasingly required new hires to have a high school diploma or GED. It was unclear whether the sudden addition of this education requirement was necessary for the job's competency requirements or whether it served to justify discriminating against certain job seekers. In any case, although GED training had not been offered in Faith's earlier program, she expected to receive GED training and support at Hospital-PA. Support she received, but not specifically for the GED:

> I had enough training, but I didn't wanna just stop there. I wanted to move on and keep goin', and I feel as though welfare was tryin' to provide that service. But they was supposed to help me get my GED, and that's something they didn't give. So that stops a lotta things when you don't have your diploma or GED.

Faith was surprised in her prior training program to learn that she had tested at college reading level: "I was shocked when I seen my assessment test come back, because they said that I had a college readin' level. . . . But I was kinda upset with my math scores, because it was like a temporary level and since I didn't do it so long, fractions just killed me." She discovered a job in home healthcare that would pay "$16 an hour with good benefits and everything, but I didn't have my GED and that stopped me from getting the job," even though she was already certified as a CNA. Instead, Faith was on track to be offered $7 an hour ($14,000 a year; $23,700 in 2021 dollars), even though she had CNA certification and prior job experience in healthcare. Seven dollars an hour in 1996 was several dollars above minimum wage, but still below 200% of the poverty level (U.S. Department of Health and Human Services 1996).

Ebony: Healthcare Training, Later 1990s, Philadelphia

Twenty-five-year-old Ebony, an African American participant in the Welfare-to-Work Study at Hospital-PA, noted that she had found high school challenging because "it was hard for me to concentrate—it was hard for me to pass. My attention span was a little short. I just couldn't concentrate." Ebony's concentration problems began in ninth grade when her parents separated and, although she described her mother as supportive and helpful, she did not find her teachers helpful enough. As a result, she left high school after completing 11th grade. Soon thereafter Ebony enrolled in a GED course and passed some of the tests but did not complete the testing. She enrolled again in a GED course concurrent with enrollment in the welfare-to-work program but reported that "math is just something hard for me." She had been tested for a learning disability in high school but did not provide any information about the result.

Although the welfare office directed Ebony to housekeeping and dietary positions in healthcare facilities, Ebony held out for a healthcare training program and critiqued the "work first" mandate of welfare reform that required participants to take the first job available, contending that it was really important to like your job: "When people are hired, they should be comfortable with they job and love to be at they job. Being in a job only for the money doesn't work for me." Ebony was particularly interested in working with children with disabilities. During the welfare program, Ebony passed two of the GED tests and needed to pass three more, one of which was mathematics, her nemesis. She was optimistic, however, knowing that she could retake a test if necessary. She also wanted further education to improve her ability to work with disabled children. Overall, the healthcare welfare-to-work programs like Faith's and Ebony's were notable for their general healthcare preparation but insufficient in helping participants pass the GED tests. In fact, Ebony did not complete her GED while in the program, which was a common outcome in workforce development programs at the time (Iversen and Armstrong 2006). General healthcare competency training took priority in the programs while employers were simultaneously increasing their education and certification requirements. Consequently, the misalignment between program focus and employer priorities hindered program participants and employers alike.

Faith's and Ebony's stories are two of many that show how occupation-targeted welfare-to-work programs aimed to improve the lives and earnings of young workers. Some program participants found healthcare jobs that paid more than the cash assistance they had received, though, in many cases, their wages, even though well below 200% of the poverty level, were high enough to put them just beyond eligibility for needed work supports such as SNAP and childcare subsidies. Even the wages of those who had or gained credentials through the program did not reach 200% of the poverty level. Certification levels beyond CNA and LPN became increasingly necessary for new hires to earn anywhere close to sustaining incomes. The wage and salary hopes of healthcare workers moving off welfare remained hindered by prior education debt, credential inflation, also known as credential creep, and low wages. The mobility hopes of middle-income healthcare workers were also constrained by these factors, which were magnified by the opportunity cost in lost wages when returning to school for RN or higher certification.

Healthcare Jobs in the 2000s

Moving forward a decade, healthcare jobs by the 2000s were considered well paid, but a recent report qualified the general situation. "Opportunities are only available to those willing [and able] to put in the time and money to retrain" (Searcey, Porter, and Gebeloff 2015, A1). The Searcy et al. also emphasized that much more knowledge of sophisticated technology and multidisciplinary coordination is expected of nurses in the 2000s than was the case in the 1980s and 1990s. Another article stated that "increased demand likely won't help America's most vulnerable job seekers because many of the new jobs will require advanced degrees and continued certifications" (Huffington Post 2012), as Faith's and Ebony's experiences foretold. In fact, almost 58% of registered nurses in 2015 had a bachelor's degree or higher, in comparison with about one-third in 1980 (Searcey et al., A7). The story of Martina at the end of this section is a typical example of the new pattern. As the Teen Study Follow-Up women and those attending welfare-sponsored healthcare training programs later in the 1990s illustrated, even in the early 2000s most pathways did not lead to RN certification. Some participants were lucky to obtain GEDs.

Tasha: Pediatric Nursing Goals Dashed, 2000 to 2005, New Orleans

Twenty-one-year-old Tasha, an African American participant in the Ethnographic Study at the New Orleans, Louisiana, site, had a long-term goal of becoming a pediatric nurse. After graduating from high school in 1999, Tasha enrolled in a federal job training program outside Louisiana, where she received training in business office technology. She chose business training rather than a nursing curriculum despite her goal of a healthcare career. Her reason was that the nursing curriculum "was uninteresting." Family health problems necessitated Tasha's return to New Orleans before she completed the office training. She enrolled in a preemployment healthcare training program soon thereafter, in fall 2001. After she went through six weeks of general "soft skills training, such as how to write a proper résumé, dress appropriately for a job interview, and how to get to work on time," that also included learning a few healthcare competencies, the plan was for Tasha to be placed in a local community college in a challenging and competitive LPN program. But the healthcare program's partnership with the college had not been sufficiently negotiated, so the option of pursuing LPN training was not open to Tasha. Instead, the healthcare program placed Tasha in Hospital-LA as a dietary service worker at a wage of $5.58 an hour ($9 in 2021 dollars). Her pay was substantially below the $7-an-hour wage minimum ($11 in 2021 dollars) that the healthcare program expected graduates to earn. A program staff member explained that "90% of healthcare job placements for graduates were in food service, housekeeping, and patient escort, positions that traditionally offered low wages."

After three months at Hospital-LA, and finding her supervisor's peremptory changes of her schedule problematic because of her need for childcare for her 2½-year-old, Tasha left her job and located a housekeeping job at Historic Hotel through her extensive strong-tie network (Granovetter 1973, 1983) of New Orleans relatives. Her wages, however, fell just below the federal poverty level for her family of two. Tasha's plan at that point was to take an interim job as a security guard at Security Company and wait for a medical coding training program to begin. The coding program was seeking permission from the state to certify graduates, a process that resulted in months of start-up delay, a common problem that ultimately disadvantaged many job seekers (Iversen 2000). In her Security Company position, because Tasha refused to use a firearm, she was assigned the 10:00 P.M. to 6:00 A.M. shift at a wage of $6 an hour ($9.46 in 2021 dollars)—less than she had anticipated.

Despite this period of tacking from job to job while waiting for what ultimately turned out to be a nonexistent program, Tasha reiterated her ultimate goal: "I want to be a nurse. That's all it is. And I think I won't be satisfied with myself until I just go and be it." Because Tasha had good grades and test scores from one of the few strong high schools in New Orleans, she finally explored the nursing program at her local vocational college on the advice of a long-time friend. The problem here was that the vocational college's 18-month LPN program was unaccredited, which meant that credits earned would not transfer to an RN program. Also, staff at Tasha's earlier healthcare preemployment program had not realized that program graduates, even those with good records like Tasha, would end up being assigned to a large number of remedial courses before they even began official nurse training. A healthcare administrator with the preemployment program explained how this problem came about: "We severely underestimated the need our students who enrolled in the community college had for academic remediation. We need to do a better assessment to decide who needs to go to the community college, who to the vocational college, and who to a coding class."

After a few more twists and turns during 2002, including a period living out of state, in March 2003, Tasha contacted the LPN program of a local technical college and planned to start its 18-month LPN program taking night classes. At program completion, she would be eligible for certification and, she thought—but was not sure—that her LPN courses would be accepted later by an RN program. Four years after high school graduation, Tasha's future opportunity in healthcare remained uncertain.

Shanquitta: CNA Work and Hospital Efficiency Changes, 2000–2005, St. Louis

Thirty-seven-year-old Shanquitta, an African American participant in the Ethnographic Study, had relocated to St. Louis from another southern state around the time we met her and her three children, two to 13 years old, in March 2001. After working for a period outside the healthcare field in a grocery, (see also her food service experience in Chapter 5), Shanquitta wanted to restore her CNA certification and practice nursing assistance in a St. Louis hospital. Shanquitta explained that the people with whom she had contact in the grocery were different from those with whom she had had contact as a CNA in the hospital:

> You can see there [in the hospital], you can tell that you make a difference. It is people that you don't know and, when they leave, they hug you and they say thank you because you help them while you were there and that way you know you're helping somebody. At [Food Store] people come in with an attitude and like you have got to do this and I just like nursing better.

Nursing seemed to like Shanquitta as well. When the research team visited her at the suburban Hospital-MO, where she hoped to work after her workforce program internship, it was clear that she felt comfortable with the work that was assigned to her and enjoyed working at that particular hospital. Shanquitta's clinical training instructor had consistently given her scores of "very good," the second-highest possible score on evaluation reports, which assessed punctuality, attendance, appearance, organizational capacities, overall performance, and initiative. After her internship, Hospital-MO offered Shanquitta a full-time CNA position working the day shift on a medical unit. She began on the 6:45 A.M. to 3:15 P.M. shift, earning $10.20 an hour [$15.50 in 2021 dollars] with full benefits—over $1 more per hour than she anticipated and $3 more per hour than any previous job in her long work history, even earlier CNA jobs. Shanquitta described her usual work duties as follows:

> We get a lot of people that have broken hips and broken knees and all that. We get them up and walk them around and make sure they are in a certain way so they won't hurt themselves. You get some kids having they tonsils out and some young guys with back conditions and stuff. It is really not complicated.

Very quickly, Hospital-MO staff recognized that Shanquitta had expertise beyond that of the usual nursing assistant, which led to her having more duties than in any previous job, as she explained:

> I don't need a lot of training [on a new task] and so they kind of got comfortable with me and let me do a lot of extra stuff that I really didn't know I could do, and so it is all right. I didn't know that we do oxygen and like they bring somebody out of surgery, they just tell us to go down there and put them on five liters, I didn't know we did that, I mean we went over it [in training], I know how to do it, but I didn't think, being a CNA, we were supposed to do that, and messing with their IVs and stuff. I asked the aides about it and they said once a nurse knows you can do it, then she just send you down there to do it. So that was pretty good too. They kind of call out my name a lot. One day I am like, "Oh is this really my name?" They was calling me for everything. I was like, "OK. Tomorrow I am going to change my name" (chuckle).

At the same time, Shanquitta's experience in St. Louis in the early 2000s was emblematic of changes in hospital policies and procedures across the country. As healthcare expenses for patients and facilities continued to rise across the United States, hospitals found it difficult to support their entire array of services. In response, many hospitals undertook efficiency and quality analyses in the early 2000s, essentially "using rigid corporate improvement techniques in a patient model" to cut costs (Gabor 2004, 4). In late fall 2001, about six months after Shanquitta started at Hospital-MO, her hospital was one of several in St. Louis that engaged consultants to do similar analyses. Shanquitta described the consultant team in measured terms:

Well, we got some people who came in trying to change everything and increase our workload. They are going to be there [until] February and, when they came in turning things upside down, you start going to work and they start sending us home saying they had too many employees. We had this big whole list of job openings and they put a freeze on all that. Normally I have like six patients to take care of but now I have like 10 or 12. So [the last] three days [we worked] hard because we had a full house. We had 30 patients.

As it turned out, Shanquitta's CNA position was greatly affected by the efficiency analysis. Despite a newly doubled workload, Shanquitta's wage remained at $10.20 an hour. Worker morale was low:

Well, the nurses are all up, they don't like it. They [the consultants] don't know [what we deal with]. They try to have us put down on paper what we do. They are not there following us eight hours to see what we are doing and we might be doing one thing and then something come up and you have to do other things, and they can't see that. Then it cuts you back and you end up being short. They don't realize the patients are the ones that are suffering from the things they are doing. Like tomorrow I might have 10 patients because it is Saturday and it is only two of us working. If I am there and this person calls me for something and I am doing that and then somebody else calls me, I just can be all day [running around].

The consultant strategy on staffing efficiency had a doubly negative effect, as it translated into higher workloads when the patient census was up and the possibility of cutbacks in hours when the patient census was low. Shanquitta was able to supplement her income through a temporary agency when her hours at the hospital were cut back, but when the census was high, she had to refuse extra hours at the temporary service, which paid more money.

By February 2002, Shanquitta's work status had substantially changed. Her hours had changed and she had been given a small wage increase from $10.20 an hour to $10.45 an hour ($15.50 to $15.89 in 2021 dollars). At the same time, the changes in schedules and wages that resulted from the external efficiency evaluation caused many disruptions and transformations within the organizational structure. Shanquitta reported that many employees quit working at Hospital-MO when the hospital instituted new 12-hour shift requirements for all. She said, "A lot of people quit or went to 12 hours, [so we are now] understaffed [and] overworked. I don't know exactly how many [quit], but it [seemed] like the whole hospital. They lost a lot of employees because of the 12-hour shifts. Some liked it and some didn't."

Although the new schedule of three 12-hour days followed by four days off enabled Shanquitta to tend to her family and augment her income with temporary work, over time she noticed that she was getting especially fatigued from standing on her feet for an extra four hours a day on her 12-hour hospital shifts. Equally problematic, Shanquitta figured out that despite giving her a raise, Hospital-MO had reduced the hours for full-time workers from 40 to 36 hours a week, which meant that in every biweekly paycheck, she ended up eight hours short of pay, even though she was also periodically able to work overtime. Shanquitta reported that a recent 72-hour take-home paycheck was for $650, while her regular 80-hour take-home pay had been $700. Thus, the opportunity to work extra hours seemed a way of concealing a pay loss such that her supposed raise was actually a reduction in overall pay. Neoliberal strategies like this became typical in the age of managed care, when cuts in the name of efficiency were surreptitiously enacted on the backs of lower-wage flexible workers like Shanquitta. Although CNAs had begun to organize at other hospitals across the country, Shanquitta was unaware of any union activity at Hospital-MO in February 2002.

A year later, in early 2003, Shanquitta said she was less satisfied with the climate at Hospital-MO. She felt that the patients were getting less good care. She worked the same schedule of three 12-hour days and her wage was now $11.12 an hour ($16.29 in 2021 dollars), but she was seriously considering switching hospitals to one nearer her home in the city. Without time, opportunity, and funding to take upgrade courses, which had been eliminated as a result of the efficiency analysis at Hospital-MO, Shanquitta was finding her career opportunities limited to a series of minimal wage increases and the need to work two jobs to even come close to making ends meet. Such worksite and policy changes, even those reaching back to the 1980s, persisted into the second decade of the 2000s.

Healthcare Jobs in the Great Recession and Beyond

Annie: Visible Changes in the Healthcare Industry, 2008 to 2015, Philadelphia

Annie's story exemplifies some of the changes in the healthcare industry in 2008 and beyond that were visible only at the periphery in the 1990s and early 2000s. Industry employment practices placed workers in equally precarious positions in both periods.

The 2008 interview with Annie, a 38-year-old white participant in the Family Study and mother of two children, age 11 and 13 years old, was conducted in her home shortly after she had knee surgery. She had worked as a computerized tomography (CT) scan technologist for an area hospital's inpatient and outpatient center for the previous seven months, which was some distance away from her suburban Philadelphia house: "Pretty far. It's about 25 miles and it takes me about 40 minutes to get there in the morning and about an hour to get home. Otherwise, it's the perfect situation for me. I work Monday through Friday, eight to four thirty, no weekends, no holidays. That's what I need to be working with the kids." Other than its problematic commute, Annie described her current job with obvious pleasure:

I do CT scans on people, anybody. I can do MRIs [magnetic resonance imagings] too; I am certified in MRI. But our place is just CT scans. I love my job, love my job. It's just so different from being in a hospital. I didn't want to let them [the new employers] down. The longer-than-expected recovery from my surgery wasn't the plan, but they were really good about it. And I'm lucky because I actually worked under my supervisor before, so they know me, and I know them.

Trust and respect on both sides, employer and employee, seemed to make up for the fact that Annie was away from work for four weeks rather than the one week than she and her supervisor expected.

In her previous hospital-based job, Annie was required to work weekends. She also found that workplace policies on coverage of other employees' shifts were changing rapidly:

Where I was before things were changing and they were gonna rotate me. If, say, the four o'clock-to-twelve o'clock person called out or the night person, I was gonna have to cover it. And, when I went there, I was told that wouldn't need to happen, but as time went on, that's what I was told. So I was, like, I need to go. I need to find something else. And I was very happy that I made that choice because it was happening more and more. I had to cover people's vacations and everything, and I was like, I'm not doing this. Who do you have as a babysitter for two kids? You can't leave them alone at night. That's just not realistic. And they'd say, "Well, that's not our problem." But luckily, I was very lucky to find a position that had the exact hours I needed. Timing, timing is everything.

Earlier, Annie had earned an associate degree and began her healthcare career as an X-ray technician, which she practiced on weekends. A year later, she went to school for CT scan and MRI certification and eventually went back to work full-time, which was "midnight to 8:00 A.M. or 11:00 P.M.

to 7:00 A.M., and my husband didn't like it." When Annie and her husband divorced, she was grateful she had completed her education: "I was very glad I had the education behind me to be able to be self-sufficient and support me and the kids in the same house we'd always been in, because just because things didn't work out between me and him, I didn't want to pull them out."

In 2009, Annie reported that she had actually been out of work for seven weeks during her knee recuperation. She had received some disability pay, but it only amounted to about half her salary. She determined that she went "three and a half weeks without getting paid." Annie also reported some changes at her workplace, in line with McCall's (2000) finding that many workers experience employer-initiated flexibility as job insecurity or forced wage reduction:

> With the hours, they asked us to do what they call flextime, which is if you're not busy in your area, to go home early and you can either use vacation time or basic leave, they call it, but you don't get paid for it. So, when I take that, I'm the only one who does what I do there, so the most amount of time I could take in a day is a half an hour early. I couldn't be leaving like four hours early and not getting paid for it.

Annie also explained that the national economy during the Great Recession had influenced the new flextime practice: "In the past year, the facility, and healthcare you know, has been affected by the economy. You know, people lose insurance, and they can't go and pay for a scan. So, they started the flextime. Another big company in the suburbs had layoffs, but our center didn't." Even so, Annie periodically lost a substantial amount of income per month from the two and a half hours of lost pay per week and additional lost pay when she had to leave work for meetings at her son's therapy facility (and chose not to use basic leave or vacation pay, which the center euphemistically called flextime).

Annie also had a long history of working and taking classes at the same time:

> Initially when I started doing what I do, I went to school for two years full-time. I didn't want to go to college for four years and my girlfriend laughs at me because she's like "You didn't want to go to college for four years, but you went to a two-year school, you worked full-time, and then you went back to school at night and continued to go on and get more certifications in different areas. . . . You did way more than four years, girl. What are you doing?" I said, "But I did it my way," and she just shakes her head and laughs. But you

know, there's so many different areas that I could move into. I'm not stuck in one area. I have four different certifications to work in different areas in a radiology department, so it's something that I learn easily. I have to keep updated. I have to do continuing education on my certifications. I may go back for one more, but not right now. My certifications are in general radiography, cardiovascular intervention, which is like cardiac catheterization, and intervention procedures. You go and do all kinds of icky stuff. You don't really want to know. And CT scan and MRI.

Annie had taken several steps to ensure that she was always going to be employable. Even so, she was somewhat concerned about being laid off:

Of course. Nobody's immune to it. There are periods, you know, you look at the numbers. Everybody looks at the bottom line, looks at the numbers, and some months I'm lower, some months I'm higher. It just all depends. Lower or higher in terms of volume. But I'm in an area where we have doctors who are capitated to certain facilities [capitation refers to doctors being paid a set amount for each person enrolled to them], so they can't all come to me anyway. It's not like you can just go wherever you want. It depends on the insurance and all that kind of stuff. So, we're working with trying to get more patients capitated for us. Some months are more steady and others are very slow. But I don't just do the CT scans. When I'm slow, I help out in X-ray, I do DEXA scans [Dual-energy X-ray absorptiometry is a means of measuring bone mineral density using spectral imaging.] I learned how to do DEXA scans by being where I am now because I've had the time to learn it and do it and it makes me more marketable.

At the same time, if she were to be laid off, Annie was not confident that she would find another job. "Because if healthcare is laying off," she said, "healthcare is laying off. Like I said, the big center did layoffs, so they're not going to be hiring. If anything, they'd bring those people back. So, if other places are laying off, I'm not going to be hired, or you'll have 50 people [applying] for one job." This pattern further reduced opportunity for healthcare workers such as Annie when elective surgery was virtually stopped during the COVID-19 pandemic.

Regarding her future work plans, Annie planned to stay put: "I have no plans of changing. I've worked at different places and when you find a good group of people to work with . . ." Her voice trailed off. Annie had seen a friend recently who asked about another work setting, to which she responded as follows:

You can go anywhere and be in a worse situation. I've done it before. I didn't have a choice because they were forcing me to go on nights and I couldn't do that as a single parent. So, when I got this job, I applied, I saw it online, I applied for it and was hired within 10 days. It was like everything fell into place and it was like God was pushing me, pushing me. And, you know, if I didn't leave where I left, I would have been laid off, because my facility was part of that large center.

Martina: Credential Creep in Healthcare Work, 2008 to 2015, Philadelphia

Martina's story, like Annie's, derives from her multiyear participation in the Family Study during and after the Great Recession. Martina's is an example of how changes in the healthcare system in the form of credential inflation (also called credential creep) became especially punishing to workers during the Great Recession. In fact, between 1990 and 2010, credential creep for healthcare work expanded from primarily affecting lower-earning workers to also affecting more educated, solidly middle-income earners, such as Martina.

In 2008, Martina was 48 years old, married, white, and the mother of four children between nine and 16 years old, plus an older, married daughter with her own home and family. Having achieved RN certification, Martina worked during the school year as a school nurse and also worked in a nursing home doing nurse supervision every other weekend. In the summer, she added days during the week to help cover for vacations. During the school year, school nursing usually required working four days a week, which gave her one day off during the week. Martina described her two jobs in vivid detail:

My school nursing job is screening heights and weights and stuff like that, and also the kids come in and taking care of them, assessing the situations, does mom need to be called? We did some health routines. We'll do diet, nutrition, or diet plans. We do health and hygiene for puberty things. In coordination with the dental program, we'll be involved with that. That's kind of a nice job. I like it because I work with my children. When they get off school, and when they get out early, I'm off, too. My other job, at the nursing home, that's where I take care of old people. They have great stories and I love talking with them.

At the nursing home, I work the weekends, so, typically, I'm the only RN in the facility, which means that if somebody's getting sick, I would be on top of it. We have a 120-bed facility and there'll be two

LPNs on one side with 60 and two LPNs on the other side. When I go in, I take a report on all patients right away so I oversee what's going on. Then you prioritize what has to be done. I go into the dining room maybe because somebody has to be in there in case somebody chokes. It's not really high stress, but a lot of times with the elderly there's a question of whether you really want to send them out, because if you send them out, diagnostic testing could kill them, they're so fragile. Anytime you can keep them in the facility, which is what we try to do. We actually try to get an order from the doctor and the family to say no hospitalization, just take care of their comfort. Obviously, if they need treatment, if something's going on and the person's pretty viable, I would call out and get them treated. So, that's my job. I think they call it triaging, where you see who needs what, which they would do in the emergency room. That's the bulk of it and there's a lot of paperwork.

I also manage the LPNs. They do a wonderful job. They're my buddies, but, if anything would go wrong, with me having a license, I would be the one liable. So, if they ask me, I usually say, "Yes, that's what I would do." Or, if I think maybe I can think of something that might be a little better, I'll tell them. It's kind of like we work together, but I know ultimately my license is hanging on what's going on. You just do the best you can. You make a decision based on what's best for the patient and that's that, and you are careful. You don't want to go overly and you don't want to go underly.

I like both my jobs, I really do. I've always liked working with the elderly and working with well children is wonderful. I like it. When my second-oldest son was nine, it looked like we needed money, so I said, "I think I'm gonna see if I can get something for evenings." They had an ad in the paper for somebody to work 7:00 P.M. to 11:00 P.M., and I thought, well, geez, nice for a couple nights a week. Then you only had to give them one weekend a month, three-to-eleven shift. I said, "I can do this." That's how I started out. Then when the youngest went to kindergarten, they would call me up and say, "We need a nurse to go on a school trip." I'd say, "OK." So, they kind of worked me into getting into the school district. I loved it and that's when they offered me a position that was part-time. They call it full-time there, but it's equivalent to a part-time position. I don't get benefits or anything. I fill in. I'm hourly paid.

At this point in 2008, although Martina felt the economy was problematic, she expected that she and her husband Jim, who ran a small construction business, would keep their jobs: "It feels like we're in a little recession right now with the war and all, but maybe these times are better than they were in my mother's generation in the Great Depression. I have a job and my husband has a job." Nevertheless, family finances, the Great Recession, and teenagers nearing college age all played into Martina's concern about her earning power:

In the early days, it seemed like we were OK, but I think my husband made a couple investments with properties and they're the kind you have to wait for it to come to fruition, so right now we're just paying out things. I'm feeling it. What I would like to do, because I don't have benefits and because both of my jobs are kind of part-time status, I'd want to get a job Mondays through Fridays with benefits.

By 2009, Martina's desire to earn more money was even stronger. But she'd waited until recently to begin the search for a new job:

I'm looking for another job that offers benefits, so I'm kind of out there, career searching. My husband has definitely taken a hit with decline in business, so he's trying to pick up extra stuff here and there, but it's not really what he likes to do. He gets one here and there, one every six weeks maybe, but not like he would get two or three a week before. I was thinking about looking [last year] and then I just stayed where I was for one more year. But this year I told them I'm not coming back in September, so over the summer I'm trying.

As the Great Recession deepened and lengthened, Martina tried to do further coursework in order to be eligible for benefits as a school nurse, illustrating the broader trend of credential inflation in the U.S. labor market and its close connection with the state of family finances, particularly in a period of recession:

I went to a local college for about six months and got a couple of credits and then I stopped. I pursued that originally because I wanted the benefits. At our school district, if you want medical benefits, you have to be nurse-certified. And school-nurse-certified is you have to have your bachelor's and then you have to be five classes away from your master's, so it's a little bit more schooling. So, I went there and started taking courses, but then I stopped because it was kind of expensive. Most of the people that went there worked for hospitals or something that will pay their tuition, and so they were able to stay. But it was like $950 every six weeks, and I had like

$5,000. I put that up front, then I thought, well, I'll work an extra weekend, and it started to get to be too much. Plus, I had to do the homework. It was all papers. You had to do papers, and I did them all at night, like I started them at ten at night and sometimes it was due the next morning. I wasn't getting it done until six in the morning and then I was going to work for the school. It was a little too much.

I still don't have my bachelor's degree. I would have to go to five or six more classes after that to be school-nurse-certified, which all the nurses that work for the school district are kind of up in arms about, because I worked in a hospital for 10 years and I was trauma-certified and intensive-care-certified and I have my verification for that and everything, and, when you work as a school nurse, you're not allowed to do anything. You put a Band-Aid on, what you do is call the parents. Unless I have a doctor's order with the medication and it has to be renewed and everything has to be just so, then I can give them medication. But if a kid needs anything, aspirin, we're not even supposed to put Neosporin on a cut because it's considered a medication. I don't like it. I feel like your hands are tied.

In one situation, Martina treated a child's cut anyway with the kind of Band-Aid that can be used instead of stitches. Two days later the wound was healing very nicely. One of the teachers said, "You know, Martina, you are their primary care physician." Martina responded, "I know, but it's so funny because I can actually get in trouble for doing all that. The point is, I would like to do more than I do, but what we do is education."

Martina had discussed her role as health educator in an interview in 2008:

In fact, I was teaching first-grade health. They had this prefabricated whole big curriculum just on their level, but it has this nice board that you turn and it told you what to get involved in, and I could add my own stuff and everything, and I loved that. So that was cool. I loved it. And boy, they were so smart and they would raise their hand. It was so cute. Like they were good.

I loved the teaching. Actually, I think if I really, really did what I want to do, which I'm getting old now and I don't have the education, it would be teaching nursing. But I think they want you to be almost to your doctorate and you see where I am. I have a lot of experience and everything, but I should really pursue more schooling along the way because I'm so behind to pursue a career like that. But yeah, I do like the teaching. I like people.

In fact, Martina gave an ultimatum to the school district about not returning in order to goad herself into searching for another job. But, in 2009, she
indicated that she had left the door open to remaining where she was.

Making use of her social network, Martina mentioned that a friend who
was a nurse consultant for a firm and who was already moving up to training other people was checking to see whether the firm needed someone like
Martina. At this point, most of the opportunities there involved working on
the weekends. But even though Martina wanted a weekday job, she felt she
could at least get her foot in the door in a job that would draw fully on her
training and substantial experience, without needing to invest time and
money in additional education:

> This new job if I get it, I'll love it because it has some maneuverabil-
> ity. Once I get to know the ropes a little bit, they give you a laptop
> and I could do a lot of the work at home. I want to be home as much
> as I can with the kids. And Jim, when he gets a job, he's like gone. I
> mean, being that he's the one that's the basic breadwinner in the
> family, I want to be the one that has the flexibility. So, I said, if I can
> get a job where I get a lot done on the weekends or whatever, if I'm
> doing it at home, maybe one day in the week I'll come in and do the
> school nursing. So, I left it open.

Because Martina had kept her credentials up to date and never officially
resigned from the school district nurse position, she felt she was still employed there and could work more or less as a substitute.

Martina also shared her perspective on the puzzling situation of the widespread call for more nurses in the United States at a time when there were
actually fewer positions available, especially for those without bachelor's-
level credentials (AllNurses 2012):

> This friend of mine, she just came back and applied at a few places
> and there were some places that were laying off. I think they're lay-
> ing off the girls or men, whoever, the veteran nurses, because they're
> the higher paid and they might be hiring new people. You'll see that.
> They're getting rid of everybody and then hiring. It's not like we're
> getting rid of them and then we're downsizing, because they're still
> going to have the same volume of patients coming in and more pre-
> dicted. Plus, they're hiring for the generally less-desirable hours. My
> friend is working 7:00 P.M. to 7:00 A.M. That's kind of heavy duty.
> That's a 12-hour day.

Martina did not realize that one additional reason for hospital cost cutting
was the many patients who postponed or avoided having elective surgeries

during the recession and its many-year aftermath because they feared taking time off work or losing their jobs during a protracted recovery (All-Nurses 2012). Elective surgeries are the "bread and butter" of hospital income, which meant that the patient population during the recession period tended to be shorter-term and pay less or not at all. Thus, replacing higher-paid skilled nurses with people from lower-paid, lower-skilled nursing positions helped hospitals and medical facilities weather the income losses of the recession. Such practices were repeated, even magnified, at the hospital level during the COVID-19 pandemic when all beds were allocated to virus patients.

All in all, Martina conveyed considerable satisfaction with her working life as a nurse because of the content of her jobs and being allowed to have input into her schedule (Lambert, Fugiel, and Henly 2014):

I have been more than happy with the flexibility of the job of nursing, because when I had my older two children, I was a single parent for 14 years and I was able to work the schedule around them. When Jim became my boyfriend, he watched them for me on weekends while I worked. And then, during the week, I worked in a hospital pool and I didn't have to be there until after the kids went to school, because usually a day-shift nursing job is 7:00 A.M. to 3:00 P.M. But, if you're in the pool, that means they're going to use you wherever they need you, so they don't really know if they need somebody for about another hour or so after work starts. I loved the flexibility of hours. I actually liked my career. I like helping people, and even when I get down at the end, even though it's grueling sometimes, I feel like I made a difference, so I like that. And I like it because it has a lot of variety. When I work at the nursing home, I'm supervisor, but you're dealing with different things all the time, different tasks. It could be dealing with the doctors, the families, the patients, the pharmacists. It's paperwork, it's hands-on care, seminars where you keep up on the latest medical improvements and products and different things they do, which I think is really interesting. So as far as my career, I have never regretted it.

What Martina would have liked, however, is even more time for community service. She participated in neighborhood civic groups, taught a weekly catechism class for her church, and, together with Jim, supported their children's enrichment activities. With their level of community activity and its meaningfulness for her family, Martina began to wonder about the demands of her nursing schedule:

I'm starting to get where I don't know if I want to do the weekends anymore. I've been a nurse for 23 years, so I've been working on weekends and holidays. I'll usually work Christmas Eve, which isn't too bad. But I'm kind of getting away from it and I may try to find another job.

Four years later, in 2013, despite being generally better off financially because Jim's construction business had made a comeback, Martina and Jim were both still concerned about the continuing effects of the economic downturn on their lives, as Martina explained:

My husband being a general contractor, he has leads of where he gets his business from, and two of those places went out of business. And they were doing really well. They used to invite us to their Christmas parties and it was like, wow. And when I heard, I mean that one person in particular went under like that, I said, "Wow." So, I was a little concerned for Jim, although he does other things, so then he picks up more [work] with the other stuff—like roofing, hardwood flooring, decks, additions, bathrooms, kitchens—he's able to do all that.

And, although Martina was still pleased with her school nurse job, she was least happy about the pressure of credential creep. Nevertheless, between 2009 and 2013, Martina had returned to school and earned her bachelor's degree in nursing (BSN), feeling that "needing the degree is something that has changed over the past few years," as Rushing (2019) and others have reported in relation to the increasing intertwining of jobs, wages, and education. Martina described her situation as follows:

Actually, in the last couple of years, nurses—well, LPNs—are not getting accepted almost anywhere but in a nursing home, so they have to advance. Everybody had to go back to school or you might be out of a job. With the job I'm doing now, this private duty nursing, it's [a BSN is] actually not required. But I don't want to limit myself. I want to be able to work, walk into the hospital, and have them say, "OK, we have a job for you," which is what I used to do.

I finished, but I have to get back on the stick [and get more education]. I was paying every six weeks. It was a lot, and I started saying, "This is too much, I think I'm going to switch to something else." So, I'm actually looking at two options right now. One is an online deal that one of the girls had done. They said it's not too bad financially. I don't know if I could handle that being online. I might prefer going to a classroom one night a week, which was what I was doing when I did my BSN, and which is what my daughter is doing at an area university. And she's saying she'll get it in two semesters. She said for two semesters the whole cost is about $6,000, and I was paying every six weeks $1,200. For two years. And I was working extra weekends to pay it because I hate having bills over my head. I can still transfer my credits.

Martina was likely referring to the RN-to-MSN (master of science in nursing) track, which is offered broadly today by various nonprofit and for-profit sites, in person and online. At the same time, four of Martina's children would soon be needing support for postsecondary education programs and she did not want to go into debt. Her sense was that "I need it [the MSN] but I don't need it right now. I can work my way towards it."

Finally, since Martina's occupation of choice was teaching nursing, she might have pursued an adjunct position in a nursing program or taught in one of her credential areas—for example, trauma management—to nurses, social workers, and school teachers and counselors, for example, at a local community college or community learning center. Such opportunities might have been available in the evening, which would have enabled her to retain her school nurse position. After 2013, as the financial challenges of the Great Recession faded somewhat and the coronavirus had not yet appeared, Martina might have had the opportunity to contribute her nursing expertise to schools and a nursing facility, as well as to the community learning center through compensated civil labor. In the meantime, Martina's work has paid off somewhat more than that of many of the healthcare workers whose stories appear in this chapter. But, with several children now in college and her later-in-life attainment of a bachelor's degree, she may still struggle to finally secure a salary commensurate with her decades of experience.

Healthcare Jobs beyond 2020

Healthcare jobs currently account for almost 18% of the U.S. economy (Deutsch 2020). As noted throughout this chapter, the greater number and higher proportion of older persons in the United States in the foreseeable future will continue to have an impact on healthcare employment, particularly in the areas of hospitalization, nursing home care, physical therapy, occupational therapy, and home healthcare. Most employers in these areas, however, have instituted new advanced education requirements that many less-educated, lower-earning health workers do not have the money or time to pursue. The ongoing problems of debt-producing healthcare training programs, the use of credential inflation by healthcare employers to exclude potential employees otherwise capable of doing a job, employee-punishing cost containment strategies used by hospitals and medical facilities, and unjustifiably low wages are expected to persist into the 2020s and beyond, if not to increase. Such problems will limit the pool of healthcare workers, particularly if current criminal justice policies—which do not allow persons who have been imprisoned for minor drug crimes, such as the low-level possession or selling of drugs, to work in healthcare—remain in place. For many, working in healthcare is both a job and a passion. Greater attention needs to be given, however, to humane and predictable scheduling practices, compensated time for upgrading one's education and capabilities, and wages that convey recognition of the need for healthcare workers and the respect their work is due. The challenges revealed in this chapter will be further magnified by the impact of the coronavirus pandemic on virtually all aspects of the healthcare system as the 2020s proceed.

5

Can I Help You?

Work in the Retail Trades, 1980s to Today

R etail trade is a large industry sector comprising hundreds of subgroups, according to occupational employment and wage estimates
from the Bureau of Labor Statistics (BLS 2019j). Occupational subgroups for the workers whose stories appear in this book encompass food
service and drinking places (BLS 2020f), food and beverage stores (BLS
2020e), and clothing stores (BLS 2020a). Person-to-person engagement is a
critical element of virtually all jobs in these subgroups, which to some extent explains the longevity of these groups in the retail trade industry, even
now in the face of more online shopping.

Cashiers and retail salespersons in general are the two largest job categories in the country and were common among the workers in this chapter.
In December 2019, just before the coronavirus pandemic, together they accounted for about 8 million workers (BLS 2020i, 3). Cashiers were paid less
than retail salespersons (see Table 5.1), but neither of these jobs pays a living
wage for a family of four. Likewise, neither occupation's annual wage amounts
to twice the poverty level (see Table 5.1), even for individuals working 40
hours a week and 52 weeks a year, which the BLS considers "typical" (BLS
2020i). Although the average workweek for all employees in all occupations
in December 2019 was 34.2 hours (BLS 2020i, 9), none of the workers in this
chapter worked that many hours a week. Thus, while the Bureau of Labor
Statistics calculates the annual wage figures shown in Table 5.1 according to
40-hour weeks, because most workers' workweeks are around 34 hours, the
median annual wage figures are likely overestimates. This means that the

poverty level calculations shown in Table 5.1 also may be higher than is actually the case.

At 12 million employees, the food service and drinking places subgroup of retail trade was even larger than the cashier and retail sales subgroup, and median hourly and annual pay were larger as well. A similar pay pattern held for the food and beverage store subgroup, although the subgroup was smaller, at 3 million workers, than the other food subgroup. In both food-related subgroups, there were considerable differences between the number of employees and wages of supervisory and managerial employees and production and nonsupervisory employees (see Table 5.1). Nonsupervisory employees, such as waitresses and bartenders in food service and drinking places, outnumbered supervisory employees 7 to 1 and their annual wages were about 40% lower. In the food and beverage stores, nonsupervisory employees, such as delicatessen clerks and food preparation workers, outnumbered supervisors 9 to 1 and their incomes were just 61% of those held by supervisors and managers (see Table 5.1).

The category of clothing and clothing accessory stores was the smallest of the three retail trade areas that employed the workers whose stories appear in this book. In December 2019, this sector accounted for about 1.5 million employees, though all but about 130,000 worked in nonsupervisory positions, such as store design and sales. Managers and supervisors worked 25.5 hours a week on average, in contrast with those in design and sales roles, who averaged 22.4 hours per week and earned under two-thirds of their supervisors' earnings (see Table 5.1).

Of critical importance, considering how recessions have historically challenged workers and businesses in the retail trades, is the reality that the worst may be ahead for all workers because of the coronavirus pandemic. By August 2020, more than 22 million jobs had been lost in the United States and only 9 million jobs had been regained. The unemployment rate had risen to 10.2% from 3.5% in January 2020. Those in retail trade occupations felt these declines strongly. Overall retail sales during March 2020 were down 8.7% from February, which was the largest monthly drop ever recorded and more than twice the 4.3% decline in November 2008 during the Great Recession (National Retail Federation 2020, Apr. 13, 1). By August 2020, however, retail had gained back almost two-thirds (62%) of the jobs that had been lost earlier (Bartash 2020), but with e-commerce positions dominating over store positions.

As Table 5.1 shows, in these common occupations in the retail trade industry, only the supervisors and managers earned close to a sustaining wage for a family of four, and only if they worked full-time. Annual wages for only one of the nonsupervisory and production workers in the industry, most of whom were food services workers, reached above the federal poverty

TABLE 5.1 FULL-TIME EMPLOYMENT AND WAGES—OCCUPATIONAL
SUBGROUPS IN THE RETAIL TRADES

Occupation	No. employed	Median hourly wage	Median full-time annual wage	Percentage of federal poverty level for family of 4 (2020)
Cashiers	3.6 million	$11.37	$23,650	90%
Retail sales (general)	4.3 million	$12.14	$25,251	96%
Food services and drinking places	12 million			
Superv./mgr.	1.5 million	$15.47	$32,178	123%
Nonsuperv.	10.5 million	$14.02	$29,355	111%
Food and beverage stores	3 million			
Superv./mgr.	300,000	$19.95	$41,496	158%
Nonsuperv.	2.7 million	$12.19	$25,355	97%
Clothing and clothing accessory stores	1.5 million			
Superv./mgr.	130,000	$18.67	$38,834	148%
Nonsuperv./sales	1.2 million	$11.68	$24,294	93%

Table 5.1 was constructed by the author using data from BLS 2020a, c, d, e, f, i, and the standard
hourly-to-annual wage formula of 40 hours × 52 weeks (2080 hours)
Note: Superv./mgr. indicates supervisory or managerial position. Nonsuperv. or Nonsuperv./sales
indicates nonsupervisory production or sales position.

level for a family of four, and then only slightly. Overall, these BLS figures,
even though likely overestimates, tell a numbers story about the retail trade
industry. Workers' experiences doing these jobs provide a fuller story.

Part of the fuller story rests with the increase in involuntary part-time
jobs starting in the mid-1990s and expanding in the 2000s. Because wages
across industries remained stagnant, employers could pay part-timers less.
Part-time workers overall, women and men, earned 29% less per hour
worked than full-time workers with similar demographic characteristics
and education levels (Golden 2020, 1). Further reducing the financial security of part-time workers, employers have made use of federal tax rules that
exclude part-time workers from many types of benefits (Golden 2016, 12).
Golden (2016, 1) has characterized employers' actions as "an ongoing structural shift toward more intensive use of part-time employment by many
employers [that] is driving the elevated rate of involuntary part-time work."
Problematically for the workers in this chapter, "increased employer use of
part-time positions is particularly evident in industries in which part-time
jobs are already more prevalent, such as retail, hotels, and food service"
(Golden 2020, 2). Specifically, retail trade stores, hotels, and restaurants of

all kinds contributed more than 54% of the growth of involuntary part-time employment between 2007 and 2015 (Golden 2020, 3), and prime-age workers, persons 25 to 54 years old, such as those featured in this chapter, comprised 58% of all involuntary part-time workers (Golden 2020, 4). To survive economically, some held two or even three jobs at a time, often interfering with their sleep.

A second part of the story is that many workers found themselves searching for the stability of full-time employment and a meaningful career, which resulted in their moving from sector to sector of the retail industry in their attempts to find stable, meaningful work. The worker's sector often involved geographic relocation that negatively affected the family and children's school stability, as Tom's story illustrates in this chapter. Overall, the general volatility in the retail trade industry meant that many workers we interviewed experienced financial and emotional strain. Their strain was even evident among workers in retail or food service management. The workers' stories here are presented chronologically within the three retail trade sectors in which they worked: food services, food and beverage stores, and clothing sales and service. In a few cases, workers had briefly held cashier positions in the three sectors.

Food Services and Drinking Places and Food and Beverage Stores: 1980s to Today

In general, the food and beverage jobs of the men and women in this chapter preceded their eventual occupational landing point, although Hard Working Blessed entered food service when he left his manufacturing position after being downgraded when he incurred a serious injury and did not return to manufacturing. As a rule, and as is common nationally for food service work, with its turnover rate of 75% in 2018 and 80% in the recession period of the early 2000s (Grindy 2019), the narratives in this section show that food service may serve as a training ground for a first job (for example, Newman 1999), a way station after unsatisfactory employment, or a place saver until a preferred career can be started or restarted. The industry overall employs a large proportion of high school and college students in seasonal positions, such as summer jobs or winter vacation jobs, and is also the "economy's largest employer of teenagers, as one-third of all working teenagers in the United States are employed in a restaurant" (Grindy 2020, 1).

Noel: Food Service Management, 1990, Philadelphia

Noel's family was part of the Great Migration of African Americans to Philadelphia in the late 1880s, drawn by the promise of jobs (Wolfinger 2013).

However, deindustrialization after World War II slowed the flow of good employment for racial minorities and left many without the middle-class incomes they had achieved. Reports indicate that Philadelphia lost textile, metal manufacturing, and electronic production jobs by the tens of thousands from the 1950s to the 1970s (Wolfinger 2013, 5).

In the 1989–1990 follow-up of the Teen Study, Noel was 26 years old, married with no children, and employed as a manager in the food service world. She reflected on the positive value of having had a job in high school: "I learned early on that to work means to survive. Work taught me discipline and I became more well-rounded. I avoided drugs." She earned a high school diploma and spent three years in college at a university outside Philadelphia, where she majored in sociology and criminal justice. She did not finish college for financial and family reasons, common problems for students like Noel who have little financial backup or frequent health or related challenges in their families:

> I stopped at that point because I was three credits short of my senior year loan and there were family problems. My grandmother was ill and my mother couldn't work. I studied sociology and criminal justice, received loans and grants, and I still owe about $5,000 on the loans. My husband and I live in his parents' house, which they say they will sign over to us but haven't yet. I'm looking into finishing my BA but I have outstanding loans. I hope that they'll hold off collecting those until I can finish. I'll probably go back in 1991, about a year from now. I don't know exactly where, but I plan to finance this with grants and loans.

Unfortunately for Noel, outstanding loan debt and not having completed the original program for which she was awarded the loan meant that her grace period for paying back the loan would soon end and she would be required to start paying on it. Her only option then for continuing her education would be to apply for a high-interest loan from a for-profit loan organization, and that would add significantly to her debt. In the early 1980s, Noel had expected to have a doctorate by 1990. That goal was "hindered by family problems, as before I went to college, and like now," even though her family was emotionally very supportive of her educational goals. "They have high aims; they say I'll go far; they have high standards."

By 1990, though, Noel was employed full-time as a comanager of one of the national fast-food restaurants. Having been there for 15 months, she discussed her job responsibilities:

I manage 36 people. I do payroll, food costs, and ordering. I work with the assistant general manager. The job doesn't require any computer work. The specific training I needed was provided on the job. I have been working 48 to 50 hours a week. I earned $899 last year (1989) [$1,500 in 2021 dollars] every two weeks before taxes. That would have been enough to meet my expenses and bills if I were alone. I'm somewhat satisfied with my job. I could work part-time, and when I go back to school, I will want to work part-time, but now I want to work full-time.

Noel's anticipated income of $22,475 for 1990 (about $46,400 in 2021 dollars) was right at the median for a food service manager at a fast-food restaurant, but it was low when compared to medians of $26,000 for food service managers in all restaurants and $32,000 for managers in restaurants with table service (BLS 1990).

In the early 1980s, Noel had quite different goals for herself from what became her reality seven years later. As Noel explained, "Philadelphia high schools emphasized going into military service versus going to college. I thought I wanted to go into the air force after I graduated from college and then back to school [for a doctorate] on the military's program. But my goals changed. I was in ROTC and I changed my mind. I wasn't the type for ROTC."

Food service management did not seem to be Noel's goal, either. She had looked for other work, "trying to see if I could get into what I want to do, but I need the degree. I took the city test for probation officers a year and a half ago"—a content area consistent with her college major of sociology and criminal justice and thus a potential mobility direction for her (Iversen 1995). But once again she was caught between rising educational expectations, student debt policy, and family responsibilities. Her mother had died a few months earlier, which Noel attributed to "living in poverty because she had no health insurance and only a minimum wage job." Noel was both terribly sad and angry about her mother's plight. Her husband's father had died a month before her mother died. Both events reinforced Noel's career desire for something more meaningful than food service management: "Nobody thought I'd be working in food. They [the family] wanted me to do anything else. Food service is the slum of slums." Noel's wish was to "get into a helping profession in some way," but the loss of two supportive family members reminded her that she still needed to complete her college degree. As Boushey (2005, 2) has noted, "Highly indebted graduates may have little flexibility in the kinds of jobs they must take in order to afford their debts and may choose to postpone marriage, buying a house, or starting a family while they pay off their loans." Noel was having to postpone both having children, which her husband wanted at that time, and getting further education to increase her career opportunities.

If Noel had continued as a food service manager until today, she would likely earn at least the median annual pay of $32,178 a year, or $15.47 an hour (BLS 2020f). She would need to have computer competency, which she didn't have in 1990, and to have finished her bachelor's degree, which was already the expectation for managers in 1990 (BLS 1990). The job outlook for 2016–2026 indicates a 9% increase in the number of food service manager positions, which the BLS considers average (BLS 2019g), although that estimate was made before the COVID-19 pandemic had such a devastating effect on restaurants.

Joseph: Hotel Food and Beverage Service, 2000 to 2001, New Orleans

After Joseph, an Ethnographic Study participant, experienced challenging entry-level conditions in the New Orleans construction industry (see his construction story in Chapter 2), he chose to use his construction expertise and his food service capabilities at Boutique Hotel instead of struggling further with the pattern of race discrimination in a local construction union. Joseph worked for a year (2000–2001) at Boutique Hotel as a concierge, maintenance person, and room service attendant, focusing more on the latter as the year proceeded. Even though he preferred doing construction work, he felt the hotel experience provided him with "valuable customer service skills" that would help him later as a construction contractor. Joseph's description of his hotel work suggests that he made the best of the situation:

> All of the placements in construction were gone, so I went and got another job at [Boutique Hotel]. But, while I was working there, I was doing stuff for people. If they needed some steps fixed, I fixed those steps, or if they needed a door fixed, I fixed that door. I still used some of what I learned, but when I worked at the hotel, I wound up doing that job over a year because I maintained it, even though people was on my nerves there. This was hotel food and beverage, and I was in room service, learning how to greet people and listening to people. Keeping everything going, knowing the right words to say at the time. I was happy because for one reason I could keep a job, and it put a smile on my face. Even though I still wanted to be in construction, I wasn't just wasting my time.

Joseph earned $10 an hour ($15 in 2021 dollars) but no benefits at the downtown New Orleans hotel—a good wage, but one that still left his family of three at 138% of the federal poverty level.

Hard Working Blessed: Manager
at FastFood, 2002, Chicago

In spring 2000, Hard Working Blessed, a 40-year-old married African American participant in the Ethnographic Study and father or stepfather of two teens and an infant, had completed a manufacturing training program in Milwaukee, Wisconsin, and been hired by Steel Mill and Foundry as a crane operator. Soon thereafter, he also drove a forklift truck, mixed sand, and worked as a grinder. Although he started at a low wage in the late 1990s, after he worked there for 20 months his wage increased to $13 an hour (almost $20 in 2021 dollars). Unbeknownst to Hard Working Blessed or the manufacturing workforce organizations in Milwaukee, the manufacturing industry there was about to crash, largely as a result of the spring 2001 economic recession, in which many goods-producing establishments across the country closed their doors.

Between this situation and major injuries Hard Working Blessed had sustained at the foundry, after which he was demoted and his wages were slashed, he moved to Illinois, where he worked two jobs for about the same pay he'd earned at one job in Milwaukee. One of his jobs was manager at FastFood for $6.25 an hour ($9.34 in 2021 dollars), where "I was sometimes a store closer, other times an opener, and sometimes I went from store to store to help or teach people to do the opening and closing." Hard Working Blessed's FastFood supervisor soon identified that Hard Working Blessed's capabilities were far greater than those required by FastFood. The supervisor said, "This is a dead-end job and Hard Working Blessed is not a dead-end person." Hard Working Blessed's position on the issue at that time, however, was "I needed a job and I was willing to take whatever I could get." Late in 2002, Hard Working Blessed moved back to Milwaukee and took a truck-driving job at Wholesale Company, where, in spring 2003, "I have been promoted to a truck driver with responsibility for running a warehouse, at $12 an hour [$17 in 2021 dollars] with full benefits."

Hard Working Blessed's experience vividly attests to the widespread— even global—result of earnings loss after job displacement from injury or job loss (Quintini and Venn 2013; Jacobson, Lalonde, and Sullivan 1993). Such losses lead to greater likelihood of finding reemployment either in a lower-level position in the same or a similar industry (as Tisha's experience showed in Chapter 2) or in finding reemployment in a different business or industry where a worker's capabilities are underutilized. Hard Working Blessed's reemployment experience illustrates both loss pathways. As manager at FastFood he earned nearly $11 less per hour than at his prior foundry wage. When he moved to his job as truck driver and trucking establishment manager, he still earned $3 less per hour than at his foundry wage.

Michelle: Waitress Work, Later 2000s, Philadelphia

In 2008, as part of the Family Study, 42-year-old Michelle was a white woman in a second marriage, had four children, and was self-employed selling a brand of home furnishings and decorations offered by individual franchises. She described her current job this way:

> So I'm like, "Hi, my name is Michelle, thanks for inviting me in." I go into people's houses and they shop through a catalog and they order and I make money, and they get free products for having a party. I can make that schedule however I want, when I want to work that's good. I did waitress for a year and a half and I just quit that job in the spring.

Michelle then detailed how she had earlier struggled with the pain, problems, and occasional joys of being a waitress in a low-end restaurant:

> OK, I'll give you the short version of my experience as a waitress. I worked there for a year and a half. I had my set days—Tuesday night, Friday night, and Wednesday, Thursday day. And I worked and my body hurt, my feet hurt, and everything hurt, so I'm kind of glad that I quit. But I used to do everything. I would buy things for the store and not turn receipts in. I would clean the bathroom floors, scrub the floors, things that the younger girls didn't do. I'm a mom, I do that, you know. So, I kind of took them under the wing and did the extra things. So, I felt like I was an asset to them, and they knew that.
>
> I worked on a Tuesday night and we waitressed, we did the cashier, the bussing, the serving, we did everything. I was the only waitress. And then there's one girl that answers the phones. So that was it, and the cooks. So, I had 16 tables that night and I'm in, do, do, do, in, out, in, out. Well, I didn't show any desserts, like we have a dessert tray. By the time you show the tray and you go around through the 10 desserts, that takes time. I'm thinking of these people that are waiting to be seated for 15 minutes. So, I decided not to show the desserts. So, when I went in the next day I told my boss, "I'm really sorry I didn't sell any desserts." He said, "Because nobody wanted them or you didn't show the tray," and I said, "I didn't show the tray." I said, "I had people waiting to be seated," so that was it. I went away a couple of days, and when I came back and looked at my schedule Tuesday night, they had another waitress on with me. Never had another waitress. And Friday I wasn't even on the sched-

ule. This is where my husband works, too, he delivers pizza there. He still does. So, I wasn't on Friday night and when I questioned the lady who's in charge, the front-end manager, who we really don't click good with. . . . I don't take her crap and that bugs her. So, anyway, when I called [the boss] to find out what happened with Tuesday, he said, "Oh, well, you were so overwhelmed last week that we thought we'd put another waitress on." OK, I get it, I understand. I said, "Well Friday I'm not even on the schedule. What's that all about?" He said, "Oh, we pulled your shift because you weren't doing your job." I'm like, "What?" He said, "Yeah, we pulled your shift." I said, "OK, goodbye." And I called the boss back and explained to him and he's like, "Well, you know, because of the dessert." I said, "You know what, forget it, I'm done. I'm done, goodbye," and I hung up and I quit. And I shouldn't have done it that way but you know what, I put a hundred fifty percent into that place. I went in there, for heaven sakes, on Valentine's Day because my husband was delivering pizza. I stopped by and they were so busy, going out of their minds, but I worked two hours. Not on the clock. I didn't get paid—not even a thank you, nothing. A thank you from the waitresses and the cook but not a thank you from the boss the next day, nothing. So, you know what, you don't appreciate me, you don't deserve me, so I quit. And I feel better now I'm home.

The details of Michelle's story were typical of many waitress reports we heard across the country and were also reminiscent of some of the waitress stories in Studs Terkel's *Working* (1974). It would seem that being a waitress in a food and beverage establishment today has not changed noticeably since the 1970s and may not have changed since long before that. Waitress stories have generally featured a server's pride in doing a necessary and thorough job and being attentive and helpful to customers and coworkers. At the same time, waitresses have reported being misunderstood, overworked, underpaid, and often exploited by the people in charge, as Michelle described.

In contrast, Michelle went on to have a long and successful sales history with home product franchises and several direct sales jobs where she felt competent and appreciated: "I've gone on trips, I've gone to Hawaii with my husband through one of the organizations [because of her sales]. I've gone to the Bahamas. All free, paid." She made a conscious choice to direct her own schedule, only working at the parties when it suited her and her family. She knew she earned less than she could have if she worked full-time, but she highly valued the contribution she made to her children's school as "president of the Home and School for three years"—a role that required work flexibility and might be remunerated under a system of compensated civil labor (see Chapter 7).

Shanquitta: Grocery Deli Worker, Early 2000s, St. Louis

In 2001, Shanquitta, an African American participant in the Ethnographic Study, was a 37-year-old divorced mother of three who had just moved to St. Louis from a southern state. Through the 1990s, Shanquitta had held multiple food store and food production positions for short times between periods of employment in her chosen field of nursing (see the story of her work in healthcare in Chapter 4). She had worked as a part-time cashier at a restaurant for a year, then spent 18 months as a full-time chicken processor at a food company, and then worked for four years at another chicken processing plant until September 2000. She had earned the equivalent of $10 to $11 an hour in 2021 dollars in all three jobs.

Early in 2001, Shanquitta had moved to St. Louis to reconnect with her family because her sister lived there. New to the city, she worked part-time in the delicatessen department of a nearby food store—part of the biggest grocery store chain in the area—and earned $7 an hour ($10.50 in 2021 dollars) with no benefits. Although the job was a placeholder until Shanquitta could resume nursing training, she enjoyed the setting and her coworkers. Her typical tasks relied on her ability to multitask, as is customary in delicatessen work (Christiansen 2018) and in nursing. Her specific delicatessen tasks included handling and preparing multiple orders, making sandwiches, packing foods, slicing meats and cheeses, and preparing food trays for special orders. Sometimes she helped cook the food that was sold throughout the day, such as rotisserie chicken, salads, and macaroni and cheese. When the 2001 recession began, however, the store cut Shanquitta's hours from 20 to 16 and then to 12, with no explanation. "They just do that sometimes," Shanquitta said. Gaining recertification as a nursing assistant through the Ethnographic Study's nurse-training program partner ultimately enabled her to leave the food service position.

Clothing Stores and Clothing Accessories: 1980s to Today

Retail was the most significant economic industry in the second half of the 1900s. But the 2000s saw dramatic closings of hundreds of branches of major retail establishments, particularly department stores, which the media characterized as the retail apocalypse. Branch closings of national establishments, as well as the reduction or closing of hundreds of smaller clothing, electronics, and office supply retailers, indicated that the retail boom had turned into a bust (Thompson 2017) with only an occasional respite, the pace

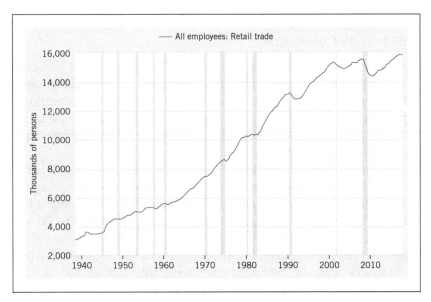

Figure 5.1 Number of employees: retail trade, 1940–2010
(Credit: Federal Reserve Bank of St. Louis [2017]).

of retail store decline was rapid in the 2000s, influenced strongly by an increase in online retail shopping, an oversupply of malls, and a shift in consumer spending away from clothes to traveling and dining out (Thompson 2017). Traveling and dining out, of course, fell sharply during the pandemic.

As Figure 5.1 shows, from 1940 to 1990 the number of persons employed in retail work in the United States increased from about 3 million to about 13 million, and the rise increased until 2000, when it topped out at about 15 million. Retail trade and service jobs accounted for three-quarters of the nearly 19-million increase in jobs in the 1980s (Plunkert 1990), although much of the overall growth was attributable to part-time positions (Haugen 1986, 9). The number of retail jobs dipped in the early 1990s recession but climbed again until 2000, when the pattern changed sharply. Between 2000 and 2010, the retail job plot looked like a roller coaster—mostly up but with downward dips. However, after reaching a record high of 15 million in 2009, 2010 saw a sizeable decline before it rose to nearly 16 million just before 2020. Time will likely show that the coronavirus pandemic, with its months of shuttered nonessential businesses and state requirements for people to stay at home worsened the existing in-person retail decline, despite the increase in online retail sales, even though the workers in online retail were predominantly warehouse packagers and package delivery persons, not retail salespersons. The changes to come were not visible, however, to workers in the late 1980s and early 1990s.

Tamicka: Retail or Legal Assistant?
1980 to 1990, Philadelphia

Twenty-two years old and African American, Tamicka graduated from high school in 1985, took a course or two in a community college, and then studied criminal justice at a local university for 18 months. Her educational expectation during the initial phase of the Teen Study in 1982 was to earn a "professional degree. I want to go to college for like eight years. I want my master's degree in teaching or child psychology."

In 1989, Tamicka admitted she had gotten "less education than I'd originally expected because I changed my mind. I was told that childcare doesn't pay so I decided to shift to legal work." In September 1989, Tamicka had completed a six-month paralegal training course that cost $5,000 ($11,000 in 2021 dollars), which she paid up front with a loan. Her completion of the program resulted in a paralegal certificate. Tamicka also acknowledged that she "was sick of school. I'm taking a break and will work for a while, earn money, and then maybe go back in September 1990."

Tamicka's need to earn money for her schooling led to a position of "checker-marker" in the receiving department of a local department store starting in 1986, which she held for four years throughout the paralegal course. She described her job as follows:

> I mark merchandise. I originally started as a cashier. I work 37.5 hours a week, full-time, and I earn $230 a week [$500 in 2021 dollars] and $11,500 a year [$24,500 in 2021 dollars]. I don't feel the job offers opportunity for advancement, because (1) it's prejudiced, (2) kids butt in, and (3) I don't like the job. Most people in my job are in school and I definitely feel underemployed. I would rather work part-time because I want to get a job in my field or work there at management. In five years, I'd like to be a paralegal in a law firm, possibly getting them to pay my tuition for law school. To do this I need to find it first—a job with tuition reimbursement for four-year degrees. I'd hope to earn $35,000 a year [$75,000 in 2021 dollars] at that job. . . . They now start at $22,000 [$47,000 in 2021 dollars].

Tamicka's assessment of the starting salary for a paralegal was on target according to Fowler's (1990) analysis of the rising need for paralegals between 1988 and 2000 and May's (2017) contention that the paralegal profession was one of the fastest-growing fields in the 2000s. Tamicka believed that a law firm might subsidize paralegal training, which may occur in a few cases, but the main route to becoming a paralegal is through an associate degree plus a paralegal certificate (BLS 2019k). As of 2019, the job outlook for paralegal and legal assistants for 2016–2026 was extremely robust, with projections showing a 15% increase in need, in comparison with a 7% increase for all occupations. Tamicka's goal in 1989 also included the possibility of department store management, which she did not think required a four-year college degree. A 2019 report, however, indicated that a bachelor's degree would be increasingly necessary, at least for a managerial position in sales (BLS 2019l, 1), which suggests there would be further struggles ahead for Tamicka.

Adele: Moving around Different Retail Jobs: *1990s to Early 2000s, Philadelphia*

After attending a welfare-to-work program in the late 1990s, and a white participant in the Welfare-to-Work Study, Adele was hired by a city club for a job that she described as "cooking and fast-paced." She liked her working environment: "I liked the way I was treated, although sometimes customers could be rude." But she did not like the hours or her transportation situation: "The hours. They were too late. I didn't want to work at the club late at night. I didn't feel safe and, at the time, I didn't have a car, so I had to take the bus at four thirty or five in the morning." She left the job after a period of time because "I wanted something better."

The better job she got was in a retail clothing store, which she liked particularly for "the discount on clothes." She got the job through the "referral of a few friends," showing that a strong-tie network (Granovetter 1973, 1983) can sometimes be useful for lower-earning workers, even if the wages do not lift them out of poverty. Nevertheless, Adele struggled with some aspects of the job:

> Dealing with people. Sometimes you don't feel like it. Some people don't like your help, but the supervisor wanted us to harass the customers, and people don't like that. Plus, standing on your feet eight hours and you had to constantly look busy even when customers were not in the store.

During the time she worked at the retail job, Adele had also added part-time work at a package delivery firm, and, when the firm offered to increase her hours, she quit the retail clothing job. Adele's enthusiasm for the package delivery firm position was evident: "I like the fast pace. I can't really keep still. I like the benefits—that's mainly why I'm there. I'm being treated nice. Me and my supervisor are close and I like the work. It's hard work for the workers who load trucks, but I don't do that." Adele's job tasks in the

warehouse were mainly to pack and unpack products and sort them into geographic delivery areas. Adele also reported that she had already accepted an
advancement opportunity and pondered trying for a supervisory position,
though she would be required to quit the union if she became a supervisor:

> I did get an advancement to pick off [a trade term for picking items
> off a list and packing for a customer's mail order]—$1 an hour
> more—and I've been thinking about being a supervisor, but I some-
> times come in a little late because of my other job. Plus, you can't be
> in the union as a supervisor, and in case something happened you
> wouldn't be protected. But I'd like to make more money and
> wouldn't need other jobs if I did. But I wouldn't have the benefits like
> I do now. I heard it comes out of your paycheck. I have to see. I'm
> thinking about it. This is my third time working at the package de-
> livery firm, but I have gotten sick in the past. I was first there in 1998.
> I do like it there. There's really nothing I don't like about it.

Because Adele's job at the package delivery firm was typically four to six
hours during the night, she had recently taken a second job at a retail inventory firm that provided inventory services to retail, healthcare, and com-
mercial and industrial establishments. Her work there involved the use of
wireless electronic scanners and custom-designed computers to accurately
calculate and report grocery, clothing, hardware, and medical equipment
stock. Adele described this second job as quite variable in the number of
hours she worked:

> When there are items to inventory, such as groceries or retail cloth-
> ing, I make a lot of money. Some weeks some stores cancel inven-
> tory, like this week I worked two days, but last week I worked five
> days. Depends on the stores, which offered varied clothing and
> home-improvement products. I'll probably be busy during the holi-
> days, but I haven't worked one yet.

Adele also described advancement opportunity at the inventory firm: "Yes,
you can become a supervisor or a trainer. Supervisor is just a part-time
position. I haven't really thought about it there." She wasn't happy with the
hours, describing times when she would "leave the package delivery firm at
5:00 A.M., go home and change, and then go to a store at 6:00 A.M. when they
start inventory. It's a lot. I barely get sleep. I catch up on the weekends. During the week, I get two to four hours a night."

Adele's situation overall is emblematic of the earlier-discussed need for
part-time workers to hold at least two jobs, since a 20-hour workweek at any

single retail occupation does not result in a livable wage. Adele wanted to have just one job: "I'd like to have one job that paid enough. Maybe as supervisor," even though she had just described one supervisory possibility as "a part-time position." During the recessions and downturn in retail that came about in the 2000s, the opportunity to support herself doing just one job probably did not materialize, despite Adele's demonstrated willingness to work hard and reliably.

By 2020, Adele's situation might have become even more difficult. Golden and Kim (2020) challenge the BLS definition of underemployment that focuses solely on part-time workers wanting full-time work. Expanding the underemployment metric to include "any part-time worker who prefers more work hours, not just those who want a full-time job" (Golden and Kim 2020, 1) would result in an underemployment rate of 8% to 11%, nearly twice the rate of 6% associated with the narrower BLS measure.

Tom: Retail Work in Women's Fashion, 2008 to 2013, Philadelphia Suburb

In 2008, during the initial phase of the Family Study, Tom was a 34-year-old white, divorced, single parent of three children for whom he had sole custody. Tom explained what he did as a merchandiser (technically, a floor supervisor) in three different women's fashion chain stores. His story captured the fluidity and unpredictability typical of work in major retail clothing establishments, with variable scheduling practices for employees (Lambert, Fugiel, and Henly 2014) and a stronger focus on price than on the product or on employee mobility. These are characteristic of most retail clothing chains, including Tom's, especially with the increase in outsourcing and often frantic price competition:

> Tom: I just put my two-week notice in. I'm a merchandiser for a women's fashion chain [chain 2], been there for two years—no, one year—and I used to work at another women's chain [chain 1] and I did the merchandising and hiring there, and I'm going to a third women's chain [chain 3]. A merchandiser lays out the floor, all the clothes, makes sure they give us floor set documents. We're supposed to match it to that. When stuff sells in between two floor sets, we're able to remerchandise and refigure the store. I have other jobs, too, like that would be my main job to start—to look at how things are selling and reintroduce it to be more appealing for people to buy. You know, more things around the store, the lighting, the fixtures, the mannequins, windows, all that kind of stuff . . . to make sure that everything

flows nice and that everything is where it is supposed to be and sized in.

INTERVIEWER: What is your work history?

TOM: I went right from high school into a job. I was in sales here and there and then I was working for a bank and working part-time at [men's clothing store] and then a position opened up in a women's store, so I went there. Going into high school, I was always an art major, so I was always into fashion. I went to hairdressing school. I did all that kind of stuff so I kind of fell into women's fashion by accident, but I was good at it.

INTERVIEWER: Did you need any special education or certificate?

TOM: Everything is from experience with me. I learned from a lot of good people, but there is degrees that you can get and then move on like out of the store. Instead of doing just the store level, you can actually move on and do, like, the whole district level. Like you would lay out and be the one to put together the manual and then send it out to the stores.

INTERVIEWER: Why are you switching stores now?

TOM: To be honest, [chain 2] is not what I'm used to. I mean, you look at [chain 2] and [chain 1], two different extremes and two different groups of customers. I went to [chain 2] because [chain 1] at the time was closing locations and condensing everything down. [Chain 2] was growing; it's a growing company, so I jumped over to them because I figured I could move up faster, but they don't really do that—they only care about the price point. They don't really care about what the product looks like. They're not really into the merchandising and marketing; they just figure if they stock a price that's cheap enough, the kids will buy it, and that's what they do. I mean, if you ever saw 15 girls come shopping, it's like a small tornado and they just rip through the store. For me, being a visual person, I'm very kind of anal where it comes to making sure everything stays in place, and, when they come ripping through the store on a Friday night and there's like 50 customers to one associate, you kind of lose that one-on-one. So, I'm going to [chain 3], figuring it will be the best for me. [Chain 1] was a little slow for me, but [chain 3] is a little bit more fast-paced and they're visual, like [chain 1] was. Their ticket price is a little lower, so they move more units than [chain 1] did. I haven't started yet, but I'm hoping it's like right in between [chain 1] and [chain 2]. I hope it's a good fit. I like being in retail. I wish I could have done more, but at this point, going back to college, trying to start a whole new career is just over for me right now, so I'm just trying to find a niche with a company where I can move up quick. My schedule now is crazy. We have two rotating days off, so for the most part I work one Sunday a month. So, I'm off three Sundays and then my other day will float. Like I'll have one week I work on Saturday and Sunday, but then I'll have maybe a Wednesday or a Thursday off. My hours are nine to six most days or one to close, which is one to ten or eleven.

Tom explained that the different chains also had different policies on vacation, sick, and personal days:

At [chain 3], it's gonna be different. They give you so many personal days to use in a year. It's included in sick day or vacation day or whatever. At [chain 2], it was different. You got unlimited sick days but you had to be the one who was sick. You had your personal day, one a month, and that's usually configured with your weekend off, so this way they would be able to give you a four-day weekend. So, you would be off, like, Thursday would be your personal day and then Friday and Saturday would be your days off that week and Sunday was the next week, so, [if your child was sick,] you would have to lie. Now if someone gets sick, I would have to call out and I could just say I need a personal day.

Like many other lower-wage workers, Tom had to travel a fair distance for work opportunity:

I'm working out in [distant suburb] starting in the new store, so it's about a half-hour drive home, so it's going to delay it a little bit for me to get home, but I had to go where the money was going to be. I wish I could do more [for my children]. . . . Like, I get jealous working in the mall, especially seeing all the families come in shopping. As it is, dragging three kids to the mall is something I don't want to do on my day off.

More problematic than a half-hour or more drive was Tom's feeling that he was starting at the bottom again. He had hopes for mobility, but they sounded a lot like they were based on the old mobility pathway, which was rapidly disappearing:

I'm working my way up. I'm gonna have to start at the ground level again with [chain 3], but the reason I went there is because they're gonna give me my own store within a year, so that's gonna be at least a $5,000 pay hike again on top of the money that they're giving me now. And then, as long as I keep moving up, I guess, I hope by the time I'm 40 I'm at least a district manager where I'm running multiple stores rather than just one. When you're a district manager, your hours are about the same, so no matter what position you hold you still have that balance between work and life, so it's still 40 hours. You could do a lot more traveling back and forth to your stores if you're district manager.

Disappointed with the slow and unpredictable pace of mobility, Tom also felt stuck in his field because he saw no alternatives:

Yeah, I've thought about doing something that's nine to five, but there's nothing. At this point, I'm not qualified to do anything. I did office work about nine years ago and then I got out of it and I've been in sales ever since, so it would be hard for me to go back to it. And to start in an office, you're looking at a lot less [money] than I would be making now. I used to sell cars, and those hours were a lot longer, but I made a lot more money. Because of the hours now, I just can't do it. I mean, if you don't sell a car, you don't eat. So, if you're scheduled nine to five that day and four forty-five comes rolling around and you haven't sold a car that day, you're either taking a gamble you're going to sell two the next day, or there's a chance you won't have a paycheck on Friday. So, you end up staying until you sell one and then your conscience falls into it because you prey on the first victim that rolls across the lot. That got too bad [for me]. I like what I do now, but I wish the hours were different. I wish I had more time in the day to do things.

At this point, Tom was not very happy with the direction and pace of his life. He felt it might have been different had he had more education:

INTERVIEWER: How do you feel about pace of your life?
TOM: Um, not too happy. I feel like a lot of things have passed me by and I'm kind of stuck in a rut. I'm stuck where I live, stuck in the kind of career I have, and I can't really get too far without working experience and putting the time in because I don't have a college degree to back me up. I guess it is what it is. I try to manage it.

Five years later, in 2013, Tom reported he had moved to another suburb in 2011 and had been with chain 3 for four years. After he moved, he left chain 3 for another fashion retailer and in 2012 became a senior manager at a major national department store chain. The timing of his work schedule remained important to Tom, as he still had two children at home: "My hours at National Department Store Chain are more day work than night. I rotate every other weekend, but otherwise I'm seven to four Monday through Friday, usually." He was relieved to be rid of the erratic schedule he put up with at chain 3.

Employment precariousness still exists in national department stores, and Tom was concerned about being laid off:

> There's always constant fear of position, title changes, whether they eliminate or add positions, and you can be laid off. And, at the same time, this national department store isn't doing well financially. It's how long we're going to be in business, even though it's been around for over 100 years.

Tom explained that the department store chain had had a large shake-up several years earlier, hired a new chief executive officer, and "wanted to revolutionize the way the company presented itself to its customers, and its merchandise, and everything else. And the company lost a lot of money in the past year, especially in construction alone. We're trying to get back. They've since let the chief executive officer go and brought back their former chief executive officer who was with the company for some 30 years. So, they're trying to get back to basics, plus trying to change to go forward a little bit better. So, they're going through a big transition."

One widespread transition in the 2000s was the risky trend of shifting company-provided benefits, such as pension plans, to workers, who then had to establish their own retirement plan, such as an Individual Retirement Account (Hacker 2008), if they had enough money to do that. In Tom's case, his large department store employer offered a retirement plan, but it was a "paper plan" rather than a fixed plan, since job tenure was so insecure: "It's just a basic plan and it expires if I leave," he said. Explaining that he would "probably be working until I'm dead" in lieu of planning for retirement, Tom still hoped for the opportunity he imagined in the company: "There's talk of possibly me getting my own location. Right now, I'm comanager at [location]. So, there's talk of maybe in January that I'm gonna have my own store, coming in sometime in 2014. So, from there, who knows what could happen." Tom was not, however, willing to relocate, having recently established his children in new middle and elementary schools.

In 2013, Tom earned $25,000 a year more than he earned in 2008 and felt that financially "I was a lot better off than I was before." At the same time, the precariousness of work in his retail setting plus the cost of medical bills and therapeutic services for his children who had learning and behavioral disabilities meant that "sometimes I live paycheck to paycheck or day to day. But I'm not struggling like I see a lot of other people and I'm a lot better off than I was before." Although the Family Study did not ask for specific wage or salary information, in his 2013 interview, Tom referred to having earlier earned about $52,000 a year, which, with three children, he said, "was barely enough." Adding the $25,000 he mentioned, it is possible that in 2013 Tom earned upward of $75,000 a year. With the federal poverty line in 2013 at $23,550 for a family of four, Tom's income was about three times that of poverty level, which could be a relatively comfortable financial position.

As Tom explained, however, retail clothing is a somewhat volatile occupational field. Productivity, for example, went from 4.7% in 2015 to 2.2% in 2016 and from −1.8% in 2017 to 4.3% in 2018 (BLS 2019b, 14). Tom had some residual debt but did not have a retirement plan or much in savings, and so real opportunity in the retail world for him was still somewhat uncertain.

Retail Trades after 2020: As the World Turns

Despite earlier warnings about the demise of the retail industry because of the continuing growth and appeal of e-commerce (Rosenblum 2017), predictions for retail in 2020 were initially more optimistic (BLS, 2020a; Petro 2020). In fact, the coronavirus pandemic in 2020 had been hardest on fashion apparel establishments, food and beverage establishments like Noel's, and department stores like Tom's (Danziger 2020). Even before the pandemic, though, the problems that caused many chain stores to close had been developing for decades, largely because they did not keep up with the times in terms of style and access or they did not invest in technology for customer service and enhanced delivery (Rosenblum 2017). Similarly, hotel rooms that were too large and too expensive, especially those without amenities such as self-service markets and in-room refrigerators and microwaves, found themselves in competition with boutique hotels that specialized in personal services, such as the room service Joseph's hotel offered to millennial and Generation Z travelers, who often travel for work as a family with young children. Personal and on-site extended services, such as in-hotel markets, some of which connect with online delivery services, are especially useful for working parents who leave a crucial item at home or whose child needs cereal in the middle of the night.

Scheduling challenges that interfered with workers' sleep and child-rearing activities, few and inconsistent hours and low wages, and general industry volatility were constants throughout the 40-year period represented here. Overall, such factors had a negative effect on workers' quality of life.

Technological improvements and macroeconomic volatility, however, seldom disrupted respectful service relationships with customers unless the employer and employee had competing priorities and values. For example, Michelle created a welcoming service environment for customers and had pride and satisfaction in her work as a waitress until her boss devalued those aspects in favor of what he viewed as a higher priority. Tom, similarly, found the "price-point" boss at chain 2 created a disrespectful and uncomfortable workplace for his capabilities, expertise, and personal well-being. Perhaps the disruption to traditional supply chains and ways of conducting business resulting from the coronavirus pandemic will lead employers to develop more respectful relationships with their employees, making worksites more satisfying and productive for the millions of retail trade industry workers like those featured in this chapter. In addition, opportunities for compensated civil labor (see Chapter 7), especially for retail trade workers who are part-time or inconsistently scheduled, could protect such workers from the historic income volatility in the industry that will likely continue well beyond the pandemic.

6

Homes, Buildings, Cars

Real Estate, Architecture, and Automotive
Service Work in the 2000s

W hile the chapters in this book so far have illuminated the daily
experiences of workers in lower-wage occupations, the Family
Study focused on workers with middle incomes[1] during the Great
Recession. Alex's, John's, and George's positions in real estate, architecture, and
automotive service, respectively, show that jobs considered professional and
semiprofessional, largely from tradition or because of education and training
requirements, are no less immune to the economic swings of recessions and
pandemics than are the jobs of workers described in the preceding chapters.
The technical and relational characteristics needed for real estate, architecture,
and automotive service positions are as vulnerable to technological change,
economic downturn, credentialism, and job loss from position restructuring
as positions in manufacturing, clerical, retail, food, and healthcare are. We see
this in Alex's, John's, and George's work experiences in this chapter.

Real Estate and Architecture Work

Alex and John, 2008 to 2015 and Beyond, Philadelphia Suburb

Alex and John, a white male couple, had been together for over 20 years as
of summer 2008 during the height of the Great Recession. They had two

---

1. Because there is no universal definition for "middle income," in the Family Study, we
used the range other scholars employ, which is family income that falls within 75% to 125%
of median family income (Gauthier 2015; Birdsall, Graham, and Pettinato 2000).

adopted children, ages 12 and eight, both of whom had learning disabilities. The family had recently moved from center-city Philadelphia to the suburb that was the site of the Family Study.

In 2008, Alex, 49 years old, was a licensed real estate agent and office coordinator in a center-city real estate firm. As background for Alex's field, owning a home became one of the main symbols of the American Dream by the mid-1900s. Fewer than half (43.6%) of U.S. residents owned their homes in the 1940s, but two-thirds (66.5%) did by 2010. The surge in homeownership after World War II was aided strongly by the GI Bill of 1944 and related investments in suburban expansion. Owning one's home rapidly became a symbol of middle-class status across the United States, even though homeownership was—and arguably still is—strongly unequal and segregated by race. The surge in homeownership influenced development of the real estate industry in both the residential and business sectors (Wake 2019).

Alex described his real estate position as follows: "I'm part field agent, part scheduling coordinator. I'm sort of the front man in the office. Anyone that calls the office usually goes through me, so I'm sort of in the middle of everything." John, 55 years old, characterized Alex as "the glue that holds the office together." During the Great Recession, Alex's firm had implemented cost-cutting procedures that began to affect his job and its security:

I'm not working at my office. I'm working at home, which is my vacation. That's the way it is. Because my company's trying to save some money, they've only got a certain quantity of employees doing a certain quantity of work, and I can't find anyone to be my replacement. So, since I can't, no vacation.

In essence, Alex's firm employed a cutback in pay rather than a cutoff strategy for coping with financial downturn, which some suggest is more equitable and productive and which preserves employees' jobs in the long run even though it reduces their income in the short run (Stites 2014). Alex described his usual day in the office as follows: "So my day in the space of two minutes just descends into absolute chaos, because I schedule the rentals, I schedule sales appointments, I coordinate other agents, I coordinate inspections, so I've got five, six telephone lines and I'm continuously on." Alex was salaried, and he had always worked 60-hour, six-day weeks, especially at the point that the real estate market was challenged by the housing and financial crisis that led to the Great Recession. Even so, he said he liked his job, despite the days when he got stressed out: "I like the people that I work with. I've basically been working with them for 13, 14 years." Alex also described the recession's effect on his office:

The economy is in such a state of turmoil right now. Because we're a
real estate office, we're running things very close to the vest right now
as far as money coming in. Right now, things are fine, but we don't
know what it's going to be like in November and December when
nobody is buying houses. Am I going to have a job in three months?

Alex's partner, John, was an architect who specialized in healthcare facilities. As background to John's field, buildings such as hospitals that required
broad-based knowledge of human beings, human behavior, and human
needs benefited greatly from architectural workers' expertise, until reducing
booming healthcare costs in 2008 started to dominate public attention. At
that point, architectural firms that specialized in healthcare buildings became less sought after than before. Even so, John said he loved his chosen
career:

Professionally, I have a wide range of experience, from doing offices
and office buildings to pharmaceutical laboratories to healthcare
facilities to MOB stuff [new models of medical office buildings].
When you're an architect, it's kind of a way of life. Some people call
it a disease. Experiencing space, experiencing concepts as to why a
grand staircase was designed the way it was, or the buildings that are
extremely cantilevered, how do they get them to stay the way they
are? It's the whole spatial experience of architecture. Ornamenta-
tion. That's what I like about architecture.

The couple had health insurance through John's office because it offered
domestic partner insurance. Health insurance was important, as both men
had encountered relatively serious health challenges in the past couple of
years: prediabetes that turned into type 2 diabetes (Alex) and a heart problem requiring stents (John). But, in summer 2008, in contrast to Alex's concern about the stability of his job, John expressed complete confidence in
the security of his job: "Well, I'm going to have a job, because, one, I've been
there for 10 years; two, we do healthcare facilities and there are always
healthcare facilities. Thirdly, I can also teach, so there you go."

By January 2009, Alex and John had both become unemployed. They
had characterized their joint annual income in 2009 as about $60,000
($74,000 in 2021 dollars), which was the same as they reported in 2008. But
after the change in employment status in 2009, their income was actually
only about $45,000 ($56,000 in 2021 dollars). In 2008, their joint income
had placed them at around 300% of the federal poverty level for a family of
four, whereas in 2009, their joint income barely reached 200% of the federal

poverty level—bare self-sufficiency. John's architectural firm did not close in 2009, but there was a significant layoff:

> The firm let 16 people go. The problem was that it was 16 people across the spectrum. There were two principals that had been there for 22 years. I was there for 10 years. Another person was there for 18 years. There were some that had been there for two years. Two were here on green card status. The design practice part of the firm was about 75 people, something like that, spread between two cities: Philadelphia and New York.

Despite his supervisor's earlier assurance about the stability of John's position, he was very suddenly laid off, although he was not totally surprised about it:

> I went back in November [after health troubles]. Things were starting to slow down in November. I went to my supervisor and actually said, "What's going on?" And he said, "Don't worry. Don't worry. You're too important. You will never get laid off." That wasn't the answer I was expecting, because that told me that, one, he was just trying to make me feel good and, two, something's up.

John then described the healthcare industry and its financing more broadly, which amplified the reasons for his layoff:

> I'm an architect, but I specialize in healthcare facilities, and even though healthcare is the last to contract, it's also the first to expand. What happened was, especially in November [2008], I saw it coming a year ago when the bond market started going down the tubes. But I knew things were really up when the daily loans that companies and banks loan to each other froze, it just froze. When that freezes that means the economy freezes and the healthcare systems were particularly hurt, because the healthcare systems only make some of their money by doing healthcare. A good chunk of their money comes from investments and stuff and their investing was going down the tube. When their investing goes down the tube, they're not going to expand. They're not going to renovate. They're not going to renew. So, when that happens, there are no projects!

John also attributed his layoff to a one-month bout of illness, including two weeks in the hospital, when "all my projects were shuffled to other people."

Alex had earlier shared the story of his layoff, which involved only slightly more advance notice:

I had worked in a small family-run real estate office. Basically, what happened is the market just completely dried up. Since I was the front desk person, I would be the one that would handle all the telephone calls. So, you know we were getting calls from utility companies, saying, "By the way, the building you have over on X street, we're cutting the power on that because the electric bill hasn't been paid." So, I was seeing stuff like that. This would have been last August, September [2008], because our market was near a university. It's a very nice neighborhood and the houses are reasonably expensive, but there wasn't nearly the traffic we had, say, two years ago. We had an office staff of myself, two principals, our rental agent, our contract person, and our property manager, so that's like six people. They're down to three right now. They let me go, let the rental agent go. Their business just dropped off to a point of where nobody's making any money. The people there are basically on commission, so if you don't sell anything, you don't make any money. They can't even collect unemployment because they're self-employed. Even though I'm a licensed agent, I've been working as an administrator, which is why I can collect unemployment.

Irrespective of the Great Recession, Alex also described gender and age factors in the real estate business, which protect certain agents and disadvantage others:

Real estate is one of the industries that has a lot of women in it, and you'll find a lot of agents do it kind of part-time, or they're full-time but they also have a spouse who's working, so the money they bring in is sort of extra for the household. There are a lot of younger agents that are out there that had not seen an economy like this, so I think a lot of them are in very bad shape. The ones that survive have their own investment properties, so if you're not making commission, you have income coming in from that. Unfortunately, we [John and he] don't have any properties because we made a conscious decision that we didn't want to have to deal with the rental thing. We've done it before and the money's nice, but the maintenance headaches kind of consume you.

Alex's view about future possibilities in real estate was quite pessimistic, which both discouraged him and pushed him toward joining a collaborative that John was starting:

Agents don't really have need for administrative staff right now, because they just don't have the volume to do it. The people that they have, they're maybe keeping them or they're working part-time, or they're just handling their own business themselves. For me, there's not a lot out there right now. It's kind of frustrating, and plus I've also found that I'm falling into that category of the older worker, which also has its issues. You end up feeling completely useless, like you have no skills whatsoever.

Even though I've got a tremendous amount of experience, it's just that nobody seems to really care for it right now. My background actually is also interior design and architecture, so I've started to sit in on some of the collaborative meetings. I'm thinking of going back to school and getting my AutoCAD [computer-aided design software] skills up to date. I've discovered that the local community college is surprisingly diverse. There's a lot there and I'm thinking that maybe what I should do is see what other degree I can get and maybe kind of rebrand myself.

Vallas and Penner (2012) have said that the concept of rebranding a person is one way that illustrates Kalleberg's (2011) views about labor market precariousness. On May 10, 2017, googling the phrase "branding yourself to get a job" yielded 510,000 results. On May 3, 2020, googling the same phrase yielded more than 51 million results. The tightening labor market in 2019, particularly at the upper end, may be represented in that figure.

Alex and John both showed entrepreneurial resilience, planning a new career in which they would each participate, as John explained:

Since we became unemployed in January, we've pretty much set our offices up here. Actually, I learned how to network our two computers together. After I got laid off, I started doing things that I've always wanted to do, or had planned to do, such as set up my own website and stuff like that, and start LinkedIn. We became part of a collaborative; well, we're still looking for employment but we're also looking for clients. With that we could potentially, instead of finding employment, create employment. Right now, the collaborative is two interior designers and two architects. The other architect was a partner in an architecture firm that had been around for around 30 years, and it imploded two months ago. So, you got eight AutoCAD stations sitting in his basement right now. AutoCAD is a computer with an AutoCAD drafting program. So, that's basically what we're doing. And they're doing active marketing with hospitals and hospital healthcare systems and the like, and my job is to market to contractors and people that would potentially require consulting services. We'll just see what happens.

John's comments here prefigure our discussion about the need to expand ideas about work and consider compensated civil labor in Chapter 7, as do Alex's comments below about John's and his ability to contribute to their children's school.

Alex also commented on the Great Recession. Earlier he noted that he and John had weathered previous recessions but that this one was different, as others (Porter 2016) have also reported:

What's different about this one is it's a broad-based recession that people who two years ago were solidly middle-class people with nice houses and car payments and so forth, suddenly there's nothing. In these classes that I go to, it's amazing to see people who were obviously high-end professionals who did business all over the world, in some cases, being laid off and not being able to find anything.

If there was a silver lining to Alex's and John's unemployment, it was that they had become active in their children's school in ways that had been impossible before. Alex said, "It has given us the freedom to do things. Like, our daughter had an end-of-year concert, which normally we wouldn't have been able to go to, because it was at one in the afternoon." On the downside, some of the children's community activities exceeded their budget: "Last year, we had them in the local Y summer program, but we can't afford to do that this year." Alex and John had also been staunch supporters of a Philadelphia theater, support that they had to put on hold because of their finances, thus affecting the theater's income and its audience as well. They were eagerly looking forward to passage of "the president's health insurance initiatives" [i.e., the Affordable Care Act], believing that "we won't be able to afford health insurance if we're not employed by the end of next year" [2010]. Their unemployment insurance and rainy-day fund would suffice with budget trimming until then.

Overall, demographic and economic factors challenged Alex's and John's futures. First, they were older workers—a demographic that, together with very young workers, was particularly hurt by the Great Recession. Second, even by 2016, the real estate market and the building trades, which are critical for architects, had barely recovered at all. Both career areas had been influenced by technological changes, such as more online home searching versus use of live realtors, so resuming their prior occupations looked like an uncertain prospect. Setting out on their own without unemployment insurance or their rainy-day fund seemed equally ill advised.

The couple's prescient views about further labor market changes in the following five years evidenced a mix of pessimism and reluctant acceptance with only hints of optimism. John's views were reminiscent of our discussion in Chapter 1 about how employers are increasingly contracting with contingent workers for specific work tasks rather than hiring more full-time employees (Sweet and Meiksins 2017):

[We're experiencing] an economic transition into something we've never seen before. I don't know what it is yet, but it might be what we're doing right now, where we're basically all becoming independent contractors coming together to do projects, at least in architecture. Various specializations. Firms might be hiring independent contractors and independent consultants instead of hiring employees. . . . Instead of hiring architects as employees to run their projects, they may hire architects to do certain elements, like hire an architect to run the creation of contract documents, and then hire another architect to do the contract administration out in the field. But instead of them being employees, they would be independent consultants and therefore they would be responsible for their own health insurance and their own billing and the like.

John's assessment of the future of architecture is in line with current research, which suggests that the need to build more senior living and related healthcare facilities to accommodate the increasing number of aging persons will not necessarily resurrect opportunity for all architects, largely because younger architects describe wanting variation in their projects (O'Donnell 2018). If architects are used at all in such building projects, they will likely be relegated to small contracts and will not run the whole project.

Alex's even broader reflections on social stratification seem consistent with Autor and Dorn's (2013) polarization hypothesis:

I think there's going to be—I'm not sure I want to call it a groundswell—but I think people's perceptions of what it takes to be middle class are going to be changing. I really get the feeling that we're sort of evolving into a two-tier society. You've got those at the top that just don't have to worry. They've got money coming in from all over the place. They don't have to deal with the day-to-day realities of putting groceries on the table and stuff like that. And there are going to be the rest of us who are going to be caught between healthcare and living expenses and stagnating wages and continuing outsourcing of jobs. So, there's going to be, I think, a lot of economic uncertainty. People are going to really cut back on things and get used to living with less and not move up from one house to the bigger house and go on one or two expensive vacations every year. It might be every other year, and you'll stay in the same house and try to cut your expenses wherever you can because you have to. So, I think the middle class is going to become increasingly stressed over the next five years.

Conversations with both men in 2013 showed remarkably alignment with their earlier predictions. Neither had been employed full-time since the 2009 interview, although John's consultant contract with an architecture firm that he signed the day after that interview had lasted for 18 months. Since then, John had had a few contracts but no fixed employment. Of value to both his field and his community, John got involved in pro bono work for the American Institute of Architects: "I've joined the community group design collaborative, which does architectural projects free through the AIA, so I've been involved with that. And I'm also on the historical architectural review board of my town. I've also become part of many, many Meet-Up groups, networking groups for entrepreneurs and business owners." Both organizations could be generative sites for compensated civil labor (see Chapter 7), which have many community benefits.

Because John was a registered architect, he planned to sign papers that afternoon to become a limited liability corporation. By incorporating, John, at the time uninsured, would become "an independent businessman," which would then enable him to buy reasonably priced health insurance. Signed into law in 2010, the Affordable Care Act had made more reasonable insurance possible for people like John and Alex who had significant preexisting health conditions.

Alex had remained self-employed as a real estate subcontractor since 2009 and had not held a position in a company until early 2013. Alex lamented the couple's financial struggles: "We have been surviving, but at great cost to any 401Ks that we have. Like everybody else, that's the first thing that goes." The real estate market began to pick up in 2013, though, and Alex was offered a job. He said, "I am still developing my client base, but I'm with a good company." Even so, his work income was skeletal and uncertain, nothing the couple could count on. They also believed that their ages affected their prospects of being hired anew, now that John was nearing 60 and Alex was in his mid-50s. John reported he frequently received the euphemistic explanation that he was "overqualified for the job," which he interpreted as thinly disguised ageism. Employers rehiring after recessions often prioritize younger, less expensive workers even if they are less experienced, and both factors may have affected John's postrecession employment situation (Quintini and Venn 2013). Alex, too, held health insurance that was provided through the Affordable Care Act to independent business-people. Without that categorization, neither Alex nor John would have been able to afford health insurance.

Retirement income for both men, however, remained uncertain. Alex vividly described how the old employment contract of guaranteed retirement funding was being replaced by employer-centric practices:

> If we were government employees, you know, then we'd have like 30 years of service and you get these very nice retirement packages. Or what happened to a person that I know, he was like six months away from retirement and he got laid off. Because companies are just doing all kinds of tricks like that to get out of funding stuff. Unfortunately, it seems like the only way. The only people that can actually retire are those that have an independent income to begin with.

Alex's and John's experiences may also constrain future opportunity for their children. Eliminating some of the children's educational enrichment activities (Iversen, Napolitano, and Furstenberg 2011), as the parents mentioned earlier, could have particularly adverse effects on them, with their learning disabilities. Alex also described the impact the couple's tenuous financial situation had on their daughter's possibilities for a college education:

> We have no money for loans. We'll help Jasmine [then entering eighth grade] in trying to get grants, get loans, get some stipend, something, but as far as us paying for it, unless we win the lottery, that's out of the question. At one point, we planned to invest in college savings, but when your income goes down, and when it goes down drastically, you sort of need every nickel. Just to stay alive, you know, make sure we got gas and electric on.

Alex and John then segued from speculating on the children's future to their own and to what they saw as the current pattern of employer hiring:

> JOHN: In my profession, most firms hire children right out of college and the reason is that they can, they're cheap. If they hired someone like me, they have to pay a bit more, but they get the experience. The other side of the track is that I hear from clients when I'm doing my marketing for this company that I'm starting up, they say, these big firms, they're sending out these children that don't know the first thing about how to construct a building much less run a project. But you know, the big firms are not hiring people my age and experience.

ALEX: The big firms are basically run these days, unfortunately, with companies that I think it's across the board, really, with just about anything. It's not the product you produce that's important. It's how much money do you make for the shareholders. That's the overriding goal. So, with architectural offices, they can hire students immediately out of college and sort of factor in the fact that, OK, these people are going to screw up and it's going to come in over budget, but we'll still make money off the deal.

John's and Alex's comments accord with findings in business literature about firms' tendencies to hire younger, cheaper workers instead of older, more experienced ones (Cappelli, Barankay, and Lewin 2018), and about the need to maximize shareholder satisfaction over improving workers' wages or long-term corporate investment (Perlstein 2013). Although Alex and John accurately described current employment practices in many areas besides architecture and real estate, their presumption that it would be easy for college-age youth to be hired in 2020, when their children were that age, was off track. As of July 2019, the national unemployment rate was around 3.7%, but the rate for people 20 to 24 years old was 6.8% (BLS 2019c). Alex and John had not lived that experience yet with their own children, even though they had certainly lived their own unemployment.

In line with their financial constraints, the couple had adopted practices they never thought they would, as John explained:

A lot of us who I guess you would call members of the former middle class, you end up doing a lot of stuff that you never really thought you would end up doing. Like shopping at Goodwill. I used to buy at a department store, but not anymore. Like, we actually share food with our neighbors. What happens is every now and then they get these bags of chicken legs from Philabundance and they bring a bag of chicken legs over for us. We split it into three packages and we can get three to six meals out of it. And we do a lot with beans.

Alex and John remained optimistic about their economic future when asked what they anticipated over the next five years, although their sentiments in 2013 were nearly word for word the sentiments they had expressed in 2009, and both views preceded the effects that the coronavirus pandemic ahead in the 2020s would likely have on both men's job areas. Realistically, Alex also identified that "The social contract that was sort of developed in the 1940s and 1950s, you know, in many ways, I think, has become kind of shredded." Even so, in 2013, John and Alex were both looking toward an improved economic situation. As John said, "That's why we're doing what we're doing. It goes in line with my mantra, if you can't find employment, you've got to create it. And we've been here before. Back in the recession of the 1990s, I was unemployed for four years."

If Alex has remained connected to real estate, he might find today's market more hospitable than it was in 2013, even though the median annual pay for real estate brokers and sales agents in 2019 of $58,770 (BLS 2020j) was below both the median household income ($63,700) and the median family income ($75,500) in 2019. Moreover, the projected rate of job growth for real estate agents between 2016 and 2026 was 6%, which was considered around average (BLS 2015). As for John, O'Brien (2014, 1) reported that "employment in construction and architecture are up from their lowest points, but there's a long way to go to reclaim the ground lost in the Great Recession." The median annual pay for architects in 2018 was $79,400, but job growth between 2016 and 2026 was projected at only 4%, which is slower than average for all occupations (BLS 2019m). Although some project a great need for architects to build smaller-scale healthcare and senior living facilities as the size of the aging population surges (O'Donnell 2018), the need for people with John's specialty of building larger general service hospital facilities was decreasing.

Automotive Service Work

George: Automotive Service Work, 2009 to 2013, Philadelphia Suburb

Looking first at the background context for twenty-first century automotive service work, George initially benefited from the surge in the U.S. automotive industry that began after World War II, when steel and other metals necessary for cars were repositioned to general versus wartime use. The automotive industry was dominant in the United States from the 1950s to the 1980s, but car manufacturing became increasingly threatened by foreign manufacturers in the 1980s (Singleton 1992). As Singleton has noted, "The auto industry affects, both directly and indirectly, the job prospects of hundreds of thousands of workers" (1992, 18). As a result, the downturn in the 1980s affected the broader economy as well as the industry itself, such that all automotive-related players recognized that major industry change was necessary. Thus, the industry resurgence that followed in the 1990s (Cutcher-Gersenfeld, Brooks, and Mulloy 2015) resulted from new and expanded collaborative efforts between the United Autoworkers Union and the three main U.S. car manufacturers: Ford, General Motors, and Fiat/Chrysler. This resurgence lasted until the two recessions in the first decade of the

2000s: 2001–2002, and the Great Recession of 2007–2009 and its extended aftermath, as George's experience illustrates.

George's story could be aptly named "The Old Employment Contract Meets the Great Recession." In the mid-2000s, just before the Great Recession, George, 47 years old and white, was a highly experienced director of service and parts at a successful automotive dealership, earning a six-figure salary. His wife Mary was employed at a high-end healthcare facility as a certified nursing assistant (CNA). George, Mary, and their five children (one newly graduated from college and employed as a financial planner, two in college, and two in middle school) were living a comfortable "middle-class life," as George described it. Within a period of a year or so, between 2007 and 2009, the family's life was turned upside down. First, Mary had to stop working because of health problems stemming from lifting nonambulatory persons. Second, George's automobile dealership closed down. The closure may have been attributable to automotive industry compensation costs for blue-collar workers in 2008 that were higher than compensation for similar workers in other manufacturing industries (Wallick 2011). Relatedly, during the 1980s and 1990s, the automotive industry in the United States was experiencing fierce competition from foreign carmakers, which resulted in "fluctuating output and employment growth for the U.S. motor vehicle industry" (Singleton 1992, 18). Over time, such competition may have weakened the stability of George's dealership. The closure meant George lost his job and was not eligible for carryover health insurance because COBRA requires an employer contribution, which was impossible because the dealer had closed down. Third, the family became eligible for the federal Supplemental Nutrition Assistance Program (SNAP), previously known as food stamps.

George's experiences graphically illustrate the precariousness of many middle-income families today, even though his job seemed like a perfect example of the security of the old employment pathway (Kochan and Dyer 2017). George said,

> I loved my job. I really enjoyed it, enjoyed dealing with the people, with the technicians. That's what I started doing. I started as a gas pumper way back when and then moved on to working on cars, became a technician, went to school for that, and just progressively moved my way up. I'm not somebody that could do the daily grind of going to an office. Though I was going to the same establishment, it wasn't like sitting at a desk every day, doing the same thing. For me it was different people every day, different situations, circumstances that you have to deal with that makes it more enjoyable. What I can do to help people, basically, is what it comes down to.

Nobody looks forward to getting their car fixed; it's something that everybody dreads. To be in a position to be able to take care of them and satisfy their needs, that's what I like.

This past year [2008–2009] has been tough, both economically and on a personal level. I lost my job five months ago, so that was basically adding insult to injury because, as you know, everything's getting more expensive and then to find myself jobless didn't help any. So, it's been a trying year. The automotive dealership I worked at going on 14 years closed. It was a family-owned and -operated facility, since 1994, I think, and they didn't have the ability to fall back on other stores. They'd been trying to upgrade their facility for the past year and a half, but they got behind the ball. The economy started going down, sales started going down, service started going down, and I think it all just caught up with them. They got to the point that they couldn't meet their commitment to [a major automobile company] on a monthly basis. I've been working since I was 12. I've never been jobless. It's a tough thing. Do I see it more around the neighborhood? Absolutely. Do I know friends that have been laid off? Absolutely. It's hitting everybody. It's a broader scope. . . . It was something that you see what was going on, but in the back of your mind you think, "Oh, it can't happen. It can't happen." Then you see the state of the dealership that you were working in. You didn't want to believe it, until it got to the point when I came home and said, "You know what, I'm done. It's not gonna get any better." So, I left a week before they closed. I could see, like car sales, we were doing between $140,000 and $120,000 consistently, month-in, month-out, and all of a sudden it was in the hundreds, then the seventies, and you could just see business dropping off. I could see service business dropping off.

Going back to school is something I'm looking at. I'm not certain what the auto industry is going to do, especially with the big national companies. I think it's time for a change, and I'm gonna have to go into something else, whether it be customer service, or something other than that. Healthcare field doesn't ever seem to be affected by the economy, so that may be something that I'll have to look at. They're always going, always looking for people. Or advertising, your news, radio, your TV stations, stuff like that. They just keep on going. You don't see them collapsing and folding and looking for bailouts and handouts.

The future of work in the healthcare and advertising fields was not quite as rosy as George imagined. While it is true that healthcare jobs tend to be less adversely affected by recession, as we saw in Chapter 4, the majority of healthcare jobs pay low, below-poverty-level wages. For example, home health aide employment was predicted to increase 47.3% by 2026, but the median annual wage for home health workers in 2018 was only $24,200 (BLS 2019a). As to advertising, although internet publishing was relatively unscathed by the recession, publishing overall lost nearly a half-million jobs, and jobs in all media still had not recovered by 2014 (O'Donovan 2014). The change in projected employment for advertising, public relations, and related services between 2016 and 2026 was 4.1%, lower than the 7% average for all occupations. The Bureau of Labor Statistics (2016) projected a 34.4% decline in newspaper publishing between 2016 and 2026.

George reported checking electronic and print job sources of work every day. He had been to the area Career Link, the federal workforce development center, but had not yet figured out what alternative to follow. In the meantime, he was living on unemployment insurance income, which, he said, "isn't a lot, but it's something." He particularly benefited from the unemployment insurance extension begun in 2008, ultimately to 99 weeks instead of its usual 26 weeks. Later research on the effects of extended unemployment insurance benefits found that "the phasing out of extended and emergency benefits [in 2012 and 2013] reduced the unemployment rate mainly by moving people out of the labor force rather than by increasing the job-finding rate" (Farber, Rothstein, and Valetta 2015, 9).

Maintaining health insurance became too expensive for George, however, since his job loss occurred before passage of the Affordable Care Act:

> When the dealership closed, I wasn't able to get COBRA because when your business closes, there goes your opportunity for COBRA, so I had to go out and get it on my own. I had it for three months, something like that. It was like $409, $411 a month, and it just got to the point I can't afford it. So, we're not covered now. We're applying for CHIP [Children's Health Insurance Program]. So, my wife is not covered either. It's not good at all. Case in point, I went down a couple of weeks ago to get her inhaler. Last time I got it I had insurance. They said, "Well it's a $35 co-pay." I said, "No, I don't have any insurance anymore." They said, "Well, that's $298, then." So, I went home and got on the website. You know they always advertise [drug company] may be able to help in your needs. You have to fill out a form and send it in. We'll wait and see. My wife has COPD [chronic obstructive pulmonary disorder] and asthma. Otherwise, our kids' health is good, though last year Connor was playing for a minor league football team and ripped his bicep tendon and Brady had

appendicitis and had to have that removed. You hope and pray that nothing happens while you're running around with no insurance.

Clearly, the limitations of COBRA for workers whose companies close is one that demands serious policy attention, especially with the expected volatility of the labor market ahead due to technological changes, automation, trade policy challenges, and, most recently, the coronavirus pandemic and the accompanying deep economic downturn.

In addition to health and job direction struggles, George was concerned about losing his house: "It's always something that's in the back of my head." He had already refinanced and grouped the college loans for his children into one bundle that didn't come due until they graduated, but not having a job "always gnaws on the back of my mind all the time." The family's savings were gone, and he'd made payment arrangements with both his mortgage lender and the local electric company, which he found willing to help to some extent. He thinks this was due to the scope of the nonpayment problem. He expected it to be a year or two before the economy got going again, which was overly optimistic, as history has shown.

In 2013, when we asked George how things had been for him and his family since 2009, he responded with a cracked voice:

Declining rapidly. That was the start of everything going awry with the automotive industry. I was unemployed beginning of 2010 almost an entire year until almost '11 and then it's just been spotty because you have to remember every car manufacturer was doing the same thing. . . . To give you a for instance, [his national automotive company] had 6,685 dealerships nationwide. The beginning of this year [2013], they're less than 2,300. That's how many dealerships closed, so you can imagine that many people are out in the workforce doing the exact same thing that I was doing, looking for jobs. I was going on interviews and you'd have 15, 20, 30. I mean, one time I went into an owner's office, he's sitting there interviewing me, and he said, "Just put your résumé there and we'll get to it." I was number 78, so the last five years have been extremely hard for myself. My wife was unemployed. Her unemployment ran out. For me, all of a sudden, you've got this huge explosion in the workforce of people available to do jobs. So, what that does is it knocks down agreeable pay. My pay has in the last five years been cut basically in half. I am by the skin of my teeth holding on. Extra money, spare money, vacations, everything just ground to an absolute halt. It's a huge life lesson, plus the family can't stop. In the middle of that my oldest boy was halfway through college, my next son was going into college. Since then, they have both graduated, as did my older daughter. If it wasn't for government funding, FAFSA, PHEA, the College Board, I would never have been able to afford sending them into schools.

Since 2011, I've moved around. I tried going in the aftermarket, I went with [automobile parts supplier], which was a huge mistake, but I gave it two years to try and see how far I could progress in their company, because they're a huge company, they're nationwide. There's great room for improvement and advancement, but it's your typical aftermarket, it's just a grunt—they work you to the bone. I was in six different stores between here and Delaware. It was ridiculous. Now I'm down the street at [another] auto dealership and that was just . . . I happened to be passing and I knew I hadn't applied there because I'm basically [another automotive company] background. I went in there and they were actually looking for somebody. Three interviews later, I was hired. May was one year, so I've been there a year and a couple of months.

George's situation illustrates how job loss and job displacement, which signify permanent layoff for workers with long tenure on the job (Davis and Von Wachter 2011, 1), have resulted in lower pay in the next position, if one has even been located, which is similar to the situations of many of the workers in previous chapters, regardless of their occupational area. At best, George's income was cut in half. At times over the four years between 2009 and 2013, he earned less than that, even when he held multiple jobs. Most employers during that period considered him a production and nonsupervisory worker, not a director-manager as he had been in 2008 and earlier. Despite his general optimism in 2013, George also expressed a new sense of employment insecurity and precariousness that scholars report is common today in many occupations (Kalleberg 2018). In George's words,

You know, layoff is always in the back of my mind, because really what happened between the banks and the automotive industry has changed everything. You can't take anything for granted, and I don't. It's just one of those things. Is it something that gnaws in the back of my mind? Absolutely, because you really don't know. I have really zeroed in on paying attention to a couple of different things where I've been working: number one, the stability of the company, and number two, how they are as far as corporate looks at them. I've just seen how corporations will look at something and, if your customer satisfaction isn't high, your sales aren't good, your service isn't good, they'll pull their point and you're done. I've seen it. I won't get caught again like I got caught before, but the problem is, and it's going back to what I said before, what's out there and the going pay rate aren't what they used to be before.

Despite George's general concerns about job stability, he reported feeling somewhat secure at his new jobsite:

> Yeah, I feel my job is generally secure right now. I hit the one-year mark and I've had plenty of discussion with my boss, as far as how is everything here. Because I've been in my fair share of places when you think everything's good, and then you walk in and it's like you're done, gone, and out of here. It's family-owned, it's only one store, they don't have a bunch of different dealerships. I deal with on a daily basis the director of parts service and body shop and the owner, so I think it's working out nicely.

Even so, George continued to look for work in a dealership franchised by the national automobile company he worked for earlier. He felt, however, that for the positions he'd want, more education would be necessary:

> My background is heavy in [national automobile dealer], but anything that I try and get into, like an area service manager, because I know from the top down in [national company], in their dealership world you need to have a college education, which I don't have. Do I have the experience? Absolutely. Have I been trained by some of the best in our area? Yeah, I have been. But is it something I can get into? Unfortunately, not. I mean, I've applied, I put in my résumé, and ultimately it comes back to we want bachelor's of science, a BA, some kind of college education. I just don't have it. Honestly, it's just something I can't do right now. Not only can I not afford it, I can't afford the time.

Interestingly, online ads for the position of director of automotive service and parts that the research team examined in August 2019 did not ask for a bachelor's degree. Even positions with salaries up to $100,000 required at least three years of experience but did not ask for a college degree. One wonders, then, whether mention of the college degree George reported as required in 2013 was a tactic to screen out an experienced, potentially higher-wage applicant.

At the end of the day, George still considered himself "middle class . . . but just a harder-working middle class." He anticipated "a lot of hard work" over the next five years: "Every day's going to be a battle. Is it going to stop?

Absolutely not. I can't stop. Am I going to do everything in my power to improve where I am right now? Absolutely!" Automotive mechanics and electrical repair and maintenance is an occupational area that was projected to grow 10.4% between 2016 and 2026 (BLS 2015). But the growth would be in service rather than in managerial positions such as the one George held before the Great Recession. Both types of position would also likely become cut back significantly in the 2020s because of the coronavirus pandemic's effects, such as less driving and shuttered automobile service facilities.

Service Industry Workers Share Common Fates

For a decade or so after World War II, many working families—particularly if they were white—belonged to unions, had at least a high school degree, and were able to make ends meet relatively comfortably, even if only one person in the family was employed. That pattern changed dramatically after the 1970s with the downward shift in unionization, the shift from well-paying manufacturing jobs to lower-paying service jobs as noted in Chapter 2, and the increase in the number of people earning college degrees. Described as polarization of employment by education and capability level (Autor and Dorn 2013), by the 1990s, technology and corporate leadership positions became increasingly highly paid while most service industry jobs remained low-paid. By the 2000s, the incomes of some who formerly had higher or middle incomes (often because they had two earners in the family) began to fall, and many workers, like Alex, John, and George, lost their jobs during one of the recessions between 2000 and 2010. The examples in this chapter alert us to the fragility and precariousness of jobs and occupations previously considered well-paying and stable. The examples throughout the book also show that the incomes and job insecurity of many workers have become more similar, regardless of education, gender, or income. These workers also expressed having alternative capabilities and desires that were not being met in their labor market jobs. The final chapter offers some new possibilities for *real* opportunity for these workers.

7

Turning Struggles into Flourishing

Creating Real *Opportunity through Compensated Civil Labor*

D espite the massive changes in the labor market between 1980 and today, few creative or effective policy or practical solutions to the work struggles of the workers in this book, and millions like them across the United States, have been offered. The persistent belief in the American dream—that opportunity and prosperity are available to all through labor market jobs—has resulted in workforce development and work support policy solutions aimed at changing individual behaviors rather than improving economic and labor system structures and practices. Specifically, more education has been the proposed mobility solution for lower earners and unemployed persons for decades. This solution emerged from the dominant belief that persons with lower-paid jobs need more education and training to contend with technological advances and changes in job content in today's labor market. With the exception of New Deal work programs in the 1930s, the default belief in education has undergirded federal workforce training programs since the 1960s and reached its pinnacle in the early 1990s.

At that time, evaluation findings from a major national study conducted in the 1980s were interpreted broadly to indicate that "job training doesn't pay" or even help most participants (Orr et al. 1996). In response, federal workforce training policy patterned itself after the 1996 welfare legislation to emphasize "work first." As it turned out, most "work first" programs were only a few weeks long, dealt only with résumé construction, interview techniques, and computer job searching and generally didn't help participants find stabler work situations or living-wage jobs. In contrast, studies that evaluated participants' employment results several years after training program completion, in contrast to the typical six- to 12-month timeframe of "work first" programs, found decidedly positive results on the programs' effectiveness (Acs, Phillips, and McKenzie 2001; Hebert, St. George, and Epstein 2003).

More recently, scholars, the press, and the public have vigorously debated the question of how much education is actually necessary for today's jobs. The debates have focused on the education necessary for family-supporting jobs, the real monetary returns associated with additional education and training for high-school-educated workers or those who are stuck in dead-end jobs, and whether credentials, or the reputation of the education or training provider—what economists call the "signal effect" (Ehrenberg and Smith 2018), might matter as much as or even more than actual capabilities. At present, however, the main changes to the workforce development and welfare systems, as to the labor market itself, have come about as the result of tinkering with existing policies, systems, and practices. In reality, there simply are not—and, if we maintain the status quo, in the future there will not be—enough labor market jobs in the United States for the millions of people who want work. Also, most occupations projected to grow over the next decades offer wages that are too low for families to be able to avoid debt or save. The coronavirus pandemic and economic downturn in the United States beginning in 2020 has magnified these labor market inadequacies (Manyika, Smit, and Woetzel 2020).

But a future filled with debt and dead-end jobs is not the only way forward. By expanding what we think of as work, we can shape a future filled with opportunity for more than just those in the high-middle and top of the wage and salary scales. Expansion could also dramatically improve the quality of life for millions of workers whose capabilities and passions are not being utilized in their labor market jobs. If people's passions and capabilities were viewed as civil labor, and compensated accordingly, it could benefit millions of workers, their communities, and, in the case of infrastructure improvements, the nation overall.

Expanding What We Think of as Work: Toward Compensated Civil Labor

This chapter will offer alternatives to today's labor market challenges and aim at suggesting meaningful and adequately paid work activities for workers tomorrow and beyond. The *compensated civil labor* alternatives that will be proposed here, which extend Beck's (2000) concept of civil labor, are based on two propositions. The first involves expanding what we think of as work, how we do work, and, particularly, how we do paid work. The second involves creating policies and economic practices that make doing compensated civil labor possible. Importantly, these propositions will not ignore the dangerous work conditions associated with some labor market jobs, condone low wages, or emphasize leisure pursuits over work. Compensated or paid civil labor simply involves *expanding* the idea of work far beyond the paid jobs in labor market organizations and businesses that we define as work today.

A system of compensated civil labor would entail compensating people for their non-labor-market work. At a minimum, civil labor could include engagement in the arts, culture, communities, and politics, as well as parental labor, work with children, helping older or disabled persons, and responding to community needs. Civil laborers could partner with people working in area nonprofits, businesses, and community organizations toward economic development, neighborhood beautification, and environmental and ecological improvements such as community gardens and much-needed physical infrastructure improvements. The United States is in great need of improving its infrastructure, which only moved from D-plus in 2017 to C-minus in 2021 (American Society of Civil Engineers 2021, 2). Even so, C-minus remains dangerously inadequate when it comes to bridge, runway, and road safety. Later in this chapter, we detail how the U.S. infrastructure could be radically improved by paid civil labor. Overall, a system of compensated civil labor could offer people more varied income pathways, engagement in meaningful activities, and an increase in civic involvement. It could make possible combining different work activities rather than having to earn a livelihood from a single full-time labor market job. Many people might combine a part-time labor market job with part-time compensated civil labor.

Others have also envisioned changing labor market work, historically and recently. Initially, in *Wage-Labour and Capital,* Marx (1933) contended that reproduction of the labor force rested fully in the hands of employers and capitalists, outside the family. Engels's (1942) theory of sex stratification dealt with the division of labor within the family, which ultimately became the rallying point for radical feminism. Engels's contention about women's major role in reproducing the labor force eventually resulted in international "wages for housework" campaigns, which broadly aimed at gender equity and redefined housework as viable labor that should be compensated. This movement became a unifying aspect of second-wave feminism in the early 1970s, influencing Silvia Federici's (2012, 92) position that capitalism "must rely on an immense amount of unpaid domestic labor for the reproduction of the labor force," which she described as a position to which Marx had been blind. On a related point, Kathi Weeks (2011, 99) has proposed that we reject the following attitudes about labor market work: (1) the current ideology wherein labor market work is the highest calling and a moral duty, (2) labor market work as the center of social life and the main way individuals access the rights and claims of citizenship, and (3) the privileging of labor market work over all other pursuits. Weeks's suggested solutions were to shorten working hours yet retain the same pay and consider universal basic income, which she envisioned as "payment for our [women's] participation in the production of value above and beyond what wages can measure and reward" (230). Employer support for Weeks's idea of shorter hours might be influenced by research showing that productivity increased alongside fewer, focused hours of labor market work (Glaveski 2018). In a sense, this win-win for employers' needs and many workers' needs and desires also frees their time and capabilities for compensated civil labor—in a scenario similar what Weeks describes as "the one [life] that we might want" (232). Further connecting Weeks's position with the theoretical frame of this book, she characterizes the life issue for Max Weber (1978) as "the wealth of possibilities that the work ethic diminishes" (Weeks 2011, 233). Weeks demands consideration of alternatives to the existing world of work, which this book aims to provide through the introduction and consideration of compensated civil labor.

André Gorz (1999, 1) has similarly urged us to conceptualize work in a different way: "We must learn to see work differently—no longer as something we have, or do not have, but as *what we do*. We must be bold enough to regain control of the work we do." Applebaum (1995, 71) has discussed alternatives to the labor market work ethic, such as these: a *usefulness ethic*, based on the idea that the need to be wanted is more in tune with the human condition than the need for formal work; a *life ethic*, concerned with the full development of human beings to replace the notion that our occupation is our major contribution to society; and a *contribution ethic*, based on the belief that we can find fulfillment in doing things for others. Throughout *What Workers Say*, virtually all the workers emphasized how important it was that what they "do"—that is, what their work activities are—be meaningful, helpful, make a difference, and be a source of pride.

In solidarity with the scholars' and workers' urgings, we propose that our society could fruitfully contain both labor market work and compensated civil labor. The inclusion of civil labor would incorporate the sensibility and community-oriented values of these proposed alternatives and make all labor—not just market labor—worthy of respect and remuneration, whether by civic money, exchange, time, or other form. The value that compensated civil labor could add is also visible in parents' desire to be able to arrange their time and energy for childrearing and income production in proportions that best suit their family's priorities.

A system of compensated civil labor in the United States would likely be applauded by people in the millennial and Z generations, which is the case in Germany, where civic commitment is very high among young adults and is often aided by community and national foundation funding (Facts about Germany 2020; Beck 2000, 81). Young adults both in the United States and globally have found themselves outside the formal labor market in recent years, and some have argued that Generation Z (those born between 1995 and 2010) and millennials (those born between 1981 and 1996) have perspectives on work that emphasize collaboration and person-to-person communication among workers, firms, and communities (Annie E. Casey Foundation 2021; Future Workplace and Randstad USA 2016).

A system of civil labor might also appeal to policymakers trying to remedy structural racism,[1] particularly as we saw it in the construction industry (Chapter 2), but existing, even when not obvious, in many labor market sectors. Particularly troublesome for African American workers, the public sector jobs that enabled many of them and their families to own homes, avoid debt, and provide enrichment activities for their children contracted after the Great Recession, in contrast to the historical pattern of postrecession expansion (Laird 2017). More than 765,000 public sector jobs that were held by one in five African American workers in state and local governments, which had previously been an employment equalizer, were lost during the Great Recession. Most of these jobs had not been reinstated by the time of the economic downturn from the coronavirus pandemic, which then resulted in 1.5 million more job losses in the state and local government sector between February and July 2020 (Wolfe and Kassa 2020). These losses disproportionately affected Black and brown women and men.

A realizable vision for work expansion would involve labor market jobs and civil labor and compensation for both. For example, one way to mend the failing U.S. infrastructure would be to use many more less-trained workers on road, bridge, and airport runway improvement projects, either full-time or part-time. A small number of expert supervisors could oversee the efforts of these larger work groups rather than having the small or repetitive parts of projects directly handled by highly trained, highly paid employees. As a result of compensated labor, the less-trained workers could learn new capabilities "on the ground" and projects could be completed quicker and more effectively. Although trade unions might balk at the idea, they might also begin to grow again if they engaged this larger pool of workers. The guaranteed employment movement in the United States during the Great Depression in the 1930s, especially through the Works Progress

---

1. I thank the reviewer who underscored this suggestion.

Administration (WPA), was an early antidote to an insufficient number of jobs and is discussed more fully later in this chapter.

Crucially, compensated civil labor is designed to be focused on community and practical, as well as socially recognized, valued, and rewarded with pay that has the same status as labor market wages. Alternative or additional types of compensation arrangements could include time-based currency, goods exchanges, community government accounts, and philanthropic awards. All could enhance people's roles and opportunities to engage productively in both labor market wage labor and compensated civil labor and be recognized accordingly by their community, as examples later in this chapter suggest.

The Need and Potential for Compensated Civil Labor

To assess the overall need and potential for compensated civil labor in the United States, we used information from two main employment surveys. The Current Employment Statistics Survey (CES), also called the payroll survey, was designed to measure employment positions, hours, and earnings in nonfarm and salaried jobs, with industry and geographic details (BLS 2019c). Because the CES surveys establishments, its results exclude employment in private households and self-employment. CES provides basic information about the number of job *positions* that currently exist in the United States by industry and geographic location. Information from CES has been cited throughout chapters 2–6. In contrast, the Current Population Survey (CPS), also called the household survey, provides data on the number, social characteristics, and demographic characteristics of employed *persons* who are defined as "in the labor force" or "not in the labor force," as described in Chapter 1, as well as data on "not employed" persons. CES and CPS (BLS 2019d, i) both survey only the civilian noninstitutional population with one exception: if the CES survey respondent is in the military and also holds a nonmilitary job, both jobs will be counted. We look at the availability of labor market jobs first and then at the potential size of the civil labor force.

Are Enough Labor Market Jobs Available?

As of spring 2021, accurately assessing the number and types of labor market jobs that are available is like riding a roller coaster. When businesses began to reopen in February 2021, job growth fluctuated wildly and varied by and even within industry sector. Despite a slight uptick in job growth in April 2021, 8.2 million fewer jobs were available than had existed in February 2020 (Tankersley, Rappeport, and Smiliak 2021, A1, 6). Establishments in all industry sectors populated by the workers in this book have been affected by the lessened possibilities for employment. The reasons for the lag in employment and job growth, however, are quite contested. One side, which includes organizations such as Chambers of Commerce, argues that the government's stimulus pay has produced a work disincentive that resulted in a labor shortage, but recent analysts suggest that what some call a "labor shortage" may really be a sign that previously struggling workers are reassessing returning to poorly paid, opportunityless work (Long 2021).

The Civil Labor Force May Be Quite Large

The size of the potential civil labor force is also a critical part of overall economic well-being, so we need to know how many possible civil laborers there might be. CPS data are particularly useful for assessing both the number and composition of what could be the compensated civil labor force. We use 2019 data here to consider the potential size of the civil labor force on the basis of a statistical period more typical than that of the coronavirus pandemic.

Even if only one-half of the 10.5 million people identified by CPS as external to the number of available labor market jobs, such as undocumented persons and those, like Joseph (Chapter 2), who are paid "under the table," plus one-quarter of the 63 million doing volunteer activities wanted compensated work, that would amount to around 21 million persons available to engage in paid civil labor. This is a sizable and impressive pool of energy to tap, and doing so could improve conditions for working people and their communities. In fact, the figure might actually be higher, since many of the nearly 26 million part-time workers might want to utilize paid civil labor in order to compose full-time employment. Many of the 6 million who are officially unemployed but looking for work might also engage in paid civil labor (BLS 2019i), and the 3 million considered "discouraged" or "marginally attached to the labor force" but who "currently want a job" might, too (BLS 2019e). Estimating conservatively, adding together half the number of individuals from each of the categories above, except for only one-quarter of the volunteers, the civil labor pool could contain around 40 million persons. Moreover, combining part-time compensated civil labor with a part-time labor market job could enable workers to use their capabilities and interests in the labor market and also for the benefit of society more broadly. This possibility is suggested by 37% of the respondents to a recent business survey who "started a side business to pursue their passion and the 41% who said they did so to spend more time doing what they enjoy" (Marks 2019). The same research also found that having a side business improved some of the workers' performance at their regular jobs and offered an affordable test to assess their venture's long-term viability. In all, it seems there could be a lot of person power available to do more compensated civil labor work, which might also utilize the capabilities of those who, for reasons unrelated to their abilities, are disproportionately excluded from labor market work. The result could then be greater social, racial, gender, and economic equity.

The following groups could be added, at a minimum, to our enumeration of who might engage in civil labor: persons 55 years old and older, like John (Chapter 6), who still want to work and have important experience and enthusiasm to use for the benefit of others outside the labor market; workers in dangerous, inhospitable, or discriminatory work situations, like Hard Working Blessed (Chapter 5), who might leave, even if only part-time, to work at compensated civil labor that was safe and equitable; and labor market workers like Teresa (see later in this chapter), who want to contribute their unique passions and talents to their communities at least part of the time.

Volunteer Work or "Gig" Work and Compensated Civil Labor

Volunteer Work

As noted earlier, approximately 63 million persons (one-quarter of the adult population) are doing work outside the labor market. This work is often called volunteer work (Nonprofit Source 2018) or care work, which tends to involve unpaid activities in communities, public schools, hospitals, and other civic organizations. And while some consider volunteering to be more meaningful than paid work, rates of volunteering have been declining over the last two decades (Poon 2019). More broadly, Viviana Zelizer (1997) discusses the meaning of what she calls "multiple monies" and contests the notion that monetary transactions render social life cold, distant, and calculating.

> Zelizer shows how at each step in money's advance, people have reshaped their commercial transactions, introduced new distinctions, invented their own special forms of currency, earmarked money in ways that baffle market theorists, incorporated money into personalized webs of friendship, family relations, interactions with authorities, and forays through shops and businesses. (2)

Reflecting Zelizer's view, many workers in *What Workers Say* who struggle to make ends meet said they would relish the chance to "do good" and "do well" simultaneously. As Zelizer (1997) writes, "Multiple monies matter as powerful, visible symbols of particular types of social relations and meanings. More than that, they directly affect social practices. People not only think or feel differently about their various monies, but they spend them, save them, or give them for different purposes and different people" (211). It is important to note that civic money could be both instrumental for the civil laborers and a source of working pride. If compensation were not needed or wanted, money could always be quietly donated to the civil laborer's chosen cause, preserving the laborer's status as a working contributor. Furthermore, most workers are committed to both their job and their community. The power of one's social and geographic location means that, rational choice theory to the contrary, many people would rather supplement their labor market income locally than move to a new city, state, or country with the anticipated fiscal and familial challenges of relocation (Agovino 2020). Compensated civil labor could provide the bridge of locational stability for such workers and their families.

Teresa's Story

Teresa is a typical example of a labor market worker who also wanted to work for her community. At 43 years old in March 2000, when she entered the Ethnographic Study in Seattle, Teresa was the African American mother of an adult son and a son in upper elementary school. Teresa had a diverse employment history of nearly 25 years but described her most recent office work as "tedious and solitary." When she learned about a new 12-week automotive training program, she enrolled, hoping to find a more challenging, better-paying job. Teresa was extremely successful in the program and landed a position as utility person at Rental Car Company-WA upon program completion, a position at which she remained during our several years of research contact and beyond. Her job involved computer entry, oil changes and tire changes, and other tasks overseen by a manager of the company's fleet of two thousand to three thousand cars. Over time, she increased her income there by taking and passing automotive services competency tests. But what Teresa really wanted was time to also work at catering, which she described as her "heart-string," or what she loves to do. She catered for her local church, her son's school, and, occasionally, other community organizations when she had the time. Her church provided kitchen space and parishioners attributed an increase in church participation to Teresa's culinary contributions. Her years of catering had been voluntary other than occasional reimbursement for the food supplies she needed. But Teresa said she would love to do catering work as civil labor and be compensated by the community for her skill and expertise.

Gig Work

The official employment categories exclude workers who are working in what is currently called gig work or alternative work arrangements, which includes independent contractors, such as part-time childcare providers; on-call workers, such as substitute teachers or nurses; employees placed by temporary agencies; and digital platform workers, such as Uber, eBay, and Airbnb (Schultz 2020). Gig work may be truly independent of an employer such that autonomy and flexibility are the upside of such jobs. But, when independent contractors are affiliated with businesses such as Airbnb and Uber and similar entrepreneurial ventures, the businesses are really more like standard employers with rules, procedures, policies, and regulations that both the independent contractor and employer must follow (Chung 2019; O'Connor 2016). These businesses seldom offer health insurance, unemployment insurance, sick and vacation days, or other nonwage benefits that most labor market employers offer their workers, which substantially reduces the upside of independent contract work. A recent piece of California legislation (Assembly Bill 5; Cal.Sup.Ct.2018), which went into effect January 1, 2020, aimed to avoid worker exploitation by reducing or eliminating employers' misidentification of employees as independent contractors (State of California 2020). The California statute contains a three-part test, known as the "ABC test," to determine whether gig or independent worker, which could also pertain to independent taxi drivers and over-the-road (OTR) truck drivers: (A) the worker is free from control of the employer in connection with performing the work; (B) the worker does work that is not in the usual course of the hiring entity's business; and (C) the worker is customarily engaged in an independently established trade, occupation, or business of the same nature as the work performed for the hiring entity (Chung 2019, 2).

In addition, if twenty-first-century unions or unionlike organizations were to group workers by industry or content of work rather than by employer, as Andy Stern (2016) grouped workers as he spearheaded formation of the now 2.2 million-member Service Employees International Union, and if Congress would pass portable health insurance legislation, workers could more easily and fruitfully move to independent contracting or compensated civil labor for some part of their work lives. Mobile health insurance, for example, could be person-, occupation-, or geography-based, rather than employer-based. Although federal and state safety net supports, such as temporary cash and food assistance, will always be needed for some people even if a civil labor system exists, the extent of the need could be much smaller with compensated civil labor than without it. Part of the compensation for workers' civil labor contributions might come from a community or city's annual budget allotments. Such workers could then share their valuable talents and capabilities with their communities and beyond.

Historical Guides for Paid Civil Labor and Possible Current Day Partners

Entrepreneurial and innovative policies and practices that include "identifying new sources of income for citizens" (Brown et al. 2017, 32) could facilitate expanding civil labor. One policy solution to the lack of sufficient jobs and adequate-wage jobs might be to develop a guaranteed employment initiative. Past and current initiatives serve as partial guides.

New Deal's Public Works Administration

In 1935, the New Deal's Civil Works Administration made $400 million (just over $7½ billion in 2021 dollars) in Public Works Administration money available to finance programs of civil works (Stern and Axinn 2018, 167), which included the creation of manual labor jobs. The Civil Works program led to the eight-year Works Progress Administration (WPA) program that put roughly 8.5 million unemployed persons to work in a wide range of occupations (History.com 2019). Even though WPA jobs were temporary from the outset, whereas many civil labor jobs could be more permanent, the guaranteed employment movement resulted in new capabilities that translated into jobs for many WPA workers as the Great Depression lifted, which might also become the case for today's civil laborers.

National Investment Employment Corps

A more recent federal proposal, a national investment employment corps (Darity and Hamilton 2012, 81), would offer all citizens 18 years old and older an employment guarantee at a minimum annual salary of $20,000 ($23,000 in 2021 dollars) with $10,000 ($11,500 in 2021 dollars) in benefits, including medical coverage and retirement support. The proposal described a program that would automatically stabilize income and job creation in both bad and good economic times. Some of the corps program funds also could be allocated to compensating civil labor projects at community and national infrastructure levels. A guaranteed minimum salary and benefits could move youth and older adults into compensated civil labor, as both groups have suffered particularly severe unemployment and slow-to-nonexistent reemployment after the economic downturns of the Great Recession and the coronavirus pandemic.

Guaranteed Employment and Guaranteed Basic Income

A guaranteed employment policy would need to be augmented by some form of wage policy, especially in this era of massive income inequality. One solution might be to set a proportional cap on executive income in a company relative to the average worker's wage or the average wage of the largest worker category in the company. Additional funding for civil labor initiatives could come from a portion of the funds currently allocated to federal-state programs like unemployment insurance, which still has a temporary and limited reach. As Stone and Chen (2014, 3) report, "Since the late 1950s, fewer than half of unemployed workers have actually received unemployment insurance, except during recessions." Even the important American Rescue Plan of 2021 is intended to be a temporary stopgap until the economy rebounds more fully, although many hope that there will be permanent legislation to replace it. Civil labor funding might also come from the tax system in the form of income enhancements. Whereas today the earned income tax credit pertains only to labor market work, an expanded earned income tax credit could be made available to people doing all forms of work activity, including civil labor.

Ultimately, a guaranteed employment program, which could include compensated civil labor, might be augmented by a basic income policy, because income is still tied to the customary conception of work in the United States. Important are early findings from the Stockton Economic Empowerment Demonstration (SEED), which suggest that unconditional cash income actually enabled participants to find full-time employment (West et al. 2021). Guaranteed cash income might similarly enhance participation in compensated civil labor. Similarly, current efforts for a $15 minimum wage are useful for the many underpaid workers in minimum-wage or tip-plus-wage positions, such as the food service workers in Chapter 5, but the reality is that by the time the "Fight for $15" is won, especially in states whose minimum wage remains at its 2009 level of $7.25 an hour, the buying power of $15 will be significantly eroded. This reality is evident throughout the wage examples in this book. Time after time, translating lower- or even moderate-wage figures into 2021 dollars shows that $15-an-hour equivalencies have existed for years. The translations also show how $15 an hour is insufficient for most workers, both because they are not hired for a 40-hour week and because the dollar has experienced inflationary erosion over the decades.

Civic Money

In addition to federal and/or state government funding, because civil labor is based in communities, civil labor could be compensated locally, with civic money, via labor or time exchange or by a system of credit whereby the civil laborer would pay money or time into a community-based credit fund that could then be accessed at a later period of need. Having a variety of compensation arrangements could facilitate individual patterns of civil labor keyed to diverse and particular worker, state, and community needs. Various compensation sources could also expand workers' opportunities to participate productively in both the labor market and civil labor. In this way, the idea of work would move away from the unachievable goal of a full employment society to the reachable goal of a multiactivity society (Beck 2000, 36). In a multiactivity society, individuals participate in the labor market and do other forms of compensated work, sometimes simultaneously, sometimes sequentially, and sometimes one or the other.

Compensated Civil Labor Today

Exchanges

As one example of a compensatory exchange process, in January 2015, a Philadelphia philanthropist identified and purchased space in an economically disadvantaged section of the city for a community of artists, knowing that their work was often impossible to do without adequate space in which to work. In exchange, for every hour the artists worked on their art in the funded space, they were required to spend an hour on neighborhood projects initiated by community members, whether or not the projects were related to art. A similar initiative, the Neighborhood Time Exchange (2019), was developed in another economically disadvantaged Philadelphia neighborhood in 2018. Local and national funders supplied selected artists with studio space, a monthly stipend, and basic tools and supplies. In exchange for time in the studio, as the website noted, the artists "work within the neighborhood to bring local ideas to life." Both exchanges illustrate the expanded possibilities for lives and communities that are similar to, and might expand to, compensated civil labor. In addition, private giving for work exchanges like these could become even more widespread if tax deductions to the donors were available. Whether the gift was large or small, it could be honored as a civic contribution.

More broadly, these and related activities across the United States are examples of economist Lawrence Katz's view that "sees the next wave of automation returning us to an age of craftsmanship and artistry . . . an economy built around self-expression" (quoted in Thompson 2015, 17). Thompson reported on the Columbus Idea Foundry, a gigantic space that used to be a "cavernous shoe factory" that is now "stocked with industrial-age machinery. Several hundred members pay a monthly fee to use the nonprofit's arsenal of machines to make gifts and jewelry, weld, finish, and paint, play with plasma cutters, and work an angle grinder or operate a lathe with a machinist" (Thompson 2015, 18). Products from sites such as this are exchanged, given as gifts, or displayed on personal website videos, sharing workers' creative labor, capabilities, and cultural products for community benefit. An artist at the foundry said, "Most people I know at the foundry would quit their jobs and use the foundry to start their own business if they could" (Thompson 2015, 20). Compensated civil labor might facilitate these entrepreneurial ambitions. Although the Columbus Idea Foundry closed in March 2020 for lack of funding during the pandemic, it reopened in spring 2021 as the Idea Foundry, under new leadership.

Doing Both: Labor Market Work and Paid Civil Labor

Some firms take the form of worker cooperatives that are structured as worker-owned and worker-managed businesses or professional organizations (Pencavel 2001). Other firms have experimented with shared labor market jobs but might usefully experiment more, since studies suggest that in an eight-hour day, three to four hours of continuous, undisturbed work is optimal for productivity and lives (Glaveski 2018). The eight-hour workday was designed in the early industrial era to reduce the then-typical 10 to 16 hours a day on the factory floor. Today, whether conducted in the factory or the office, recent worksite studies of employee work habits have found that the optimal work-to-break ratio for employee well-being and productivity alike is roughly one hour on, 15 minutes off (Bradberry 2019). Schor's (2012) description of the MacArthur Foundation project on Connected Consumption emphasizes that fewer hours of work are the best antidote to high unemployment and underemployment such as the United States has experienced during and since the Great Recession. More recently, Japan, Finland, New Zealand, and Germany are experimenting with four-day workweeks at six to eight hours a day or shorter-day workweeks, both at the same pay as five-day weeks, finding that productivity, morale, and loyalty all improve (Darby 2019). Reducing workdays and workweeks could also leave time for compensated civil labor if workers wanted that.

Other work activity formats seem related to civil labor but have somewhat different structures and goals. One example is exchanges of goods, such as tools or machinery, in which temporary or permanent exchanges are negotiated by digital platform or in person. The goal of such exchanges is to maximize people's economic savings and protect the environment. A second example is participation in time banks, in which services such as rides, yard work, art instruction, or computer help are offered or debited according to hours spent (community time bank organizer, personal communication, March 25, 2019). Goods exchanges and time banks currently tend to be community-based and generally nonprofit enterprises, if they are even formalized, but, in contrast with compensated civil labor, they generally do not involve direct monetary compensation.

Typically, however, both goods exchanges and time banks involve internet platforms. Although convenient for many, this medium could exclude those who cannot afford internet service, whose internet service is unreliable, and who don't know how to use the internet (Iversen and Armstrong 2006). Such exclusions readily lead to reproduction of discrimination by socioeconomic status, race, ethnicity, gender, sexual orientation, and age. The safety concerns, potential for social injustice, and legal exposures of sharing platforms that Schor (2014) characterizes as basically invisible transaction processes may be far less likely to occur in a system of compensated civil labor because of the collaborative and local nature of the persons and organizations involved.

Goods exchanges, time banks and civil labor share both similarities and differences. All are collaboratively formulated by assessing the needs and wants of people in the local community and then pairing those needs and wants with the local persons who want to contribute their capabilities. In all three, social recognition of personal capabilities and talent is important. The main difference is that goods exchanges and time banks do not involve compensation, whereas civil labor does, although compensation may take various forms. Profit making is not the goal of any of these work activities, but the benefits of exchanges and time banks tend to be for individuals or, at most, pairs of people. In contrast, the explicit goals of compensated civil labor include civic contribution, community improvement, and infrastructure improvement.

Exciting Community Civil-Labor-Type Initiatives in the United States

The range of civil-labor-type initiatives in the United States is impressive and growing. The Mayor's Office of New Urban Mechanics (MONUM) in Boston was formed in 2010 and serves as the city's research and design lab (MONUM 2018, 1). MONUM's civic research agenda is a fully collaborative, cooperative, community-based and community-oriented initiative that could easily incorporate compensated civil labor. The agenda democratizes the participatory research process by inviting everyone in, shifting the focus to everyone's questions, and using the collective experiences, capabilities, and expertise of community members to serve the common good (MONUM 2018, 3). As its website explains, MONUM "acts as a front door for startups, universities, and residents wanting to experiment with the city . . . to improve the quality of life for Bostonians" (3). Funding for startup projects comes from MONUM, its philanthropic partners, and an area bank. Simi-

larly, MONUM's large bank-funded garden beautification project to enhance city gardens in underserved neighborhoods could provide payment
or lifetime memberships to the hundreds of dedicated garden volunteers.

Similar smaller-scale examples of partnerships between the mayor's office and the community that involve or could involve compensated civil
labor can be found in Swarthmore, Pennsylvania, a small, historically
Quaker community outside Philadelphia. In August 2019, I spoke with
Swarthmore mayor Marty Spiegel,[2] who clarified that "The town gets funded primarily by property taxes: 20% goes to the town and 80% to the school
system. Most of the funding for community services, such as fire, police,
refuse, and snow and leaf removal, comes from the twenty percent." Yet
notable beautification efforts have taken place in recent years. How did that
happen? Mayor Spiegel explained, "The structure of the government/public-
private/nonprofit business collaboration is key," as is true of policy influence
around the globe (Weible and Sabatier 2017). In Swarthmore, the application process for efforts such as town beautification is interpersonal: a local
resident comes to the mayor, or to whomever the resident knows in the local
government, with an idea. Mayor Spiegel illustrated the process with the
following example, which took place when he was town center coordinator,
some years before he was elected mayor:

A resident who had a landscaping business wanted to beautify
downtown Swarthmore. He made a proposal to me to take to the
town council. He offered to do the downtown planting himself, and
did so. The first year, he placed pots of exotic plants around town
twice a year, for free. They were very popular! The resident did the
same thing the second year, but shortly after that he came back to
the town council to say that he couldn't afford to supply the plants
and labor for free anymore. Could the town help? The town agreed
to pay half the cost of the plants and a local nonprofit horticultural
organization agreed to pay half. The resident provided his labor at a
much lower fee than he would normally charge for that work, because he continued to wanted to give back to the community. That
remains the current agreement.

In another example, the local garden society funded broad-based plant-
ings around town, having received a $10,000 endowment as seed money

---

2. Marty Spiegel and Andy Rosen both approved using their real names in this book and
each reviewed and approved their interview comments.

from a local family. Active fundraising grew the initial endowment. Most of the labor was done by volunteers or residents who wanted to learn more about gardening and horticulture. If the work were viewed as civil labor, these persons could be compensated with funds from the endowment, as "keeping the gardens tended and kept up is the much larger job than just planting," Mayor Spiegel said.

In a third example, during an interview in January 2020, Andy Rosen, manager of the Swarthmore Farmers Market, described the pivotal role of the outdoor market in providing service to the community, competency training, and small financial rewards for the town's high-school-aged youth. Rosen became market manager in 2015 with the goal of further expanding and revitalizing it. Since then, the market has doubled in size and youth participation has grown from one student volunteer to 30 volunteers. Here's how Rosen described the process, its benefits, and its challenges:

Some students come one or two times and then stop; others come all the time. I don't know whether there were a set number of hours they had to fulfill for the high school service requirements, as the students only occasionally need me to sign something that indicates how long they had worked. . . . I've reached out to area colleges but have only gotten a small number of volunteers from those sources.

A very small number of "core" volunteers come 18 to 20 times on average during the season. They come in shifts for setup and breakdown of the tents and tables and usually help vendors, who appreciate that help greatly. All I need to do is say, "Hey, could you go help that vendor set up," and the students are glad to do that. Setup requires them to be there at 7:30 A.M. until 9:30 A.M., and it is hard physical work. Similarly, breakdown occurs from around 1:15 to 2:00 P.M., which always needs additional helpers. In my view, it seems to be a way they can serve in an organization they feel good about. We give these core students a $25 gift card at the end of the season, but another quasi-financial thing is that when vendors need workers, I can often match them with a student who needs a job. Vendors will pay $10 plus all the fruit and vegetables the student can carry. One of the orchards is a big user of student help; I feel really good about that. The kids can make a decent amount of money over the season.

With a background in business and social work, Rosen has taken on the role of informal job adviser here. Parents reinforce the arrangement by telling the manager such things as "how much my daughter/son *loves* work at the farmer's market." Rosen then elaborated on how the market works:

> I also engage adult volunteers; my core is around seven or eight, but often there are more. Between students and adults, there are usually at least nine volunteers over the course of any single market, although sometimes eight or even more than ten. A new volunteer in-market role this past season is market table coordinator, who I've trained to handle all the financial exchanges, which can get quite extensive and complicated each market session. For example, the market takes EBT [Electronic Benefit Transfer] cards for SNAP and works with a food organization in Philadelphia on its Food Bucks program, which is an add-on to SNAP. For every $4 a patron uses on SNAP with their EBT card, they are given $2 free to spend on fruits and vegetables. Once a month the patron gets double food bucks. In terms of general funding issues for the market, it is independent of the town center organization but does get some funding from them. For the future, the market is working to be a zero waste farmer's market.

At the end of our conversation, the manager and I discussed the comparison of volunteer work with compensated work. Speaking personally, Rosen's view was that it would "change the dynamics if I got paid and it would change the calculus of the market. . . . It'd be a different motivation." At the same time, he recognized that this might not be a view held by everyone, especially after the recent discussions in town council meetings about paying townspeople for some of their current volunteer work. Rosen's final comments on the topic go to the core of his ideas about service, equity, and money, which also go to the heart of compensated civil labor: "In the final analysis, having worked as a compensation consultant for many years, I also recognize that too many workers in the labor market are relatively underpaid and aren't able to express their strengths and capabilities in a volunteer capacity."

Finally, compensated civil labor could as fruitfully take place in prisons as in communities. Prison inmates could learn transferable capabilities for their postprison futures, take creative pleasure in their activities and products, and benefit personally by earning a reasonable financial cushion for their return to the broader society, versus the 14 cents that is the national average for inmates who receive the least compensation for their maintenance work in prison. The highest hourly rate for inmates doing prison maintenance jobs is $2 an hour, which is offered only in two states (Moritz-Rabson 2018, 1). Doing work in a society with wage work and compensated civil labor could also shift values toward a more inclusive and generative version of the American Dream and work ethic.

A Case for Compensated Civil Labor: Susan, 2009, and Becca, 2013

One example of how civil labor could work came from Susan (see her story in Chapter 3), who in 2009 offered this view of how something like civil labor could enhance her eighth-grade daughter Becca's work pathway:

Becca's goal is a little bit different because she's also changed direction. So, whether it's broadcast journalism, and she doesn't want to be the newscaster on the anchor desk, she wants to be the director. She wants to be behind the scenes making it happen. She also really enjoys writing. She's written three 300-page novels. None of them published, so can she get a job that will allow her to pay for her finances but also pursue this passion of hers? You know, as a hobby, as enjoyment, as relaxation, whatever? So, I don't care if she's a nutritionist [another of Becca's interests] or if she goes into publishing or if she becomes an English teacher, as long as she's happy, she's successful.

In a 2013 interview with Becca, after her first year in a local community college, she talked about her passion for writing:

Writing has always been a big part of my life. I started writing in kindergarten, like short stories. I wrote my first novel in kindergarten and then I've just been writing since. And then in eighth grade I wrote a 350-page novel. And then, for my senior grad project, I wrote a 400-page novel and I'm working on my fourth novel now. That one's still kind of slow because I've been writing for school, but writing fiction is a totally different ball field. So, I have a niche for it and I get cravings to write. So, I can't really just throw that away. It's kind of like my hobby and people don't really get it as a hobby because they see it more as work. Writing papers is work to me. Writing a novel is like playing a video game. Like it's easy and it's fun.

Becca's creative talents could be fostered if she worked in the labor market part-time, to pay off her education debt, unless that could end up fully or partially forgiven by state or federal policy attention (Weeden 2015). She could also receive support from her community in the form of compensated civil labor for mentoring community youth who are aspiring writers.

From Martina in 2009 on the Need for Community Civil Labor

An example of how compensated civil labor could significantly enhance the lives of people in a community neighborhood came from Martina in 2009 (earlier story in Chapter 4).

INTERVIEWER: Do you think families like yours get a fair break in the amount of support that you get from the government?

MARTINA: Sometimes I feel a little gypped as opposed to, like, the city. I think I might have mentioned this last year. It's always irked me. There's a park right around the corner, and, when we moved in, they had tennis courts and they have a little area for the kids. They have a pavilion, but the tennis courts were never maintained and, like, grass is growing up inside the cracks and all. My husband Jim and I, well, you know, he plays tennis and, every once in a while, I will play with him, and they never did anything. Now this is 17 years later and I think, OK, the taxes have tripled, that's just my taxes, so everybody else's have tripled, and I go into these other neighborhoods where, you know, they put a lot of funding in, especially in the city and all, and I see these great areas like where the kids can play basketball and they light them up at nighttime and everything, and I think well, why are they maintaining. . . . Like, I don't think they maintained the recreational areas around here, like, even a little bit, so to me that's, like, I don't like that.

INTERVIEWER: So, you would like to have them do more for the community?

MARTINA: Yeah, for the community, yeah, even where the kids play football and everything, like, because we travel to go to other areas and I think, geez, they really have nice facilities here (laughs) and ours are, like, shabby, and we do all this fundraising and all just to keep it afloat. My husband redid the whole clubhouse up at the field and did the flooring and put electricity in and painted and put concrete and made it nice and all, him and a few other guys. And I thought, if everybody helped out, you know, and we could get the funding that should be there, there should be some recreational funds. But I don't know, like I say, I go to other areas and it's, like, wow, this is really nice and they keep it nice.

In Martina's community, a system of compensated civil labor that involved construction and building workers together with community youth could improve facilities for youth, teach youth useful competencies, and might even increase the desirability of the community's real estate. Establishing a community fund to enable community-based enhancement, whether cultural or recreational projects like the one Martina describes, could be a useful first step. Allocating a small portion of community tax dollars and establishing a regular fundraising program to compensate workers like Jim and his volunteer construction partners for materials and part of their time could be the way to start.

Making Compensated Labor Happen: Creating Real Opportunity Now

Selection and implementation processes associated with compensated civil labor involve the following considerations, at a minimum: how the local sites decide what the community needs; who decides who is selected to contribute if more than one person steps forward; how the compensation is decided; and who, if anyone, follows up on the quality and adequacy of the contributions and the conditions for contributing (i.e., what the market calls "conditions of labor"). Redefining and expanding our concept of work and developing a system of compensated civil labor could serve to activate people's capabilities for contributions to society, as well as to themselves. Implementing the system might involve a person or group in the middle, such as a local governmental representative or a nongovernmental or nonprofit community organization facilitator, for whom organizing person-to-person arrangements is part of their job. Such processes are all vulnerable to partisanship, personal preference, and bias. But, arguably, a community setting may be more likely than a market setting to have built-in checks and balances that are equitable and actually utilized, since collaboration and community well-being, rather than profit, are the aims.

The workers' stories about the struggles they have experienced in the formal labor market, as well as their occasional satisfactions; our statistics on the labor market, work, and worksites; and our examples of compensated civil labor strongly suggest that that expanding what we think of and call work, especially in the form of compensated civil labor, could be generative and possible in the United States. Our hope is that policymakers, community members, and the general public are persuaded that such an expansion is only becoming more necessary in relation to demographic, cultural, environmental, and geopolitical changes in the country and across the globe. These changes, recently compounded by the coronavirus pandemic and economic downturn, are on pace to surpass the Great Recession, and possibly the Great Depression, in negative global impact. As a result, many cities and smaller localities already are experimenting with new ways to think about work activities that are productive and meaningful and contribute to the community as a whole, as well as to individuals them-selves, as we see in the innovative examples described briefly in this chapter.

Ultimately, this book invites readers to think about ways in which work-ers in a wide range of jobs and industries affect all our lives and to actively engage with the ideas here about what could make their work pay off, pro-vide future (real) opportunity, and benefit families and communities at the same time. We underscore Gorz's (1999, 1) view expressed earlier in the chapter: "We must learn to see work differently: no longer as something we have, but as *what we do*. We must be bold enough to regain control of the work we do." Civil labor, in the varied ways it can be structured and com-pensated, could expand human well-being, help persons and communities flourish, and increase the safety and responsiveness of our country's physi-cal infrastructure. In the wake of the coronavirus pandemic that began in 2020, in which millions of everyday workers in the United States lost their jobs and millions of businesses and nonprofit organizations closed or down-sized, temporarily or permanently, communities of all sizes may be realiz-ing the importance of people's civic engagement and collaborative problem solving. Compensated civil labor seems needed now more than ever to complement labor market jobs and create *real* opportunity for millions of hard-working people.

Appendix

The People and the Research

I have always been fascinated by the sociological aspects of work—what work consists of, what processes and policies are involved, and how people experience the work they do. I've been similarly fascinated by related theory about economic mobility, stratification, and inequality. This book, however, originated from the moment in 2008 when I learned of the death of Studs Terkel, whose epic volume, *Working* (1974), had been a strong influence on my academic career. When Terkel died, I realized his book had described people's experiences with work across the United States just before the labor market changed dramatically in the late 1970s. I also realized that, by the mid-2000s, many scholars had documented these labor market changes and their effects from demographic and statistical perspectives, but few had followed workers' experiential pathways over the decades since 1980. My *aha* moment came when I realized that I had interviewed workers in various occupations about their experiences and thoughts from the 1980s to 2020, and that this material could be used to expand public and scholarly knowledge about working in common industry jobs. In *What Workers Say*, I also added analytic commentary, qualitative forms of generalization, and potential solutions to the workers' struggles, which Terkel's book had not done.

As I noted in the brief discussion of people and research at the end of Chapter 1, I view my multiple research projects on work over these decades as relating to one another within a design that I call "virtual longitudinality." Structurally, this book simulates a four-decade longitudinal study, but instead of following the same individuals over the entire period, the book draws on studies conducted during each of the decades that are connected by participants' ages and occupational pathways. That is, in each of the industry sectors, study participants were roughly the same age. Teen Study Follow-Up respondents in 1989 and 1990 were nearly the same ages (on average) as Welfare-to-Work Study respondents were between 1990 and 2000, as Ethnographic Study respondents were between 2000 and 2010, and as the slightly older Family Study respondents were between 2008 and 2015 and beyond (see Table A.1). While the respondents in each sector were not the same persons, they were similar enough demographically and worked in similar enough occupations to draw analytically founded conclusions about whether and how workers experienced labor market opportunity over the decades.

For the analyses, I first reviewed the verbatim interview transcripts and auxiliary material collected over the four decades of labor market change through a holistic and interpretive lens. I wanted to ascertain whether and how the narratives of the workers and job seekers reflected their experiences in their particular labor market industry and occupational positions—in short, how they saw it then and how I analyze it now. Second, my decade- and era-oriented questions for these analyses were different from the focus in each of the original research projects, even though all four projects attended to the working conditions, economic mobility, struggles, and inequities that the study participants had experienced. Third, I pondered what

TABLE A.1 THE STUDIES REPRESENTED IN *WHAT WORKERS SAY*

Name of study; Year(s) of contact; Location	Age range	Mean age	Average birth year	Number of study respondents
Teen Study Follow-Up; 1989–1990; Philadelphia	21–24	23	1966	$n = 95$
Welfare-to-Work Studies; mid-1990s; Philadelphia	25–30	27	1972	$n = 44$
Ethnographic Study; 2000–2006/2009+; Milwaukee, New Orleans, Philadelphia, St. Louis, Seattle	18–45	32	1969	$n = 25$ families plus auxiliaries; over 1,000 persons interviewed in all
Family Study; 2007–2015+; Philadelphia suburb	31–56	39	1971	$n = 61$ interview participants; 393 survey responses
Total number of persons interviewed (most, multiple times)				$N = 1,240+$

issues might occur from reanalyzing a set of data through a historical lens that includes the present. The conclusion I came to was that *What Workers Say* is basically a historical reanalysis (Burawoy 2009), a variant on oral history. It comprises material from individual research studies conducted at particular time points, uses original participants' voices, and examines this material in the context of work-related stratification, opportunity, and equity, both at the time of the particular study and over the entire time period.

Each of the four research projects that compose this book underwent rigorous Institutional Review Board assessment and approval at Bryn Mawr College (Teen Follow-Up Study) and the University of Pennsylvania (the other three studies). Each project employed rigorous qualitative methodology that included longitudinal inquiry, triangulation of data, and thorough peer review in the resulting publications. I have arranged the chapters in this book by the chronology of the relevant research studies within the industry settings common to many workers in the United States and populated by them. I have further identified the study and time period within which each worker's narrative belongs. Not all industry chapters reflect workers' experiences from all four study decades, as some studies did not contain participants working in every industry. All study participants had been compensated earlier when they participated in the original studies. I also gratefully acknowledge the academic colleagues who contributed to each of the studies discussed in what follows. The generous and helpful funders for each project are acknowledged in the Dedication and Funding Acknowledgments section of the book. The narrative material in *What Workers Say* from the four original projects has not been published elsewhere, unless so cited.

1. The Teen Study Follow-Up: 1989 to 1990

In 1989 and 1990, for my doctoral dissertation (Iversen 1991), I interviewed 95 women who had participated for two years in the early 1980s in a family planning clinic study conducted at a Philadelphia hospital (Freeman and Rickels 1993). The women were age 13 to 17 years old in the early 1980s and in their mid- to late twenties at follow-up in 1989 and 1990. I randomly selected 95 women from the 326 participants in the original two-year study to interview about their education and work pathways since the early 1980s, including their hopes, goals, and ideas about future education and work. The original Teen Study material from the early 1980s, to which I was given full access, together with the follow-up material, resulted in seven to 10 years of information about the 95 study participants. The follow-up sample was fully representative of the 326 women in the original study.

Because the philosophical framework for the Teen Study Follow-Up was lodged in Elder's (1984) life course perspective and Weberian (1978 [1922]) theory on stratification, each study participant and I together constructed a life history calendar (Freedman et al. 1988), which served to "jog" and organize the participant's recall of earlier life events and also allowed the participant and me to revisit what she had said during the original two-year study. The Teen Study Follow-Up narratives in this book come from the 95 audiotaped interviews, my field notes on those interviews, notes I wrote on the semistructured guide as I conducted the interviews, and notes from postdissertation analysis and coding of the interview material in the early 1990s (Iversen 1991, 1995). In the later 1990s, I destroyed the audiotapes per Institutional Review Board commitment. I focus here on the education and work experiences of the Teen Study Follow-Up participants as they met the challenges of their part of the changing work world, drawing also on their earlier hopes and goals from the Teen Study data.

As the Teen Study Follow-Up research constituted the material for my doctoral dissertation, I am most indebted to my Bryn Mawr College chairperson, Leslie B. Alexander, Mary Hale Chase Professor in the Social Sciences and Social Work and Social Research, and to Ellen Freeman, research professor in the department of Obstetrics and Gynecology at the Perelman School of Medicine at the University of Pennsylvania, for their generosity and encouragement. My friend and doctoral colleague, Jane Tausig, was also a great support. My dissertation topic was inspired to a great extent by Frank F. Furstenberg Jr.'s (1976) seminal Baltimore study. From my postdissertation years to today, I have benefited greatly from working on additional research projects with Professor Furstenberg (see, for example, number 4 below, the Family Study). Two generous dissertation grants from the Fahs-Beck Fund for Experimentation and Research, for which I am very grateful, enabled me to compensate the Teen Study Follow-Up participants.

2. The Welfare-to-Work Studies: Mid-1990s

The "work first" requirement of the TANF program, implemented after passage of the Personal Responsibility and Work Opportunity Reconciliation Act of 1996 (i.e., "welfare reform"), coincided with a demographic surge of older persons in the United States and their greater need for healthcare services. As a result, many healthcare facilities across the United States partnered with local TANF programs to provide job-related training in healthcare. In Philadelphia, as in other cities with welfare and workforce development programs, healthcare employers saw the program as an opportunity to build an expanded healthcare workforce. In this "welfare reform" context, University of Pennsylvania faculty colleagues Lauren Rich, Beth Lewis, Lina

Hartocollis, and I worked with several healthcare service organizations in Philadelphia to research and guide their healthcare job training efforts. The narratives in this book came from healthcare trainers, healthcare employers, program staff, and program participants about their experiences as the programs developed and proceeded in the mid- to late 1990s. The narratives in this book from these welfare-to-work projects have not been published elsewhere.

Subsequent publications described the structure and process of the research projects (Iversen 2000; Iversen, Lewis, and Hartocollis 1998); and a grant award from the University of Pennsylvania Research Fund in the late 1990s provided support to Lauren Rich, Beth Lewis, and me (Iversen, Rich, and Lewis 1999) for a pilot study of job retention. Supportive professional colleagues included Cheryl Feldman, Karen Hudson, Symme Trachtenberg, and Steve Wilmot. Doctoral student assistants were Mona Basta, So Young Min, Min Park, and Sarah Suh.

3. The Ethnographic Study: 2000 to 2005, and Informal Follow-Up to 2019

In fall 1999, following the kind recommendation of poverty scholar Kathryn Edin, the Annie E. Casey Foundation invited me and anonymous others to submit a proposal for an ethnographic study of parents participating in its 10-year, five-city workforce development initiative, the Jobs Initiative. The goal of the Jobs Initiative was to improve the ways that regional employment efforts help economically disadvantaged residents get and keep good jobs. Ultimately, my proposal(s) for this independent research resulted in five years of generous grant funding from the foundation.

Foundation support enabled me to gather a team of nine experienced researchers from different disciplinary backgrounds (one or two local researchers in each of the five cities, plus myself) to conduct longitudinal ethnographic research on the work and mobility experiences of parents in 25 families (five per city) who had participated or were currently participating in the Jobs Initiative (Iversen and Armstrong 2006; Giloth 2004). The research aim was to deeply explore the following: What is economic mobility for low-income families in today's America? How do those related to the working parent (family members, employers, and others) experience the parent's efforts to move up through work? How do these views, then, affect the working parent's views of their work?

To examine these and related questions, the local researchers and I conducted multiple and repeated in-person interviews with each family for three to four years between 2000 and 2005. Each family also gave written permission for the research team to talk with others that they or we felt were important in their mobility efforts. These others included parents' workforce program staff, trainers and teachers, extended family members, and friends. We also interviewed the parent's work supervisors and colleagues during extended observational visits to the 74 employment sites in which the 25 study parents had worked during the years of the research. The research team also conducted multiple classroom visits and interviews with principals, teachers, and counselors in the parents' children's schools and observations and interviews with leaders and members of families' social and religious organizations. Finally, the team observed and spent time with staff at the participants' training organizations and workforce intermediaries affiliated with the Annie E. Casey Foundation and its workforce initiative.

Well over one thousand interviews resulted in thousands of hours of audiotaped interview material and more than ten thousand pages of data. We triangulated (double-checked) the data and interpretations to maximize reliability through on-site observations, auxiliary contacts, the research families' review of their "family story," and regular conversations among all the people on the research team. We also shared field notes and audiotaped and transcribed interviews. The narratives of the workers in the Ethnographic Study are singularly focused in *What Workers Say* on how the worker's particular industry location influenced their work in the context of labor market practices of the early 2000s.

I am deeply grateful to foundation principals Robert Giloth and Susan Gewirtz for the opportunity to conduct the ethnographic research. Their professional, academic, and financial support firmly established my academic career. The views about the study participants in this book, however, as well as any errors, are mine alone and do not necessarily represent the views of the foundation.

The team of research ethnographers were Annie Laurie Armstrong, Miriam Isabel Barrios, Michele Belliveau, Melissa Burch, Käthe Johnson, Larry Morton, Cynthia Saltzman, Diane Michalski Turner, and myself. Data analysts and "family story" writers were then-doctoral students Robert P. Fairbanks II; Michele Belliveau; and Mona Basta (see the appendixes in Iversen and Armstrong [2006] for additional information about study design and methods).

4. The Family Study: 2008 to 2015 and Beyond

What we call the Family Study in *What Workers Say* is a longitudinal subset of a two-country, multisite, mixed-methods study that began in 2007 as a comparative study of middle-income families in the United States and

Canada (Furstenberg and Gauthier 2008; see also Iversen, Napolitano, and Furstenberg 2011 for more details). The larger study, formally called Families in the Middle (FIM) Study, was conducted in two sites in the United States, a large Philadelphia suburb and a large city in the state of Washington, and in five sites in Canada. Family Study participants whose stories appear in this book all lived in the Philadelphia suburb.

In 2008, I joined study principals Anne Gauthier and Frank F. Furstenberg Jr. as a senior investigator and Philadelphia suburb interviewer. The Philadelphia team included the principals, Furstenberg and Gauthier; the senior investigator and interviewer (Iversen); interviewers Laura Napolitano, Sigrid Luhr, Patricia Tevington, and Kristin Turney; and doctoral-student analysts Sigrid Luhr and Chenyi Ma.

The purpose of the longitudinal qualitative interviews in the Family Study was to document the processes and lived experiences of financial strain during and after the Great Recession to identify possible coping or management strategies that quantitative studies had not explored (Furstenberg and Gauthier 2008). To that end, the interviewers met with the study participants two or three times, and occasionally more, from 2008 to 2015 and beyond, usually in participants' homes. The semistructured interviews included numerous open-ended questions, and all were audiotaped and transcribed. Experiences and responses from families in the Tacoma, Washington, city site were remarkably similar to those from the Philadelphia suburb site. As with the other three studies, *What Workers Say* focuses on the work experiences and perceptions of the Family Study participants. Funding for the FIM research to the study principals, Furstenberg and Gauthier, went to the research team and compensation to the study families.

Theoretical Underpinning of the Research Methods

The theoretical underpinning of the research methods showcased in this book aligns with Michael Burawoy's (2009, 43, 44) concept of the extended case method, with its four dimensions that emerge from his idea of "reflexive science," which he considers dialogic: (1) they extend the observer into the lives of participants under study; (2) they extend observations over time and space—in interaction within social situations; (3) they extend micro processes to macro forces, such as from persons to social institutions; and (4) they extend theory.

Burawoy's (2009, 9) comment that "we are living history as we do research" is particularly germane to this book's historical orientation to labor market changes over four decades. During the five-plus years I've spent reanalyzing worker narratives for this book, my home office has expanded to three rooms and thousands more pages of charts, written notes, verbatim quotations, articles, press pieces, scholarly books, and commentaries on the social, economic, and political world of workers from the 1980s into the 2020s.

Only a few other scholars have engaged in ethnographic reanalysis. That fact is surprising because Burawoy (2009, 289) emphasizes it is not necessary for the original studies to be actual ethnographies; they can simply be ethnographic, which he characterizes as "seeking to comprehend an external world both in terms of the social processes we observe and the external forces we discern." Lisa Dodson, for example, combined four Boston-area life history studies in *Don't Call Us Out of Name* (1998), which focused on the experiences of African American, Latina, white, Haitian, and Jamaican women as the 1996 welfare reform legislation was being passed. Rosabeth Moss Kanter's 1989 book, *When Giants Learn to Dance*, was also a multisite, multistage study in which each study examined different parts of management in different areas with different people.

For *What Workers Say* overall, I am also grateful to my academic colleague, Naomi Farber, for generously including me in her Milwaukee Teen Study in the early 1990s. Although I have not used material from that project (Farber and Iversen 1998; Iversen and Farber 2000) in this book, working on it gave me valuable experience and understanding for my subsequent study of hard-working, lower-earning parents and their families. I am also grateful to the Moelis Family Research Program Fellow, Joanna Kamhi, for her very careful analytic work in summer 2014 and to Marlene Walk for earlier stimulating material and conversations during her independent study with me on the meaning of work in fall 2012.

References

AARP Public Policy Institute. 2019, December. *Employment Data Digest*. Washington, DC: AARP Public Policy Institute.

Academic Evaluation Services, Inc. 2020. https://aes-edu.org/website/home/index.cfm.

Acs, Gregory, Katherin Ross Phillips, and Daniel McKenzie. 2001. "Playing by the Rules, but Losing the Game: Americans in Low-Income Working Families." In *Low-Wage Workers in the New Economy*, edited by Richard Kazis and Marc S. Miller, 21–44. Washington, DC: Urban Institute.

Agovino, Theresa. 2020. "Americans Aren't Moving." SHRM. https://www.shrm.org/hr-today/news/all-things-work/pages/Americans-are-not-moving.aspx.

AllNurses. 2012. "Nursing: Not a Recession-Proof Career." allnurses, June 13. https://allnurses.com/nursing-not-a-recession-proof-career-t436280/.

American Society of Civil Engineers. 2021. *2021 Report Card for America's Infrastructure*. Reston, VA: American Society of Civil Engineers.

Annie E. Casey Foundation. 2021. "Seven Top Social Issues for Gen Z." Baltimore, MD: Author.

Applebaum, Herbert. 1995. "The Concept of Work in Western Thought." In *Meanings of Work: Considerations for the Twenty-First Century*, edited by Frederick C. Gamst, 46–78. Albany: State University of New York Press.

Autor, David H. 2015. "Why Are There Still So Many Jobs?" The History and Future of Workplace Automation." *Journal of Economic Perspectives* 29 (3): 3–30.

———. 2019. "Work of the Past, Work of the Future." AEA Papers and Proceedings 109, May, 1–32.

Autor, David H., and David Dorn. 2013. "The Growth of Low-Skills Service Jobs and Polarization of the U.S. Labor Market." *American Economic Review* 103 (5): 1553–97.

Bach, Deborah. 2015. "Blacks Hit Hardest by Public-Sector Job Losses during Recession, Study Finds." *UW News*, August 24. Seattle, WA: University of Washington.

Baily, Martin N., and Barry P. Bosworth. 2014. "US Manufacturing: Understanding Its Past and Its Potential Future." *Journal of Economic Perspectives* 28 (1): 3–26.

Bartash, Jeffry. 2020. "The U.S. Has Only Regained 42% of the 22 Million Jobs Lost in the Pandemic. Here's Where They Are." *Marketwatch*, August 7. https://www.market watch.com/story/restaurants-and-retailers-have-regained-the-most-jobs-since-the -coronavirus-crisis-but-theres-a-catch-2020-08-07.

Bartik, Timothy J., and Susan N. Houseman, eds. 2008. *A Future of Good Jobs? America's Challenge in the Global Economy.* Kalamazoo, MI: W. E. Upjohn Institute for Employment Research.

Beck, Ulrich. 2000. *The Brave New World of Work.* Translated by Patrick Camiller. Cambridge, UK: Polity.

Benmelech, Efraim, Nittai K. Bergman, and Hyunseob Kim. 2019. "What's Causing Wage Stagnation in America?" *Kellogg Insight*, December 2. Evanston, IL: Northwestern University, Kellogg School of Management.

Birdsall, Nancy, Carol Graham, and Stefano Pettinato. 2000. "Stuck in the Tunnel: Is Globalization Muddling the Middle?" Working Paper No. 14. Washington, DC: Brookings Institution, Center on Social and Economic Dynamics.

Blank, Rebecca M., Sheldon H. Danziger, and Robert F. Schoeni, eds. 2006. *Working and Poor.* New York: Russell Sage Foundation.

Boushey, Heather. 2005. *Student Debt: Bigger and Bigger.* Washington, DC: Center for Economic and Policy Research.

Bradberry, Travis. 2019. "There's an Optimal Way to Structure Your Day—and It's Not the 8-Hour Workday." *Quartz at Work*, March 4. https://qz.com/work/1561830/why -the-eight-hour-workday-doesnt-work/.

Brown, Justine, Tom Gosling, Bhushan Sethi, Blair Sheppard, Carol Stubbings, John Sviokla, Jon Williams, and Daria Zarubina. 2018. "Workforce of the Future: The Competing Forces Shaping 2030." https://www.pwc.com/people

Buffie, Nick, and Sarah Rawlins. 2017. "Declining Rate of Unemployment Insurance: Many Workers Are Unemployed Too Long to Receive Help." *CEPR.net*, February 14. https://cepr.net/declining-rate-of-unemployment-insurance-many-workers-are -unemployed-too-long-to-receive-help/.

Burawoy, Michael. 2009. *The Extended Case Method: Four Countries, Four Decades, Four Great Transformations, and One Theoretical Tradition.* Berkeley: University of California Press.

Bureau of Economic Analysis. 2018. "Services-producing Industries." https://www.bea .gov/help/glossary/services-producing-industries.

Bureau of Labor Statistics (BLS). 1990. *Occupational Outlook Handbook: 1990–1991 Edition.* Bulletin 2350, April. Washington, DC: U.S. Bureau of Labor Statistics.

———. 2011. "Occupational Employment and Wages—May 2010." Washington, DC: U.S. Bureau of Labor Statistics.

———. 2015. "The Employment Situation—May 2015." News release, June 5. Washington, DC: U.S. Bureau of Labor Statistics.

———. 2017. "Projections of Occupational Employment 2016-26." Washington, DC: U.S. Bureau of Labor Statistics.

———. 2018. "Employer-Reported Workplace Injuries and Illnesses: 2017." News release, November 8.Washington, DC: U.S. Bureau of Labor Statistics.

———. 2019a. "Automotive Industry: Employment, Earnings, and Hours." Data extracted on September 29, 2021. Washington, DC: U.S. Bureau of Labor Statistics. https:// www.bls.gov/iag/tgs/iagauto.htm.

———. 2019b. "Clothing and Clothing Accessories Stores." *Industries at a Glance.* NAICS 448. Washington, DC: U.S. Bureau of Labor Statistics.

———. 2019c. "Comparing Employment from the BLS Household and Payroll Surveys," January 2019. Last modified February 5, 2021. Washington, DC: U.S. Bureau of Labor Statistics. https://www.bls.gov/web/empsit/ces_cps_trends.htm.

———. 2019d. "Current Employment Statistics Highlights." Washington, DC: U.S. Bureau of Labor Statistics.

———. 2019e. "The Employment Situation—June 2019." News release, July 5. Report USDL-19-1137. Washington, DC: U.S. Bureau of Labor Statistics.

———. 2019f. "Fastest Growing Occupations, 2018 and Projected 2028." Washington, DC: U.S. Bureau of Labor Statistics.

———. 2019g. "Food Service Managers." *Occupational Outlook Handbook.* Last modified September 8, 2021. Washington, DC: U.S. Bureau of Labor Statistics. https://www.bls.gov/ooh/management/food-service-managers.htm.

———. 2019h. *Injuries, Illnesses, and Fatalities.* Washington, DC: U.S. Bureau of Labor Statistics.

———. 2019i. "Labor Force Statistics from the Current Population Survey." Table 8, "Employed and Unemployed Full- and Part-time Workers by Age, Sex, Race, and Hispanic or Latino Ethnicity." Washington, DC: U.S. Bureau of Labor Statistics.

———. 2019j. "Occupational Employment and Wages, May 2018: Retail Salespersons." Last modified March 29, 2019. Washington, DC: U.S. Bureau of Labor Statistics. https://www.bls.gov/newsrelease/archives/ocwage_03292019.pdf.

———. 2019k. "Occupational Employment and Wage Statistics, May 2019, 23-2011, Paralegals and Legal Assistants." Washington, DC: U.S. Bureau of Labor Statistics. https://www.bls.gov/oes/2019/may/oes232011.htm.

———. 2019l. "Occupational Employment and Wage Statistics, May 2019. 11-2022, Sales Managers." Washington, DC: U.S. Bureau of Labor Statistics. https://www.bls.gov/oes/2019/may/oes232011.htmhttps://www.bls.gov/oes/2019/may/oes112022.htm.

———. 2019m. "Occupational Employment and Wage Statistics: 17-1011. Architects, except Landscape and Naval." Washington, DC: U.S. Bureau of Labor Statistics. https://www.bls.gov/oes/2019/may/oes171011.htm.

———. 2020a. "Clothing and Clothing Accessories Stores, NAICS 448." Washington, DC: U.S. Bureau of Labor Statistics. https://www.bls.gov/iag/tgs/iag448.htm.

———. 2020b. "The Employment Situation—December 2019." News release, January 10. Washington, DC: U.S. Bureau of Labor Statistics.

———. 2020c. "The Employment Situation—January 2020." News release, February 7. Washington, DC: U.S. Bureau of Labor Statistics.

———. 2020d. "The Employment Situation—March 2020." News release, April 3. Reissued September 23, 2020. Washington, DC: U.S. Bureau of Labor Statistics. https://www.bls.gov/news.release/archives/empsit_04032020.pdf.

———. 2020e. "Food and Beverage Stores." *Industries at a Glance.* NAICS 445. Washington, DC: U.S. Bureau of Labor Statistics.

———. 2020f. "Food Services and Drinking Places." *Industries at a Glance.* NAICS 722. Washington, DC: U.S. Bureau of Labor Statistics.

———. 2020g. "Labor Force Participation Rate—Men." Accessed from FRED, Federal Reserve Bank of St. Louis, https://fred.stlouisfed.org/series/LNS11300001.

———. 2020h. "Labor Force Participation Rate—Women." Accessed from FRED, Federal Reserve Bank of St. Louis, https://fred.stlouisfed.org/series/LNS11300002.

————. 2020i. "Occupational Employment and Wages—May 2019." News release, March 31. Washington, DC: U.S. Bureau of Labor Statistics.

————. 2020j. "Real Estate." *Industries at a Glance.* NAICS 531. Washington, DC: U.S. Bureau of Labor Statistics.

————. 2020k. "Union Members—2020." News Release, January 22. Washington, DC: U.S. Bureau of Labor Statistics. https://www.bls.gov/news.release/pdf/union2.pdf.

————. 2020l. "Occupational Employment and Wages, May 2020. Washington, DC: U.S. Bureau of Labor Statistics.

California, State of. 2020. "Independent Contractor versus Employee." Sacramento, CA: State of California, Department of Industrial Relations. https://www.dir.ca.gov/dlse/faq_independentcontractor.htm.

Campaign to Invest in America's Workforce. 2019. *Investing in America's Workforce: A National Imperative for the 21st Century.* CIAW report, September 19. https://www.americasworkforce.org.

Cappelli, Peter, Iwan Barankay, and David Lewin. 2018. "How the Great Recession Changed American Workers." *Knowledge@Wharton,* September 10. https://knowledge.wharton.upenn.edu/article/great-recession-american-dream/.

Carnevale, Anthony P., Nicole Smith, and Jeff Strohl. 2019. *Recovery: Job Growth and Education Requirements through 2020.* Washington, DC: Georgetown Public Policy Institute, Center on Education and the Workforce.

Chamberlayne, Prue, Joanna Bornat, and Tom Wengraf, eds. 2000. *The Turn to Biographical Methods in Social Science: Comparative Issues and Examples.* London: Routledge.

Christiansen, Maria. 2018. "What Are the Duties of a Deli Worker?" https://work.chron.com/duties-deli-worker-19748.html.

Chung, Steven. 2019. "In the Gig Economy, Who Is an Employer and Who Is an Independent Contractor?" *Above the Law Daily Newsletter,* October 2. https://abovethelaw.com/2019/10/in-the-gig-economy-who-is-an-employee-and-who-is-an-independent-contractor/https://abovethelaw.com/2019/10/.

Ciulla, Joanne B. 2000. *The Working Life: The Promise and Betrayal of Modern Work.* New York: Three Rivers.

Clogg, Clifford C., Scott R. Eliason, and Kevin T. Leicht. 2001. *Analyzing the Labor Force: Concepts, Measures, and Trends.* New York: Kluwer Academic/Plenum.

Collins, Michael. 2016. "The Threat of Declining Wages." *Industry Week,* November 29. https://www.industryweek.com/the-economy/public-policy/article/22007283/the-threat-of-declining-wages.

Covert, Bryce. 2015. "The Slow Death of the Secretary." *New Republic,* May 4. https://newrepublic.com/article/121712/slow-death-secretary.

Currier, Erin, Clinton Key, and Sarah Sattelmeyer. 2016. *Worker Benefits—and Their Costs—Vary Widely across U.S. Industries.* Philadelphia: Pew Charitable Trusts.

Cutcher-Gershenfeld, Joel, Dan Brooks, and Martin Mulloy. 2015. *The Decline and Resurgence of the U.S. Auto Industry.* Washington, DC: Economic Policy Institute.

Danziger, Pamela N. 2020. "Retail Bankruptcies Could Go from Bad to Worse in 2021." *Forbes,* October 7.

Darby, Luke. 2019. "Why America Should Adopt the Four-Day Work Week." *GQ,* November 5. https://www.gq.com/story/four-day-work-week-is-better-for-everyone.

Darity, William, Jr., and Darrick Hamilton. 2012. "Bold Policies for Economic Justice." *Review of Black Political Economy* 39:79–85.

Davis, Steven J., and Till Von Wachter. 2011. "Recessions and the Cost of Job Loss." Brookings Papers on Economic Activity, Economic Studies Program, The Brookings Institution, 43 (2)(Fall): 1–72.

Department of Numbers. 2019. "U.S. Employment and Jobs." Accessed January 25, 2020, https://www.deptofnumbers.com/employment/us/.

Deutsch, Alison L. 2020. "The 5 Industries Driving the U.S. Economy." Investopedia, October 24, 2021. https://www.investopedia.com/articles/investing/042915/5-industries -driving-us-economy.asp.

Dodson, Lisa. 1998. Don't Call Us Out of Name: The Untold Lives of Women and Girls in Poor America. Boston: Beacon.

———. 2009. The Moral Underground: How Ordinary Americans Subvert an Unfair Economy. New York: New Press.

Douty, H. M. 1984. "A Century of Wage Statistics: The BLS Contribution." Monthly Labor Review, November, 16–28.

Dutton, Jane E., Gelaye Debebe, and Amy Wrzesniewski. 2016. "Being Valued and Devalued at Work: A Social Valuing Perspective." Qualitative Organizational Research: Best Papers from the Davis Conference on Qualitative Research, 9–51.

Eberstadt, Nicholas. 2016. Men without Work. West Conshohocken, PA: Templeton.

Ehrenberg, Ronald G., and Robert S. Smith. 2018. Modern Labor Economics Theory and Public Policy. 13th ed. New York: Routledge.

Ehrenreich, Barbara. 2001. Nickel and Dimed: On (Not) Getting By in America. New York: Henry Holt.

Elder, Glen H., Jr. 1984. "Families, Kin, and the Life Course: A Sociological Perspective." In Review of Child Development Research Vol. 7: The Family, edited by Rosa D. Parke, 80–136. Chicago: University of Chicago Press.

Engels, Frederick. 1942. The Origin of the Family, Private Property, and the State. New York: International.

England, Kim, and Kate Boyer. 2009. "Women's Work: The Feminization and Shifting Meanings of Clerical Work." Journal of Social History 43 (2): 307–40.

Facts about Germany. 2020. "Committed Civil Society." https://www.tatsachen -ueber-deutschland.de/en/chapter/society/committed-civil-society.

Farber, Henry S., Jesse Rothstein, and Robert G. Valletta. 2015. "The Effect of Extended Unemployment Insurance Benefits: Evidence from the 2012–2013 Phase-Out." Working Paper 2015-03. San Francisco: Federal Reserve Bank.

Farber, Naomi B., and Roberta R. Iversen. 1998. "Family Values about Education and Their Transmission among Black Inner-City Young Women." In The Development of Competence and Character through Life, edited by Anne Colby, Jacqueline James, and Daniel Hart, 141–67. Chicago: University of Chicago Press.

Federal Reserve Bank of St. Louis. 2017. "All Employees, Retail Trade: 1940 to 2017." Accessed July 30, 2017. https://fred.stlouisfed.org/series/USTRADE.

Federici, Silvia. 2012. Revolution at Point Zero: Housework, Reproduction, and Feminist Struggle. Brooklyn, NY: Common Notions.

———. 2013. "A Feminist Critique of Marx by Silvia Federici." End of Capitalism, May 29. http://endofcapitalism.com/2013/05/29/a-feminist-critique-of-marx.

Ferguson, James, and Tania Murray Li. 2018. "Beyond the 'Proper' Job: Political Economic Analysis after the Century of Labouring Man." Working Paper 51. PLAAS, UWC: Cape Town.

Fleurbaey, Marc. 2018. A Manifesto for Social Progress: Ideas for a Better Society. Cambridge: Cambridge University Press.

Fowler, Elizabeth M. 1990. "Careers: Reducing the Stress on Lawyers." *New York Times*, January 23, D20.

Freedman, Deborah, Arland Thornton, Donald Camburn, Duane Alwin, and Linda Young-DeMarco. 1988. "The Life History Calendar: A Technique for Collecting Retrospective Data." *Sociological Methodology* 18:37–68.

Freeman, Ellen W., and Karl Rickels. 1993. *Early Childbearing: Perspectives of Black Adolescents on Pregnancy, Abortion, and Contraception*. Newbury Park, CA: Sage.

Furstenberg, Frank F., Jr. 1976. *Unplanned Parenthood: The Social Consequences of Teenage Childbearing*. New York: Free Press.

Furstenberg, Frank F., and Anne H. Gauthier. 2008. *Families in the Middle: A Cross-National Study of Middle-Income Families in High-Income Economies*. New York: Russell Sage Foundation.

Future Workplace and Randstad USA. 2016. "Managing Gen Y and Z in the Workplace." Accessed February 5, 2020. https://www.randstad.com/workforce-insights/employer -branding/library/items/managing-gen-y-z-workplace/.

Gabor, Andrea. 2004. "Running a Hospital like a Factory, in a Good Way." *New York Times*, February 22.

Gaddis, S. Michael. 2014. "Discrimination in the Credential Society: An Audit Study of Race and College Selectivity in the Labor Market." *Social Forces* 92 (4): 1–29.

Gauthier, Anne H. 2015. "Documentation for the Families in the Middle (FIM). NIDI/ University of Calgary." https://research.rug.nl/en/publications/documentation-for -the-families-in-the-middle-fim.

Ghanbari, Lyda, and Michael D. McCall. 2016. "Current Employment Statistics Survey: 100 Years of Employment, Hours, and Earnings." *Monthly Labor Review*, August, 1–22.

Gianarelli, Linda, Laura Wheaton, and Gregory Acs. 2020. "2020 Poverty Projections." Washington, DC: Urban Institute, July, 1–12.

Gill, Rosalind, and Andy Pratt. 2008. "In the Social Factory? Immaterial Labour, Precariousness and Cultural Work." *Theory, Culture and Society* 25 (7–8): 1–30.

Giloth, Robert, ed. 2004. *Workforce Intermediaries for the Twenty-First Century*. Philadelphia: Temple University Press in association with the American Assembly, Columbia University Press.

Glaveski, Steve. 2018. "The Case for the 6-Hour Workday." *Harvard Business Review Digital*, December 11, 1–6.

Golden, Lonnie. 2016. *Still Falling Short on Hours and Pay: Part-Time Work Becoming New Normal*. Economic Policy Institute Report, December 5. Washington, DC: Economic Policy Institute.

———. 2020. *Part-Time Workers Pay a Big-Time Penalty*. Economic Policy Institute Report, February 27. Washington, DC: Economic Policy Institute.

Golden, Lonnie, and Jaeseung Kim. 2020. *Underemployment Just Isn't Working for U.S. Part-Time Workers*. Center for Law and Social Policy Report, February. Washington, DC: Center for Law and Social Policy.

Goldin, Claudia, and Lawrence F. Katz. 2018. "Women Working Longer: Facts and Some Explanations, Chapter 1." In *Women Working Longer: Increased Employment at Older Ages*, edited by Caludia Goldin and Lawrence F. Katz. Chicago: University of Chicago Press.

Goodman, Christopher J., and Steven M. Mance. 2011. "Employment Loss and the 2007–09 Recession: An Overview." *Monthly Labor Review* (April): 3–12.

Goodrum, Paul, and Manish Gangwar. 2004. "The Relationship between Changes in Equipment Technology and Wages in the U.S. Construction Industry." *Journal of Construction Management and Economics* 22:291–301.

Gorz, André. 1999. *Reclaiming Work: Beyond the Wage-Based Society.* Translated by Chris Turner. Cambridge, UK: Polity.

Gould, Elise. 2019. *What to Watch on Jobs Day: Are There Signs of Wage Acceleration?* Economic Policy Institute Report, August 1. Washington, DC: Economic Policy Institute.

Gould, Eric. 2018. "The Impact of Manufacturing Employment Decline on Black and White Americans." *VoxEU,* December 19. https://voxeu.org/article/manufacturing -decline-has-hurt-black-americans-more.

Granovetter, Mark. 1973. "The Strength of Weak Ties." *American Journal of Sociology* 78 (6): 1360–80.

———. 1983. "The Strength of Weak Ties: A Network Theory Revisited." *Sociological Theory* 1:201–33.

Grindy, Bruce. 2019. "Hospitality Industry Turnover Rate Ticked Higher in 2018." *National Restaurant Association,* May 9. https://restaurant.org/education-and-resources /resource-library/hospitality-industry-turnover-rate-ticked-higher-in-2018/.

———. 2020. "Restaurants Provide First Jobs and a Career Path." National Restaurant Association, March 6. https://restaurant.org/education-and-resources/resource -library/restaurants-provide-first-jobs-and-a-career-path/.

Guendelsberger, Emily. 2019. *On the Clock: What Low-Wage Work Did to Me and How It Drives America Insane.* New York: Little, Brown.

Hacker, Jacob S. 2008. *The Great Risk Shift: The New Economic Insecurity and the Decline of the American Dream.* 2nd ed. New York: Oxford University Press.

Hatch, Julie, and Angela Clinton. 2000. "Job Growth in the 1990s: A Retrospect." *Monthly Labor Review* 123 (12): 3–18.

Haugen, Steven E. 1986. "The Employment Expansion in Retail Trade, 1973–85." *Monthly Labor Review* 109 (8): 9–16.

Hebert, Scott, Anne St. George, and Barbara Epstein. 2003. *Breaking Through: Overcoming Barriers to Family Sustaining Employment.* Baltimore: Annie E. Casey Foundation.

History.com. 2019. *Works Progress Administration (WPA).* June 10. https://www.history .com/topics/great-depression/works-progress-administration.

Hochschild, Arlie Russell. 1997. *The Time Bind.* New York: Metropolitan.

Holzer, Harry J. 1998. "Employer Skill Demands and Labor Market Outcomes of Blacks and Women." *ILR Review* 52 (1): 82–91.

———. 2011. "Raising Job Quality and Skills for American Workers: Creating More Effective Education and Workforce Development Systems in the States." Discussion Paper 2011-10. Washington, DC: Brookings.

Holzer, Harry J., and Robert I. Lerman. 2009. "The Future of Middle-Skill Jobs." CCF Brief #41. Washington, DC: Brookings Center on Children and Families.

Huffington Post. 2012. "Health Care Industry Will Create 5.6 Million More Jobs by 2020: Study." *Huffington Post,* June 21. https://www.huffpost.com/entry/health-care-job -creation_n_1613479.

Hunt, H. Allan, and Timothy L. Hunt. 1986. *Clerical Employment and Technological Change: A Review of Recent Trends and Projections.* Report submitted to National Commission for Employment Policy. http://research.upjohn.org/reports/172.

Ingraham, Christopher. 2016. "Still Think America Is the 'Land of Opportunity'? Look at This Chart." *Washington Post,* February 26. https://www.washingtonpost.com

/news/wonk/wp/2016/02/22/still-think-america-is-the-land-of-opportunity-look-at -this-chart/.

Iversen, Roberta Rehner. 1991. "Income and Employment Consequences for African- American Participants of a Family Planning Clinic: A Seven-Year Follow-Up." PhD diss. Bryn Mawr College, The Graduate School of Social Work and Social Research.

———. 1995. "Poor African-American Women and Work: The Occupational Attainment Process. *Social Problems* 42 (4): 554–73.

———. 2000. "TANF Policy Implementation: The Invisible Barrier." *Journal of Sociology and Social Welfare* 27 (2): 139–59.

Iversen, Roberta Rehner, and Annie Laurie Armstrong. 2006. *Jobs Aren't Enough: To- ward a New Economic Mobility for Low-Income Families.* Philadelphia: Temple Uni- versity Press.

———. 2007. "Parents' Work, Depressive Symptoms, Children, and Family Economic Mobility: What Can Ethnography Tell Us?" *Families in Society* 88 (3): 339–50.

Iversen, Roberta Rehner, and Naomi B. Farber. 2000. "Transmission of Family Values, Work and Welfare among Poor Urban Black Women." In *Work and Family: Research Informing Policy,* edited by Toby L. Parcel and Daniel B. Cornfield, 249–73. Thousand Oaks, CA: Sage.

Iversen, Roberta Rehner, Beth M. Lewis, and Lina Hartocollis. 1998. "Occupational So- cial Work and Welfare Reform: Directions for Continuing Social Work Education." *Professional Development: International Journal of Continuing Social Work Education* 1 (3): 12–17.

Iversen, Roberta Rehner, Laura Napolitano, and Frank F. Furstenberg. 2011. "Middle-In- come Families in the Economic Downturn: Challenges and Management Strategies over Time." *Longitudinal and Life Course Studies: International Journal* 2 (3): 286–300.

Iversen, Roberta Rehner, Lauren M. Rich, and Beth M. Lewis. 1999. "Job Retention and Working Conditions among TANF Recipients in a Welfare-to-Work Program: A Pilot Study." Research proposal submitted to and funded by the Faculty Research Committee of the University of Pennsylvania, School of Social Work.

Jacobson, Louis S., Robert J. Lalonde, and Daniel G. Sullivan. 1993. "Earnings Losses of Displaced Workers." *American Economic Review* 83 (4): 685–709.

Jiang, Yang, Mercedes Ekono, and Curtis Skinner. 2016. *Basic Facts about Low-Income Children.* New York: Columbia University, National Center for Children in Poverty.

Jones-Correa, Michael. 1998. *Between Two Nations: The Political Predicament of Latinos in New York City.* Ithaca, NY: Cornell University Press.

Kalleberg, Arne L. 2009. "Precarious Work, Insecure Workers: Employment Relations in Transition." *American Sociological Review* 74 (1): 1–22.

———. 2011. *Good Jobs, Bad Jobs: The Rise of Polarized and Precarious Employment Systems in the United States, 1970s to 2000s.* New York: Russell Sage Foundation.

———. 2012. "Job Quality and Precarious Work: Clarifications, Controversies, and Challenges." *Work and Occupations* 39 (4): 427–48.

———. 2018. *Precarious Lives: Job Insecurity and Well-Being in Rich Democracies.* Med- ford, MA: Polity.

Kanter, Rosabeth Moss. 1989. *When Giants Learn to Dance.* New York: Touchstone/ Simon and Schuster.

Keegan, Caroline. 2020. "Black Workers Matter: Black Labor Geographies and Uneven Redevelopment in Post-Katrina New Orleans." *Urban Geography.* https://doi.org/10 .1080/02723638.2020.1712121.

Kenworthy, Lane, and Ive Marx. 2017. "In-Work Poverty in the United States." IZA Discussion Paper 10638. Bonn, Ger.: Forschungsinstitut zur Zukunft der Arbeit GmbH (IZA).

Kessler, Glenn. 2019. "Did Ivanka Trump Create 'Millions' of Jobs?" *Washington Post*, February 27. https://www.washingtonpost.com/politics/2019/02/27/did-ivanka-trump-create-millions-jobs/.

Kochan, Thomas A., and Stephen Barley. 1999. *The Changing Nature of Work: Implications for Occupational Analysis*. Washington, DC: National Academies Press.

Kochan, Thomas A., and Lee Dyer. 2017. *Shaping the Future of Work: A Handbook for Action and a New Social Contract*. Cambridge, MA: MITxPress.

Laird, Jennifer. 2017. "Public Sector Employment Inequality in the United States and the Great Recession." *Demography* 54 (1): 391–411.

Lambert, Susan J., Peter J. Fugiel, and Julia R. Henly. 2014. "Precarious Work Schedules among Early-Career Employees in the US: A National Snapshot." Chicago: University of Chicago, Crown Family School of Social Work, Policy, and Practice. https://crown school.uchicago.edu/sites/default/files/uploads/lambert.fugiel.henly_precarious _work_schedules.august2014_0.pdf.

Levy, Frank, and Richard J. Murnane. 2006. "How Computerized Work and Globalization Shape Human Skill Demands." *ResearchGate*, September. https://www.researchgate .net/publication/228619711_How_Computerized_Work_and_Globalization_Shape _Human_Skill_Demands.

Long, Heather. 2021. "'It's Not a Labor Shortage': It's a Great Reassessment of Work in America." *Washington Post*, May 7. https://www.washingtonpost.com/business /2021/05/07/jobs-report-labor-shortage-analysis/.

Lynn, Wayne. 2012. "Survival of the Small to Mid-sized Printing Company in Today's Chaotic Environment." *What They Think*, September 11. https://whattheythink.com /articles/59766-survival-printing-company-todays-chaotic-environment/.

Maciag, Mike. 2017. "A Downsized Public Workforce May Be a Permanent Consequence of the Recession." *Governing*, December. https://www.governing.com/archive/gov -suppressed-staffing-levels-government-recession.html.

Manyika, James, Sven Smit, and Jonathan Woetzel. 2020. "The Social Contract in the 21st Century." McKinsey Global Institute Report. New York: McKinsey Global Institute.

Marks, Gene. 2019. "The Value of Having a Side-Hustle Job." *Philadelphia Inquirer*, August 16, A9–10.

Marx, Karl. 1933. *Wage-Labour and Capital*. New York: International.

May, Douglas. 2017. "Job Satisfaction in the Paralegal Field." Accessed July 31, 2017, https://www.lawcrossing.com/article/3058/Job-Satisfaction-in-the-Paralegal-Field/.

Mayor's Office of New Urban Mechanics (MONUM). 2018. *Civic Research Agenda: So Many Questions, So Little Time*. Boston: MONUM.

McCall, Leslie. 2000. "Gender and the New Inequality: Explaining the College/Non-college Wage Gap." *American Sociological Review* 65 (April): 234–55.

McLafferty, Sara, and Valerie Preston. 1992. "Spatial Mismatch and Labor Market Segmentation for African-American and Latina Women. *Economic Geography* 68 (4): 406–31.

Mead, Lawrence M. 1992. *The New Politics of Poverty*. New York: Basic.

Meyerson, Harold. 2013. "The Forty Year Slump." *American Prospect*, November 12. http://prospect.org/article/40-year-slump.

Moritz-Rabson, Daniel. 2018. "Prison Slavery: Inmates Are Paid Cents While Manufacturing Products Sold to Government." *Newsweek*, August 28. https://www.newsweek .com/prison-slavery-who-benefits-cheap-inmate-labor-1093729.

Murray, Charles. 1984. *Losing Ground: American Social Policy 1950–1980.* New York: Basic.

MyPlan.com. 2004. "Printing: Employment." Accessed August 27, 2016, https://www .myplan.com/careers/printing-press-operators/summary-51-5112.00.html

National Conference of State Legislatures. 2021. "State Minimum Wages." https://www .ncsl.org/research/labor-and-employment/state-minimum-wage-chart.aspx

National Employment Law Project. 2002. *Long-Term Unemployment on a Par with Prior Recessions, but Unemployment Benefits Are Not—Will Lawmakers Fix the Federal Extended Benefits Program?* New York: NELP.

National Retail Federation. 2020. "March Retail Sales Plummet during Coronavirus Pandemic." News release, April 15. https://nrf.com/media-center/press-releases/March -retail-sales-plummet-during-coronavirus-pandemic.

Neighborhood Time Exchange. 2019. Mural Arts Philadelphia, accessed May 8, 2021. https://www.muralarts.org/?s=Neighborhood+Time+Exchange.

Newman, Katherine S. 1999. *No Shame in My Game: The Working Poor in the Inner City.* New York: Alfred A. Knopf and Russell Sage Foundation.

New Orleans Carpenters Training Center. 2016. *Carpenters.org.* https://www.carpenters .org/training_centers/la/.

Nonprofit Source. 2018. "Volunteering Statistics and Trends for Nonprofits." *Nonprofit Source.com.* https://nonprofitssource.com/online-giving-statistics/volunteering-sta tistics/.

Nussbaum, Martha C., and Amartya Sen, eds. 1993. *The Quality of Life.* Oxford, UK: Clarendon.

O'Brien, Greig. 2014. "Architecture and Construction Are Beginning to Dig Out from the Recession." *Architect*, January 23. https://www.architectmagazine.com/practice /architecture-and-construction-are-beginning-to-dig-out-from-the-recession_o.

O'Connor, Sarah. 2016. "The Gig Economy Is Neither 'Sharing' nor 'Collaborative.'" *The Financial Times*, June 14. https://www.ft.com/content/8273edfe-2c9f-11e6-a18d -a96ab29e3c95.

O'Donnell, Kathleen M. 2018. "Influx in Healthcare and Senior Living Means Big Opportunities for Architects." *American Institute of Architects*, May 14. https://www.aia .org/articles/195541-influx-in-healthcare-and-senior-living-mean.

O'Donovan, Caroline. 2014. *Here's How the Recession Affected Jobs in Newsrooms, Publishing, Advertising, and More.* Cambridge, MA: Harvard University, Nieman Journalism Lab.

Orr, Larry L., Howard S. Bloom, Stephen H. Bell, Fred Doolittle, and Winston Lin. 1996. *Does Training for the Disadvantaged Work? Evidence from the National JTPA Study.* Lanham, MD: Urban Institute Press.

Osterman, Paul. 1999. *Securing Prosperity: How the American Labor Market Has Changed and What to Do about It.* Princeton, NJ: Princeton University Press.

Pay Scale. 2020. "Average Clerical Assistant Hourly Pay." *Pay Scale.com.* https://www .payscale.com/research/US/Job=Clerical_Assistant/Hourly_Rate.

Pencavel, John. 2001. *Worker Participation: Lessons from the Worker Co-ops of the Pacific Northwest.* New York: Russell Sage Foundation.

Perlstein, Steven. 2013. "How the Cult of Shareholder Value Wrecked American Business. *Washington Post*, September 9. https://www.washingtonpost.com/news/wonk /wp/2013/09/09/how-the-cult-of-shareholder-value-wrecked-american-business/.

Petro, Greg. 2020. "7 Predictions for Retail This Year." *Forbes*, January 3. https://www.forbes .com/sites/gregpetro/2020/01/03/7-predictions-for-retail-this-year/?sh=5af93b378614.

Phills, James A. Jr., Kriss Deiglmeier, and Dale T. Miller. 2008. "Rediscovering Social Innovation." *Stanford Social Innovation Review* (Fall): 34–43.

Plunkert, Lois M. 1990. "The 1980s: A Decade of Job Growth and Industry Shifts." *Monthly Labor Review* 113 (September): 3–16.

PolicyLink. 2019. "An Overview of America's Working Poor." *PolicyLink.org*. Oakland, CA: PolicyLink.

Poon, Linda. 2019. "Why Americans Stopped Volunteering." *Bloomberg City Lab*, September 11. https://www.bloomberg.com/news/articles/2019-09-12/america-has-a-post-9-11-volunteerism-slump.

Porter, Eduardo. 2016. "The Bad News Is the Good News Could Be Better." *New York Times*, September 14, B1, 5.

Pressman, Steven, and Robert H. Scott III. 2010. "Consumer Debt and Poverty Measurement." *Focus* 27 (1): 9–12.

Putnam, Robert D. 2000. *Bowling Alone*. New York: Simon and Schuster.

Quintini, Glenda, and Danielle Venn. 2013. *Back to Work: Re-employment, Earnings and Skill Use after Job Displacement*. Final Report. Paris: OECD Employment Analysis and Policy Division. https://www.oecd.org/els/emp/Backtowork-report.pdf.

Radloff, Lenore S. 1977. "The CES-D Scale: A Self-Report Depression Scale for Research in the General Population." *Applied Psychological Measurement* 1 (3): 385–401.

Rank, Mark. 2014. *Chasing the American Dream*. New York: Oxford University Press.

Roberts, Robert E. 1980. "Reliability of the CES-D Scale in Different Ethnic Contexts." *Psychiatry Research* 2 (2): 125–34.

Romano, Frank. 2019. *History of Desktop Publishing*. New Castle, DE: Oak Knoll.

Rose, Stephen J. 2018. *Manufacturing Employment: Fact and Fiction*. Washington, DC: Urban Institute.

Rosenblum, Paula. 2017. "Five Reasons Why 'The Retail Apocalypse' Is a False Scare Story." *Forbes*, May 1. https://www.forbes.com/sites/paularosenblum/2017/05/01/five-reasons-why-the-retail-apocalypse-is-a-red-herring/?sh=44a297bfb1fa.

Rotella, Elyce J. 2002. "Clerical Occupations." In *Women's Studies Encyclopedia*, edited by Helen Tierney, 265–67. Westport, CT: Greenwood.

Rushing, Ellie. 2019. "In Montco, Health-Care Jobs Are Going Unfilled." *Philadelphia Inquirer*, July 10, A11–12.

Schor, Juliet. 2012. *Economic Fallacies: Wrong-Headed Ideas about Worktime*. Chicago: MacArthur Foundation.

———. 2014. "Debating the Sharing Economy." *Great Transition Initiative.org*, October. http://greattransition.org/publication/debating-the-sharing-economy.

Schultz, Laura. 2020. "Defining and Measuring Gig Work." Policy Brief. New York: Rockefeller Institute of Government.

Searcey, Dionne, Eduardo Porter, and Robert Gebeloff. 2015. "As Market Evolves, Health Care Opens Paths, Often for Women." *New York Times*, February 23.

Selbst, Andrew D., and Julia Ticona. 2017. "Supreme Court Must Understand: Cell Phones Aren't Optional." *Wired*, November 29. https://www.wired.com/story/supreme-court-must-understand-cell-phones-arent-optional/.

Sen, Amartya. 1992. *Inequality Reexamined*. New York: Russell Sage Foundation.

———. 1999. *Development as Freedom*. New York: Anchor.

Sennett, Richard. 1998. *The Corrosion of Character: The Personal Consequences of Work in the New Capitalism*. New York: W. W. Norton.

Shapiro, Isaac. 2004. *Number of Unemployed Who Have Gone without Federal Benefits Hits Record 3 Million*. Washington, DC: Center on Budget and Policy Priorities.

Shipler, David K. 2004. *The Working Poor: Invisible in America*. New York: Alfred A. Knopf.

Singleton, Christopher J. 1992. "Auto Industry Jobs in the 1980s: A Decade of Transition." *Monthly Labor Review* 115 (2): 18–27.

Sneader, Kevin. 2019. *How Asia's Rise Is Reshaping the World*. New York: McKinsey.

Soergel, Andrew. 2020. "More than 16 Million Americans Filed for Unemployment the Past Three Weeks." *U.S. News and World Report*, April 9. https://www.usnews.com /news/economy/articles/2020-04-09/more-than-16-million-americans-filed-for-un employment-the-past-three-weeks.

Staller, Karen M. 2022. "Federal and State Budget Basics for Social Workers. In *Social Policy and Social Justice*, 4th ed., edited by Michael Reisch, 225–46. San Diego: Cognella.

Stern, Andy. 2016. *Raising the Floor: How Universal Basic Income Can Renew Our Economy and Rebuild the American Dream*. New York: PublicAffairs.

Stern, Mark J., and June Axinn. 2018. *Social Welfare: A History of the American Response to Need*. 9th ed. New York: Pearson.

Stevens, Ann Huff, and Ariel Marek Pihl. 2017. *Labor Markets and Poverty in the U.S.: Basic Facts, Policy and Research Needs*. Davis: University of California–Davis, Center for Poverty Research.

Stites, Jessica. 2014. "Can We Have More Jobs and Less Work?" *Inthesetimes.com*, April 30. https://inthesetimes.com/article/more-jobs-less-work.

Stone, Chad, and William Chen. 2014. *Introduction to Unemployment Insurance*. Washington, DC: Center on Budget and Policy Priorities.

Sweet, Stephen, and Peter Meiksins. 2017. *Changing Contours of Work: Jobs and Opportunities in the New Economy*. 3rd ed. Los Angeles: Sage.

Tankersley, Jim, Alan Rappeport, and Jeanna Smialek. 2021. "Tepid Job Growth Inflames Debate over U.S. Benefits." *New York Times*, May 8, A1, 6.

Taylor, Frederick Winslow. 1911. *The Principles of Scientific Management*. Norwood, MA: Plimpton.

Teicholz, Paul. 2015. "Trends in Labor Productivity in the Construction Industry." San Francisco: Project Production Institute.

Terkel, Studs. 1974. *Working: People Talk about What They Do All Day and How They Feel about What They Do*. New York: New Press.

Thompson, Derek. 2015. "A World without Work." *Atlantic*, July. https://www.theatlantic .com/magazine/archive/2015/07/workd-without-work/395294.

———. 2017. "What in the World is Causing the Retail Meltdown of 2017?" *Atlantic*, April 10. https://theatlantic.com/business/archive/2017/04/retail-meltdown-of-2017 /522384.

Treuhaft, Sarah, and Darrick Hamilton. 2020. "Job Guarantee Now!" *The Next System Project*, January 30. https://thenextsystem.org/learn/stories/job-guarantee-now-sarah -treuhaft-and-darrick-hamilton.

U.S. Census Bureau. 2020. "U.S. and World Population Clock." Last updated March 9, 2020. https://www.census.gov/popclock/. Washington, DC: U.S. Census Bureau.

U.S. Department of Agriculture. 2001. "Characteristics of Food Stamp Households: Fiscal Year 2000." Washington, DC: U.S. Department of Agriculture.

U.S. Department of Health and Human Services. 1996. "1996 HHS Poverty Guidelines." Washington, DC: U.S. Department of Health and Human Services, Office of the Assistant Secretary for Planning and Evaluation.

———. 2019. "2019 Poverty Guidelines." Washington, DC: U.S. Department of Health and Human Services, Office of the Assistant Secretary for Planning and Evaluation.

———. 2020. "Poverty Guidelines: January 18, 2020." Washington, DC: U.S. Department of Health and Human Services, Office of the Assistant Secretary for Planning and Evaluation.
Vallas, Steven P. 2012. *Work: A Critique.* Cambridge, UK: Polity.
Vallas, Steven P., and Christopher Penner. 2012. "Dualism, Job Polarization, and the Social Construction of Precarious Work." *Work and Occupations* 39 (4): 331–53.
Vespa, Jonathan, David M. Armstrong, and Lauren Medina. 2018. "Demographic Turning Points for the United States: Population Projections for 2020 to 2060." Washington, DC: U.S. Census Bureau.
Voice of America. 2018. "U.S. Census: Americans Are More Educated Than Ever Before." *VOA News*, August 29. https://learningenglish.voanews.com/a/us-census-bureau-americans-are-more-educated-than-ever-before/4546489.html.
Vroman, Wayne. 2005. "The Recession of 2001 and Unemployment Insurance Financing." *Economic Policy Review* 11 (1): 61–79.
Vruno, Mark. 2016. "State of the Industry: Why 2016 Could Be the Start of a Printing Revival." *Printing News*, January 1. https://www.printingnews.com/digital-inkjet/digital-toner/article/12146215/state-of-the-industry-why-2016-could-be-the-start-of-a-printing-revival.
Wake, John. 2019. "History of American Real Estate Bubbles." *Forbes*, June 8. https://www.forbes.com/sites/johnwake/2019/06/08/american-history-of-real-estate-bubbles/?sh=71ab70cb48aa.
Wallick, Richard. 2011. "Auto Industry Labor Costs in Perspective." Washington, DC: Bureau of Labor Statistics.
Weber, Max. 1978 [1922]. *Economy and Society.* 2 vols. Edited and translated by Guenther Roth and Claus Wittich. Berkeley: University of California Press.
Weeden, Dustin. 2015. "Tackling Student Loan Debt." Washington, DC: National Conference of State Legislatures. https://www.ncsl.org/research/education.
Weeks, Kathi. 2011. *The Problem with Work: Feminism, Marxism, Antiwork Politics, and Postwork Imaginaries.* Durham, NC: Duke University Press.
Weible, Christopher, and Paul A. Sabatier, eds. 2017. *Theories of the Policy Process.* 4th ed. New York: Routledge.
Wenger, Etienne. *Communities of Practice: Learning, Meaning, and Identity.* Cambridge, UK: Cambridge University Press.
West, Stacia, Amy Castro Baker, Sukhi Samra, and Erin Coltrera. 2021. *SEED: Stockton Economic Empowerment Demonstration: Preliminary Analysis, SEED's First Year.* https://static1.squarespace.com/static/6039d612b17d055cac14070f/t/603ef1194c474b329f33c329/1614737690661/SEED_Preliminary+Analysis-SEEDs+First+Year_Final+Report_Individual+Pages+-2.pdf.
Weyrich, Noel. 2006. "Failing Grades." *Pennsylvania Gazette*, March–April, 51–55.
White House. 2018. "Executive Order Establishing the President's National Council for the American Worker." July 19. https://trumpwhitehouse.archives.gov/presidential-actions/executive-order-establishing-presidents-national-council-american-worker/.
Whittaker, Julie M., and Katelin P. Isaacs. 2013. "Extending Unemployment Compensation Benefits during Recessions." Washington, DC: Congressional Research Service.
Willis, Cara. 2015. "Five-Year View of U.S. Opportunity Shows Lack of Gains Post-recession." *Opportunity Nation*, October 5. https://opportunitynation.org/latest-news/five-year-view-of-u-s-opportunity-shows-lack-of-gains-post-recession/.
Wisconsin Department of Revenue. 2019. "Wisconsin Economic Outlook." Madison: Wisconsin Department of Revenue.

Wolfe, Julia, and Melat Kassa. 2020. "State and Local Governments Have Lost 1.5 Million Jobs since February. Washington, DC: Economic Policy Institute.
Wolfinger, James. 2013. "African American Migration." *Encyclopedia of Greater Philadelphia*. http://philadelphiaencyclopedia.org/archive/African-american-migration/.
Zelizer, Viviana A. 1997. *The Social Meaning of Money*. Princeton, NJ: Princeton University Press.

Index

McCall, Leslie, 48, 61, 83
McLafferty, Sara, 55
median wage, 3–4, 15n5, 60, 67, 96; in
  architecture, 127; for food service
  managers, 99; for home health workers,
  130; overestimated, 94–95
men, wages for, 8
mental health of workers, 56
mentoring programs, 20–21, 26, 29–31, 38, 153
merchandiser positions, 109–110
middle-income work, 4, 15, 60, 76, 85, 116–
  134, 162–163; and social stratification,
  123–124. See also architecture; real estate
military clerical jobs, 48–49
millennial and Z generations, 139
Miller, Dale T., 15
minimum wage: $15 an hour movement,
  13, 19, 146; legislation, 67
mobility, 17–19; and clerical work, 60,
  66–67; education tied to, 8, 11; and
  healthcare work, 76; industrial-era, 17;
  intergenerational, 4; in manufacturing
  industry, 19; retail trades, 99, 109, 111–
  112; and service work, 13
multiactivity society, 147
multiple jobs, 9, 108–109, 132
"multiple monies," 142–143
multitasking, 104
mutual engagement, 3

national investment employment corps, 145
Neighborhood Time Exchange
  (Philadelphia), 147
neoliberal managerial actions, 7; cost-
  saving practices, 11; flextime, 83;
  full-time work reduced, 81; intrusive
  surveillance practices, 10, 54; just-in-
  time scheduling, 7, 77, 80, 82, 109; and
  respectful relationships, 115
network ties, 34, 51, 52, 77, 89, 107; online
  groups, 124
New Deal work programs, 135, 145
night shift premiums, 21, 43
nonfarm employment, 6–7
non-labor-market work. See civil labor;
  volunteer work
nonprofits, 31

O'Brien, Greig, 127
odd jobs, 18
offshoring, 11, 24

oil and gas industries, 4
"old employment contract," 12, 18, 49, 58,
  125–126, 128
online job training, 91–92
on-the-job training, 50–51, 60, 98;
  manufacturing industries, 18–20
opportunity: economic criteria as basis
  for, 3; foundational beliefs about, 2–4, 9;
  industrial-era task-specific capabilities,
  17; intergenerational, 15, 26, 125; rhetoric
  of, 9, 11–12, 73
opportunity, real, 8, 10–13, 15, 25, 135–156,
  155–156; valuing of work by workers, 44,
  46–47, 90, 97, 103–104, 114–115, 124, 138.
  See also civil labor
opportunity costs, 36, 55, 62, 98; in
  healthcare education, 70, 76
oral history, 159
Orr, Larry L., 135
outdoor work, 15
outsourcing, 11, 109
overtime, 3, 59–60; in manufacturing
  sector, 22–23

Pandemic Relief Act, 6
Pandemic Unemployment Assistance
  (PUA) Act, 6
participatory research process, 149
part-time employment, 9, 55, 86; benefits
  not available, 52, 86; full-time reduced
  to, 81; involuntary, 96–97; management
  and supervisory positions, 95, 108, 109;
  multiple jobs held, 9, 108–109, 132;
  underemployment, 109
Penner, Christopher, 121
Personal Responsibility and Work
  Opportunity Reconciliation Act of 1996,
  52, 59, 73
pharmacy technicians, 52–53, 54–55
Philadelphia: Food Bucks program,
  152; Great Migration to, 97–98;
  Neighborhood Time Exchange, 147
philanthropists and foundations, 15, 140,
  147, 149, 150–151
Phills, James A., Jr., 15
polarization of employment, 7–8, 68,
  123, 132
policymaking, 3, 11–14, 45, 135, 139, 155
Porter, Eduardo, 76
positive work atmosphere, 55
postindustrialization, 17

workers of color, 11, 39; Hispanic (Latino/a) workers, 53, 55–56; unemployment rates for, 5. *See also* African Americans
work ethic, challenging, 137–138
"work first" mandate, 59, 75, 135–136, 160
workforce development programs, 14–15, 160–161; computer training, 59; for-profit healthcare training institutions, 69–70, 72; individual focus of, 11, 135; lack of knowledge about, 39–40; in manufacturing, 18, 26–27, 30–32; printing industry, 39; test-taking strategies, 36; welfare-to-work programs, 58–59, 70, 72. *See also* credentials
Workforce Innovation and Opportunity Act of 2014, 14

Working (Terkel), 12, 103, 157
working conditions, 10–11, 13, 56; 12-hour shifts, 80–81; abusive employers, 53; lack of space for workers, 56; positive work atmosphere, 55; workweek, length of, 7, 52, 94, 108–109, 138, 148
Works Progress Administration (WPA), 139–140, 145
workweek, length of, 7, 52, 94, 108–109, 138, 148

Y2K, 19, 22
youth workers, 5, 26, 126, 151, 154

Zelizer, Viviana, 142–143

Roberta Rehner Iversen is an Associate Professor in the School of Social Policy & Practice at the University of Pennsylvania. She is also a Faculty Associate in Penn's Institute for Urban Research. She is the coauthor of *Jobs Aren't Enough: Toward a New Economic Mobility for Low-Income Families* (Temple).